Y0-BCL-949

TS176
C3   2369

CAD/CAM

NEW ENGLAND INSTITUTE
OF TECHNOLOGY
LEARNING RESOURCES CENTER

CAD/CAM

MEETING TODAY'S PRODUCTIVITY CHALLENGE

Dr. Khalil Taraman
Editor

Published by:

Computer and Automated Systems Association of SME
Marketing Services Department
One SME Drive
P.O. Box 930
Dearborn, Michigan 48128

CAD/CAM:
MEETING TODAY'S PRODUCTIVITY CHALLENGE

Library of Congress Catalog Card Number: 80-69006

International Standard Book Number: 0-87263-063-3

Manufactured in the United States of America

CASA of SME wishes to express its acknowledgement and appreciation to the following for supplying some of the various papers reprinted within the contents of this book.

CIRP
19 rue Blanche
75009 Paris
France

North-Holland Publishing Company
P.O. Box 103
335 Jan Van Galenstraat
1000 AC
Amsterdam
The Netherlands

Numerical Control Society
519 Zenith Drive
Glenview, Illinois 60025

Production
Bramson Publishing Company
Box 101
Bloomfield Hills, Michigan 48013

PREFACE

New challenges dictate more utilization of computers in design and manufacturing. These challenges include the need to improve product quality and reliability, enhance manufacturing productivity, cut labor costs and reduce the effects of foreign industrial competition.

The first computer was created at the University of Pennsylvania in 1946, although the first commercially available computer was not offered for sale until 1951. Three years later, Numerical Control was announced to the public. In 1955, development of the first automatically programmed tool processor marked the premier of Computer Aided Manufacturing (CAM). Computer Aided Design appeared early in the 1960's when General Motors Corporation developed design augmented by computer and the Massachusetts Institute of Technology developed the Sketchpad system.

Early manufacturing applications using computers were high in cost and low in performance. But as costs dropped and performance improved, the computer found its way into the realm of manufacturing.

Today, CAD/CAM is finding a wide range of applications from designing and building aircraft to the design of cutting tools and dies, as well as jigs and fixtures.

The 1980 Delphi survey published by SME reveals that 10 percent of U.S. companies will integrate Computer Aided Design and Computer Aided Manufacturing by the end of 1980. However, this study shows the level of CAD/CAM integration as 25 percent in 1990.

An urgent need exists to educate persons to successfully implement CAD/CAM technology. This book represents a significant step by the Computer and Automated Systems Association of SME toward this goal. More than 1,000 papers were reviewed in the development of this book. Modifications were made to reach the current inclusion of nine chapters.

The first chapter, "Future Trends", discusses the development and eventual implementation of the computer-integrated automatic factory by the year 2000. Chapter Two, "Computer Integrated Manufacturing", explains the approach adopted by the Air Force toward integrated manufacturing.

Chapter Three, "Hierarchical Approach", presents an analysis and evaluation of some CAM systems and the future of these systems. Chapter Four, "Computer Graphics", illustrates how productivity and product quality are increased through the emerging field of computer graphics.

Chapter Five, "Future Directions", describes how CAD and CAM are being integrated into manufacturing at Pratt and Whitney Aircraft.

The sixth chapter, "Designing, Operating and Selling", discusses manufacturing systems and some of the problems that may arise when removed from the Research and Development domain and placed in the factory environment.

Chapter Seven, "Robots", addresses the question of how to successfully combine and apply proven technologies toward total automation in the manufacturing process.

Chapter Eight, "Economic Considerations", presents an evaluation for implementing CAD and CAM within the present state-of-the-art to achieve cost effectiveness over current design and manufacturing methodology and practice.

The final chapter, "Applications", presents some of the many successful applications of CAD/CAM.

Each technical paper was written by a CAD/CAM expert. I express my gratitude to each of the authors represented in this book and apologize to those authors of very fine publications which were not included due to the limitation on the size of the book.

Acknowledgement is due to the Numerical Control Society, CIRP and Production magazine for allowing us to reprint some of their material in this volume. My thanks is also extended to Bob King and Judy Stranahan of the SME Marketing Service Department for their efforts in the development of this volume. A special thanks is extended to Dr. William Spurgeon for his evaluation of my final selection of the technical papers in this book. Sincere thanks to my family for their patience while I reviewed the extensive material for this publication.

Khalil S. Taraman, Ph.D., CMfgE, P.E.
Editor

CASA of SME

The Computer and Automated Systems Association of the Society of Manufacturing Engineers. . .CASA of SME. . .is an educational and scientific association for computer and automation systems professionals. CASA was founded in 1975 to provide for the comprehensive and integrated coverage of the fields of computers and automation in the advancement of manufacturing. CASA is the organizational "home" for engineers and managers concerned with computer and automated systems.

The Association is applications-oriented, and covers all phases of research, design, installation, operation and maintenance of the total manufacturing system within the plant facility. CASA activities are designed to do the following:

- Provide professionals with a single vehicle to bring together the many aspects of manufacturing, utilizing computer systems automation.
- Provide a liaison among industry, government and education to identify areas where technology development is needed.
- Encourage the development of the totally integrated manufacturing plant.

The application of computer/automated systems must always be timely and must assure cost-effective manufacturing and quality products.

CASA is an official association of the Society of Manufacturing Engineers. In joining CASA of SME, you become a partner with over 50,000 other manufacturing-oriented individuals in 35 countries around the world.

A member of CASA benefits from a constant output of data and services, including a discount on all CASA activities and SME books. CASA's educational programs, chapter membership meetings, publications, conferences and expositions have proven valuable by updating a member's knowledge and skills and by expanding his technical outlook in the integration of manufacturing systems.

Membership in CASA is a means for continuing education. . .a forum for technical dialogue. . .a direct channel for new ideas and concepts. . .an important extension of your professional stature.

TABLE OF CONTENTS

CHAPTERS

INTEGRATING CAD AND CAM

DESIGNING, OPERATING AND SELLING

ROBOTS AND CAM

ECONOMIC CONSIDERATIONS

APPLICATIONS

APPENDIX

INDEX

CHAPTER 1

FUTURE TRENDS

Presented at the CIRP General Assembly and published in the CIRP Annals, Volume 25/2/1976, pgs. 473-476

Future Trends in Manufacturing—Toward the Year 2000

By M. Eugene Merchant
(1) Director of Research Planning
Cincinnati Milacron Inc.
Cincinnati, Ohio

Summary: A Delphi-type technological forecast of the future of production engineering, carried out by CIRP, indicated that the overall future trend in manufacturing between now and the year 2000 is that toward the development and implementation of the computer-integrated automatic factory. Analysis of this trend shows that there are very significant economic and social incentives at work today to provide the motivation for such to happen. As a result, most of the industrialized nations of the world are working toward realization of this objective well before the year 2000. The strategy being followed in their work is to develop and implement a sequence of viable, economic steps in the form of shorter range programs which will lead to eventual realization of the overall objective. These include development and implementation of such new optimization technology as integrated manufacturing software systems, group technology, cellular manufacturing, computer control and multi-station manufacturing systems. Preliminary technology assessment by CIRP of the likely future economic, social, and environmental impact of this trend indicates that is should be beneficial to future society if the work on it is properly carried out. The members of CIRP, as leading production engineering researchers, therefore have a major responsibility to see that this work is properly done.

INTRODUCTION

In 1971, CIRP completed and published[1] a Delphi-type technological forecast of the future of production engineering. The development of this forecast was participated in by CIRP members from all parts of the world. The effort resulted in 94 forecast events on which good concensus was obtained. These covered the subjects corresponding to the fields of activity of the eight CIRP Scientific Technical Committees, namely cutting (C), physical and chemical machining (E), forming (F), grinding (G), machine tools (Ma), metrology-interchangeability (Me), optimization (O), and surfaces (S).

From the 94 specific forecast events a consensus scenario of the evolving technological future of manufacturing was developed. This describes its expected steady technological progress from 1975 to the year 2000, and reveals many things of interest about that future. However, taken as a whole, one overall trend stands out above all others as the major expected technological development in manufacturing between now and the year 2000. This is the expectation that what may be called the "computer-integrated automatic factory" will be a full-blown reality before the end of this century. Of the 94 forecast events, 24, or over one-fourth, strongly forecast such a trend! Three of those 24 forecast events nicely summarize the nature and timing of that major development, namely:

1. By 1980 (median date), a computer software system for full automation and optimization of all steps in the manufacturing of a part will be developed and in wide use.

2. By 1985 (median date), full on-line automation and optimization of complete manufacturing plants, controlled by a central computer, will be a reality.

3. By 1990 (median date), more than 50% of the machine tools produced will not have a "stand-alone" use, but will be part of a versatile manufacturing system, featuring automatic part handling between stations, and being controlled from a central process computer.

One may well ask what forces and incentives are at work in the world today that provide motive power for such a major change in manufacturing between now and the year 2000. One is, of course, the fact that the technology needed for that change now seems feasible because of the rapid growth of the capabilities of the digital computer. However, equally important are the economic and social forces and incentives which are emerging in today's world. Both of these latter factors are contributing strongly to the prospects for early realization of the computer-integrated automatic factory. Let us examine each of them in turn.

ECONOMIC INCENTIVES

Manufacturing normally contributes approximately 30% of the gross national product of modern industrialized countries. Yet, in spite of that, manufacturing, although normally thought of as a highly productive and efficient activity, is not generally so. For example, this is clearly true of batch-type metalworking manufacturing, which normally accounts for about 40% of total manufacturing employment. The mass production type manufacturing systems (e.g., automotive transfer lines, etc.) account for less than 25% of metalworking parts manufacture. In fact, 75% of such parts are manufactured in lots consisting of less than 50 pieces. Carter[2] has shown that, when the life of the average workpiece in batch-type metal cutting production shops is analyzed, only about 5% of its time is actually spent on machine tools and, of that 5%, only about 30% (or 1.5% of the overall time) is actually spent as productive time in removing metal. This result is illustrated graphically in Figure 1. This situation can hardly be called economic or productive. Further, it truly pinpoints the two main areas where by far the greatest improvement in the economy and productivity of metalworking manufacturing can be made today. The first of these is reduction of time of parts in process in the shop, and thus of the resulting extremely high inventory of unfinished parts on the shop floor, and of finished parts waiting for others in process so that assembly of the product can proceed. It is evident from Figure 1 that this inventory could potentially be reduced by up to 90%. Resulting reduction of indirect capital and labor costs and improvement of productivity could be enormous. Here, indeed, is a major incentive to development and implementation of the computer-integrated automatic factory.

The second area of potentially great improvement is that of percent machine utilization. The 30% machine utilization indicated by Figure 1 must be combined with the fact that the average machine spends approximately 50% of its time waiting for parts to work on (because of the 95% time in transit shown in Figure 1).

As a result, the average machine tool in a batch-type shop is being utilized productively (i.e., is actually cutting metal) only about 15% of the time. Thus it is evident that this utilization could potentially be increased by 600% or more. Resulting reduction of direct labor and overhead costs and increase of productivity could be enormous. Obviously this provides another major incentive to development and implementation of the computer-integrated automatic factory before the year 2000. Another major economic consideration today is the rapidly rising cost of manufacturing labor (compensation per man-hour) relative to manufacturing productivity (output per man-hour). This is illustrated by the data in Table I, for some of the major industrialized nations of the world, for the period 1965-1970. It may be seen that, for all the countries listed (with the possible exception of Switzerland), manufacturing costs have been rising faster than manufacturing productivity. In the past five years this situation has become even more uneconomic than that shown in the table, due to the even more rapid rise in wages in the current inflationary world economy, and the notable failure of manufacturing productivity to increase at a comparable rate. Quite evidently, this situation can only be reversed by improving the rate of increase of manufacturing productivity, decreasing the degree of labor intensiveness of manufacturing, or both. Both of these can be accomplished by development and implementation of the computer-integrated automatic factory and therefore offer an additional major incentive to advancement of such technology.

SOCIAL INCENTIVES

Today, major social forces are also emerging which provide strong incentives for early implementation of the computer-integrated automatic factory. Among these trends, three sets of changing attitudes toward manufacturing are particularly significant, namely those of workers, those of employers, and those of government.

Concerning the first of these trends, there is a steadily increasing reluctance of workers to continue to expose themselves to the manufacturing environment. Thus today, in all the major industrialized countries of the world, there is an increasing shortage of manufacturing workers. This is heightened by the growing opportunities for and rewards in employment in the service industries. This trend is dealt with by Bell[3] in discussing the coming of post-industrial society. For example, this type of trend occurred first in the field of agriculture. In the United States, as the manufacturing industry developed, the percentage of the work force employed in agriculture declined from 90% in 1790 to 4% today. Meanwhile, the percentage of the work force employed in manufacturing rose correspondingly during the 19th Century. However, in recent years it has begun to decline - from 30% of the work force in 1947 to 24.9% in 1968. The U.S. Bureau of Labor Statistics projects that by 1980 the percentage will decline further to 22.4, and a Rand Corporation forecast projects that by the year 2000 only 2% of the labor force will be employed in manufacturing. (Bell's more conservative estimate is 10%.) Quite evidently, this trend represents a major incentive to development and implementation of the computer-integrated automatic factory.

Concerning the second of these trends in attitudes toward manufacturing, namely those of the employers, they are now clearly recognizing the human need for the nature of work to be such as to assure the worker of deep satisfaction from performing it (as well as freedom from unsafe or unhealthful conditions). Thus much attention is being directed to methods of accomplishing this. Here the pioneering work of such investigators as Herzburg[4] on job enrichment is proving most useful. Herzburg's significant finding, illustrated in Figure 2, is that, while the so-called hygiene factors of a job (i.e., company policy and administration, supervision, work conditions, salary, etc.) can cause dissatisfaction if they are not satisfactory, they can do little to provide on-going job satisfaction. Instead, such satisfaction derives from the adequacy of the so-called motivator factors of a job (i.e., opportunity for achievement, recognition, responsibility, advancement, growth, etc.). The major feature of jobs which provide such opportunities is participation in decision-making, often called opportunity for "participative management" on the part of the worker. Thus this trend provides a major incentive to development and implementation of the computer-integrated automatic factory, in view of the endless opportunities it offers for participation in decision-making through interactive type software programs and similar features. In addition, of course, the opportunity it offers for freeing workers from potentially unsafe or unhealthful conditions on the job is tremendous.

The third significant trend in attitudes toward manufacturing is the changed attitude which governments throughout the world are taking toward freeing workers from unsafe or unhealthful working conditions. In most of the industrialized countries of the world, government is no longer playing the essentially passive role of requiring that, as technology to accomplish improved working conditions is developed, it be put to use. Instead it is now playing the very active role of requiring that such technology be developed. For example, in the United States, the relatively new Occupational Safety and Health Act will eventually require such things to happen as, that:

1. technology be developed to eliminate the necessity for a worker to ever insert his hand, arm, or any part of his body into a potentially dangerous area of a machine (such as a press)

2. technology be developed to keep the average noise level to which a worker is exposed for an eight-hour period to below 90 (or perhaps even 85) dBA.

Here again, requirements such as these provide strong incentives to development and implementation of computer automation of manufacturing. This will allow the worker not only to be released from operation of the dangerous machines but also to spend very little time each day on the noisy factory floor.

PROGRAMS AND STRATEGY

Most of the industrialized nations of the world today are aware of the foregoing powerful incentives to change the character of manufacturing through development and implementation of the

computer-integrated automatic factory. Likewise, many of them
are equally aware of the potential of the digital computer to
accomplish this, and to thereby realize tremendous economic and
social national benefits. That potential lies in the capability
of the digital computer to provide both the hardware and software components of manufacturing with two essential, powerful
faculties, namely:

   1. on-line variable program (versatile) automation
   2. on-line moment-by-moment optimization.

As a result, many countries have organized research and development programs of considerable scope to try to realize that potential in their own manufacturing industry well before the year
2000. The main, long-range objective of these programs is, of
course, eventual realization, in that industry, of the computer-
integrated automatic factory.

Although realization of the fully computer-integrated automatic
factory is the long-range goal of the national programs, it is
well realized that to get from today's industrial methods, know-
how and installed equipment to that goal requires an evolutionary,
rather than a revolutionary, process. The strategy being
followed, therefore, is to develop and implement a series of
viable, economic steps, in the form of shorter-range programs of.
research and development, each having two essential characteristics, namely:

1. Potential for sufficient economic return to justify it by
   itself and to generate the capital to support development
   and implementation of the next.

2. Compatibility with eventual attainment of the goal of implementation of the computer-integrated automatic factory.

Out of the variety of such programs being pursued, the following
seem to be receiving a major part of the attention and effort,
world-wide:
1. Development of integrated manufacturing software systems,
   through development of individual software modules which can,
   in the long run, be readily interfaced with each other to
   build up full software systems appropriate to various types
   of manufacturing applications. Such work is proceeding most
   rapidly in the COMECON countries, as well as in West Germany,
   Norway, and Japan. The U.S. Air Force has also just launched
   a program of this type and CAM-I has underway a new program to
   develop an integrated software system for process planning of
   machined parts.

2. Development and application of group technology and cellular
   manufacturing as a required base for application of hierarchical computer systems and the evolution of multi-station manufacturing systems. Such work is proceeding most rapidly in
   the Netherlands, Japan, West Germany, Norway, and the COMECON
   countries. The newly launched U.S. Air Force program also
   has this as one of its features, as does the new CAM-I program.

3. Development and application of broad computer control of manu-

facturing processes and equipment, through use of computer numerical control (CNC), direct numerical control (DNC) and hierarchical computer systems. Such work is proceeding most rapidly in Japan, the United States, and West Germany.

4. Development and application of computer-controlled multi-station manufacturing systems which are, in effect, rather fully automated group technology cells. Such work is proceeding most rapidly in Japan, East Germany, West Germany, Norway and, more recently, in the United States.

5. Planning and development of prototype computer-integrated automatic factories themselves. Such work is proceeding most rapidly in Japan, which has undertaken a major national planning effort on "Methodology for Unmanned Manufacturing"[5]. However, such planning is also underway to a lesser degree in West Germany.

TECHNOLOGY ASSESSMENT

With such a major technological revolution in manufacturing underway on an international scale between now and the year 2000, it becomes of utmost importance to carry out technology assessment of the potential economic, social, and environmental impact which implementation of the computer-integrated automated factory might have. This should be done for purposes of determining whether changes should be made in the current direction of research and development aimed at realization of such factories, and, if so, what changes should be made. CIRP, as an international organization devoted to the advancement of production engineering research, is undertaking to assist in this process of assessment, and the first part of such an assessment has now been completed and reported[6] to CIRP. The method employed in carrying out this part was to make use of intuition in a manner very similar to that used in carrying out Delphi-type technological forecasting. All members of CIRP were invited to participate and were asked to assess the impact of the three key events from the CIRP technological forecast cited in the introduction to this paper. Concerning each event, they were asked to give their opinion as to whether the occurrence of this event would have a beneficial effect, a harmful effect, or no effect on:

-- the economic well-being of, in turn, factory workers, production engineers, universities, factories, countries

-- the social well-being of, in turn, factory workers, production engineers, universities, countries

-- the environment in, in turn, factories (noise, air, comfort, etc.), cities (air, traffic, crowding, etc.), the countryside (air, water, nature, etc.).

The consensus arrived at is summarized in Table II, which is a tabulation of the opinion totals or final "votes" of the group of 65 participating CIRP members concerning what effect the occurrence of each of the three key Delphi-forecast events would have.

Overall, it can be seen that there is very strong consensus that the coming of the computer-integrated automatic factory will in general have no harmful economic, social, or environmental effects, but that there is some significant doubt as to whether this is wholly true for the factory worker. Therefore, the second part of this project is being devoted to exploring the question of what action should be taken during the course of the research leading to the three events in turn (and particularly event number (2) to ensure that no harmful economic or social effects on the factory worker occur. This assessment is again being carried out by means of a Delphi-type consensus-seeking process.

CONCLUSION

It seems evident from the foregoing that the major trend in manufacturing between now and the year 2000, underway throughout the world, is that toward development and implementation of the computer-integrated automatic factory. This trend, in turn, is the result of powerful new social and economic incentives and trends at work in the world today. Further, preliminary technology assessment of this trend, carried out by CIRP, provides evidence that accomplishment of that major change in manufacturing should result in important economic, social, and environmental benefits to future society, if it is properly carried out. We, the members of CIRP, as leading production engineering researchers, thus have a major exciting challenge and responsibility to see that this work is properly done.

REFERENCES

1. Merchant, M. E., Delphi-Type Forecast of the Future of Production Engineering, CIRP Annals, vol. 20, no. 3, pp. 213-225 (1971).

2. Carter, C. F., Trends in Machine Tool Development and Application, Proceedings of the Second International Conference on Product Development and Manufacturing Technology, Macdonald, London, pp. 125-141 (1972).

3. Bell, D., The Coming of the Post-Industrial Society: A Venture in Social Forecasting, Basic Book, New York (1973).

4. Herzburg, F. "One More Time: How Do You Motivate Employees?", Harvard Business Review, vol. 46, no. 1, pp. 53-62 (1968).

5. Modeling of Computer-Controlled Unmanned Factory, Kikai Gijitsu, vol. 22, no. 7, pp. 1-124 (July, 1974).

6. Merchant, M. E., Technology Assessment of the Computer-Integrated Automatic Factory, CIRP Annals, vol. 24, no. 2, pp. 573-574 (1975).

TABLE I

RATES OF CHANGE OF PRODUCTIVITY AND LABOR COSTS IN MANUFACTURING

Country	Output per man-hour	Compensation per man-hour	Unit labor costs	
			National currency	U.S. dollars
Belgium	6.8	8.4	1.4	1.4
Canada	3.5	8.3	4.6	5.1
France	6.6	9.5	2.7	0.6
Germany	5.3	8.7	3.2	4.7
Italy	5.1	9.1	3.8	3.8
Japan	14.2	15.1	0.8	0.8
Netherlands	8.5	11.1	2.5	2.5
Sweden	7.9	10.6	2.5	2.5
Switzerland[1]	6.2	6.2	0.0	0.0
United Kingdom	3.6	7.6	3.8	0.2
United States	2.1	6.0	3.9	3.9

Average annual percent change, 1965-70

[1]Wage earners only.

Source: Bulletin 1710, U.S. Department of Labor (1971)

TABLE II

OPINION TOTALS IN CIRP TECHNOLOGY ASSESSMENT OF
POTENTIAL EFFECT OF COMPUTER-INTEGRATED AUTOMATIC FACTORY
(relative to occurrence of the three forecast events
listed in the introduction to this paper)

Effect	Beneficial			Harmful			No effect		
Event no.	1	2	3	1	2	3	1	2	3
Economic effect on:									
factory workers	48	50	53	5	12	8	13	3	4
production engineers	61	61	61	0	1	1	4	3	3
universities	37	36	36	0	0	0	28	29	28
factories	57	57	60	4	5	2	1	0	0
countries	59	59	60	0	1	0	3	2	2
Social effect on:									
factory workers	40	37	40	15	24	19	10	3	5
production engineers	57	53	55	0	2	1	7	8	7
universities	6	7	6	0	0	0	57	56	57
countries	52	53	54	3	4	3	8	6	6
Environmental effect on:									
factories	50	52	56	3	4	3	10	7	4
cities	6	8	27	1	1	2	57	55	35
country-side	3	3	2	4	6	6	58	56	57

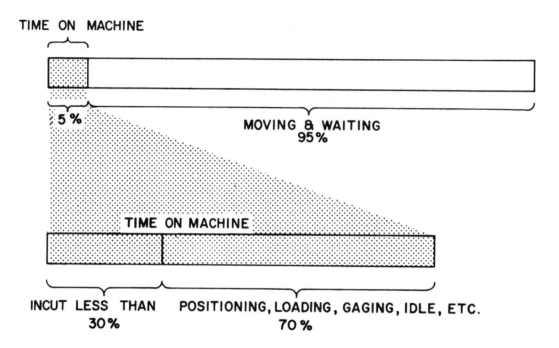

Figure 1 - Life of the average workpiece in the
average (batch-type production) shop
according to Carter[2].

Factors characterizing 1844 events on the job that led to extreme dissatisfaction

Percentage Frequency

Factors characterizing 1753 events on the job that led to extreme satisfaction

Percentage Frequency

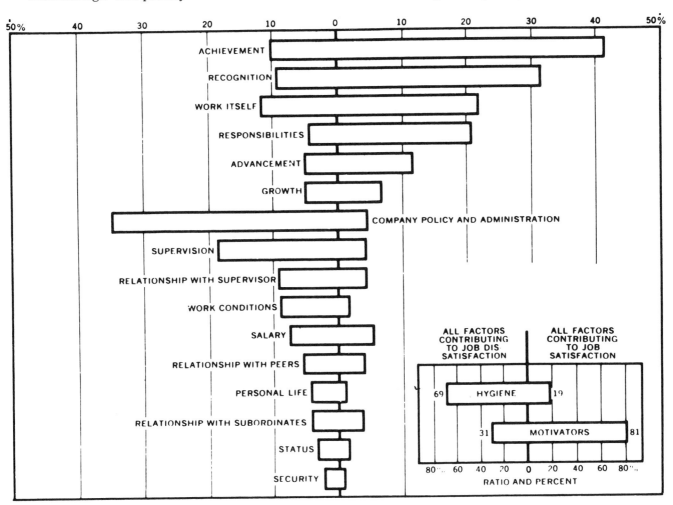

Figure 2 – Satisfaction and dissatisfaction factors in jobs according to Herzburg[4].

CHAPTER 2

COMPUTER INTEGRATED MANUFACTURING

Computer Integrated Manufacturing
The Air Force ICAM Approach

By Dennis E. Wisnosky

**Manager, Manufacturing Organization and Automation
Technology Center
International Harvester**

INTRODUCTION

The United States Air Force Program for Integrated Computer Aided
Manufacturing (ICAM) was brought about by the Air Force need to improve
manufacturing productivity in the aerospace industry. Needs and pressures
in state-of-the-art technologies, economics, human limitations, aerospace
design and manufacturing complexity, computer developments and competition
from abroad serve to complicate the ability to meet this need. Because the
government is the largest customer of manufacturing production, and because
the ICAM Program is an extension of previous Air Force work in Numerical
Control (NC), it is logical that the Air Force should lead this effort for
the Department of Defense (DoD) and that it will have a variety of spinoff
applications throughout the private sector.

ICAM is essentially a program and development plan to produce systematically related computer based modules for efficient manufacturing management and operations. Some of the ICAM technology may be individually implemented in industry, resulting in short-term gains, but the primary benefits
of the program's modular structure will be most evident in fully integrated
systems. Of particular importance to the Air Force is surge production capability, improved cost-effectiveness of weapon system production and flexible manufacturing capabilities required to maintain a credible defense pos-
ture. The private sector is heavily involved in the program coordination,
in which "wedges" (such as sheet metal parts fabrication) are being both

modeled and built to demonstrate integration by computer of all phases of design and manufacturing.

The ICAM Program is an effort to integrate the latest technologies which can provide significant improvements in efficiency, flexibility and reliability for aerospace manufacturing. The Program places particular emphasis on automation and computer aids and includes the development of universal methods and tools for that integration.

In addition to substantial direct cost savings on the manufacturing floor, the ICAM Program attacks many of the indirect or overhead areas of manufacturing productivity. Its application will, for example: improve product quality, improve production response time, shorten lead times, reduce inventory of raw materials equipment and final products and promote accurate, effective communication between all functions of manufacturing.

DEFINING THE ICAM PROGRAM

BACKGROUND

In 1973, the Air Force, with DoD encouragement and support, generated a conceptual master plan (10) that identified and grouped some of the major functions of aerospace manufacturing.

In part motivated by a memorandum from then-Deputy Secretary of Defense W.P. Clements, the Air Force continued its studies on computer-aided manufacturing throughout 1974. From follow-on communication with industry, the Air Force learned that managers' interests went beyond increased labor productivity. Industry managers qualified their interest in Computer Aided Manufacturing (CAM) concepts on the potentials of extent of Return on Investment (ROI), maintenance of competitive position, greater design flexibi-

lity and greater management control. Of these, industry considered management control as having the greatest payoff potential in CAM. The Air Force
study concluded that, in general, while the savings from separate computer-
assisted applications are substantial, the major benefits will be realized
when individually developed CAM subsystems are integrated according to a
plan that combines them into one manageable system.

A plan involving an iterative approach in developing and demonstrating such a system was presented by the Air Force starting in April, 1976, in
a series of public, industrial and professional meetings. Written reponses
from the private sector were overwhelmingly positive concerning the ICAM
Program and its approach.

This approach essentially involved (top-down) planning for Computer
Integrated Manufacturing (CIM) (11) through a model or architecture of manufacturing and (bottom-up) implementation of individual subsystems as they
are developed (12). The Program further postulated testing of its concepts
through actual implementation of an integrated set of subsystems focused on
a particular shop floor cost center. The set of subsystems was called a
"wedge" (Figure 1) through the hierarchy of manufacturing functions. This
wedge would be systematically defined (top-down) and built (bottom-up) in
the sequence: process-station-cell-center-factory (Figure 2). The initial
ICAM wedge was selected to be for aircraft sheet metal parts fabrication.
An actual operational Sheet Metal Part Fabrication Center is scheduled to be
built in the 1985 timeframe.

During 1977 and early 1978, close interaction with industry through
a Committee on Computer Aided Manufacturing (COCAM), an advisory body of
knowledgeable representatives from industry and universities, helped to
crystallize the ICAM Program. Initial ICAM projects began in 1977.

MACROVIEW OF CAM

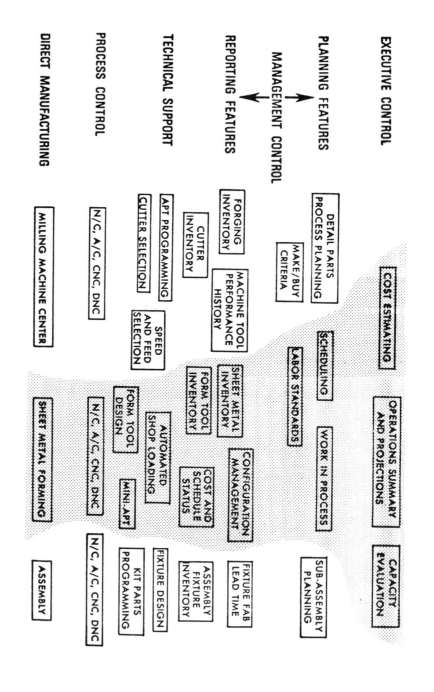

EXECUTIVE CONTROL

PLANNING FEATURES

MANAGEMENT CONTROL

REPORTING FEATURES

TECHNICAL SUPPORT

PROCESS CONTROL

DIRECT MANUFACTURING

COST ESTIMATING

OPERATIONS SUMMARY AND PROJECTIONS

CAPACITY EVALUATION

SCHEDULING

WORK IN PROCESS

SUB-ASSEMBLY PLANNING

LABOR STANDARDS

CONFIGURATION MANAGEMENT

FIXTURE FAB LEAD TIME

DETAIL PARTS PROCESS PLANNING

MAKE/BUY CRITERIA

MACHINE TOOL PERFORMANCE HISTORY

SHEET METAL INVENTORY

FORM TOOL INVENTORY

COST AND SCHEDULE STATUS

ASSEMBLY FIXTURE INVENTORY

FORGING INVENTORY

CUTTER INVENTORY

AUTOMATED SHOP LOADING

FIXTURE DESIGN

APT PROGRAMMING

CUTTER SELECTION

SPEED AND FEED SELECTION

FORM TOOL DESIGN

KIT PARTS PROGRAMMING

N/C, A/C, CNC, DNC

N/C, A/C, CNC, DNC

MINI-APT

N/C, A/C, CNC, DNC

MILLING MACHINE CENTER

SHEET METAL FORMING

ASSEMBLY

"WEDGE" THROUGH THE HIERARCHY OF MANUFACTURING

FIGURE 1

ICAM EVOLUTION

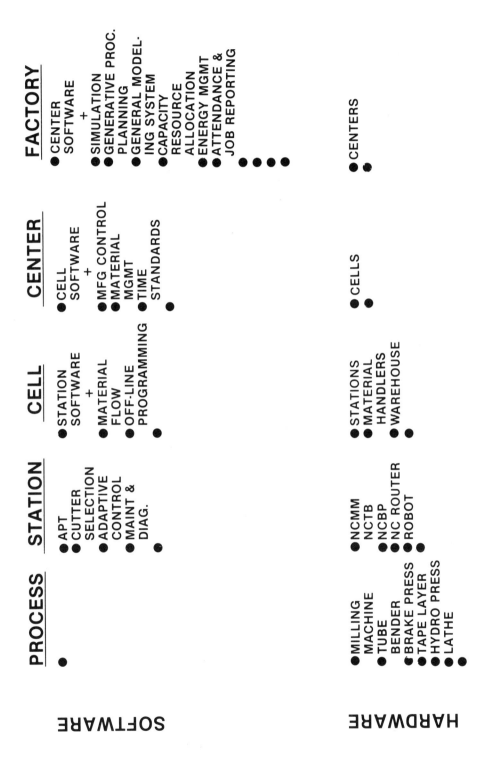

SOFTWARE

PROCESS | **STATION** | **CELL** | **CENTER** | **FACTORY**

STATION:
- APT
- CUTTER SELECTION
- ADAPTIVE CONTROL
- MAINT & DIAG.

CELL:
- STATION SOFTWARE
+
- MATERIAL FLOW
- OFF-LINE PROGRAMMING

CENTER:
- CELL SOFTWARE
+
- MFG CONTROL
- MATERIAL MGMT
- TIME STANDARDS

FACTORY:
- CENTER SOFTWARE
+
- SIMULATION
- GENERATIVE PROC. PLANNING
- GENERAL MODELING SYSTEM
- CAPACITY
- RESOURCE ALLOCATION
- ENERGY MGMT
- ATTENDANCE & JOB REPORTING

HARDWARE

PROCESS:
- MILLING MACHINE
- TUBE BENDER
- BRAKE PRESS
- TAPE LAYER
- HYDRO PRESS
- LATHE

STATION:
- NCMM
- NCTB
- NCBP
- NC ROUTER
- ROBOT

CELL:
- STATIONS
- MATERIAL HANDLERS
- WAREHOUSE

CENTER:
- CELLS

FACTORY:
- CENTERS

MANUFACTURING STAGES AND THEIR NEEDS

FIGURE 2

21

OBJECTIVES

The ICAM Program is a long term effort which includes the establishment of modular subsystems. These subsystems are designed to computer assist and tie together various phases of design, fabrication and distribution processes and their associated hierarchy according to a prioritized master plan. At appropriate times, these mutually compatible modules will be combined, demonstrating a comprehensive control and management package which is capable of continual adjustment as production needs and state-of-the-art change.

The ICAM Program provides "seed money" to advance the frontier of technology. As a large customer with great potential for gain, the Department of Defense is supplying "risk capital" for extending the technology. Industry is not geared to initiate a program of this scope, primarily because of the long term nature of the payoff. With government funding, university assistance and industry cooperation, the technology can be developed and applied in a totally open manner; industry can acquire and apply the elements freely.

The specific objectives of the ICAM Program are described in the Program Management Plan (12):

To establish manufacturing technology which will:
- Reduce defense systems costs by developing and applying computer-aided manufacturing technology to the fabrication of defense material.
- Establish a model for the integrated application of computer technology to all phases of production/manufacturing.
- Improve the long term competence, efficiency and responsiveness of American aerospace and related industries to defense needs.
- Provide a mechanism for Integrated Computer Aided Manufacturing

technology transfer to and within American industry.

- Validate and demonstrate the cost saving benefits and flexibility of ICAM for representative elements of Air Force systems production.

Benefits identified during the Air Force study validate the ability of near term ROI in CAM technology to reduce aerospace systems costs. A Return on Investment (ROI) goal of at least 25 percent for each subsystem module appears to be quite reasonable. The other objectives for industry are also attainable, but require particularly close interchange with industry in a continually evolving process.

To foster this evolutionary activity, the ICAM Program must provide near term payoff, be logically extensible and test its software methodology early in development.

For example, significant steps have been taken during 1979:

1) A robotic work station has been placed in production operation in an aerospace company (16);

2) The initial architecture, shown in Figure 3, has been used by all contractors as the basis for all subsystem definition (20);

3) Software for both architecture model building and model simulation is operational on a national computer timesharing network (17);

4) The Program methodology has served as the approach for a major aerospace manufacturer's technology modernization program (18);

5) The shop floor use of analytical equations which predict the ability to form a certain material with a certain process into a desired form has been demonstrated (19).

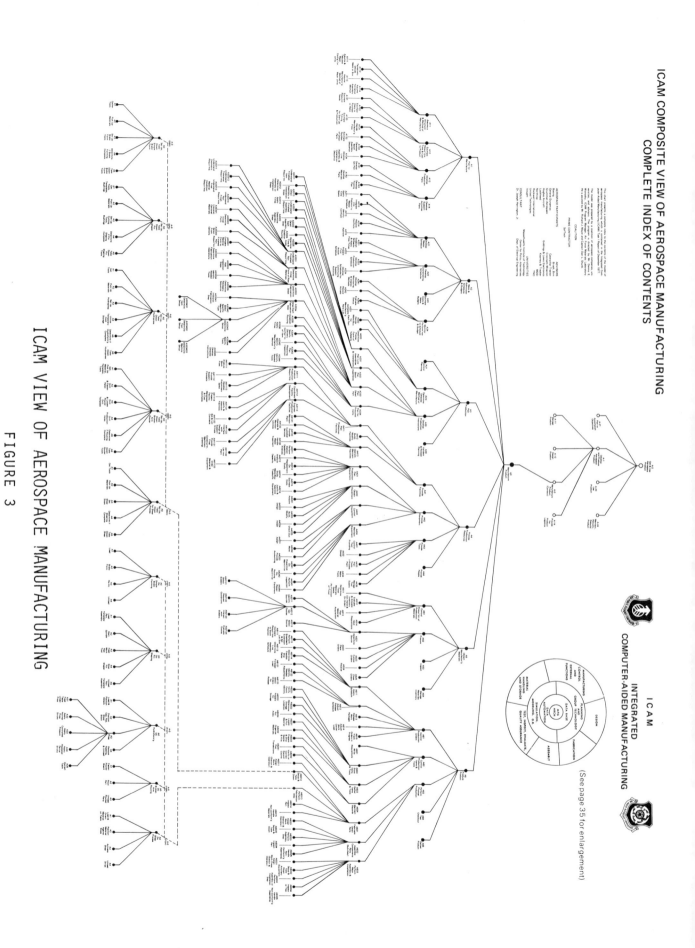

ICAM COMPOSITE VIEW OF AEROSPACE MANUFACTURING
COMPLETE INDEX OF CONTENTS

ICAM VIEW OF AEROSPACE MANUFACTURING

FIGURE 3

ICAM
INTEGRATED
COMPUTER-AIDED MANUFACTURING

(See page 35 for enlargement)

STATE OF THE ART

Elements of aerospace design, informational data banks, manufacturing technology, logistics management and human limitations are critical to implementation of Computer Integrated Manufacturing. This status, superimposed on rapid developments in computer technology, shows a clear need for an overall unifying concept of the type proposed in the Air Force's ICAM Program.

Aerospace Design

Advances in aerospace systems initially require conceptual design. For meaningful follow-on, there must be feasibility studies and eventually hardware. Both of these two latter stages require design efforts based on compatibility between desired performance specifications and both technological and materials constraints, among others. In modern aerospace systems, these design elements have become so complex that computers are now a recognized necessity to provide timely analyses and performance predictions of the many trial designs considered during a project. However, no less vital is the mutual interactive communication of such design information between interdisciplinary personnel, such as designers, scientists, engineers and project managers.

This interactive communication problem can be solved by appropriate computer software and, since 1975, has been addressed by the Integrated Program for Aerospace Vehicle Design (IPAD) project of NASA (1). However, the computer-linked coordination of design activity of this type with the materials technology and manufacturing processes (needed to translate concept images into practice) has not been addressed.

Informational Data Banks

Data banks of the type exemplified by reference libraries have long been recognized as vital resources essential to human progress in all fields, whether technologically or socially oriented. Micro-imaging techniques and computers with large storage and retrieval capabilities have been brought about by the exponential growth in information volume; storage now strains traditional library capability, and retrieval is beyond manual search methods.

Various large volume specialized data banks are maintained by government, industrial and academic institutions, both national and international in scope and location. Information stored ranges from technical subjects (mathematics, physics, chemistry, biology, medicine, engineering and materials sciences) and high density basic data (meteorological, statistical, economic, historical, demographic, etc.) (2). Although the majority of these information storage facilities do have some mode of computer searching, the communication interface with both design and manufacturing operations is still dependent upon human intervention and data transfer. This brings costly time delays, omissions and erroneous or incomplete data interpretation and evaluation.

Manufacturing Technology

The actual conversion of raw materials and shapes to end products of proper size, configuration and performance specifications is accomplished by the processes of manufacturing technology. Such technology has been advanced by techniques for faster production, more uniform output and greater performance reliability.

While improved materials, better quality control and superior design have also made their contributions (3), the ever increasing role of automation and computer control on processes and machines must be given the major credit for the advances recently observed. Numerical Control (NC), Computerized Numerical Control (CNC) and Direct Numerical Control (DNC) concepts use preprogrammed instructions. These instructions control complex machining operations which create highly reproducible tolerances on widely available equipment with minimal human operation. The extension to automation of entire assembly operations has already begun through the increasing proliferation of "robots" in metal working and electronics industries throughout the world (4). However, there is still too much human involvement with set-up time, raw materials selection and feeding and product removal. In addition, most automation efforts have been rigid and intended for mass production. The flexibility required for quantities typical of aerospace production has only barely been considered.

Logistics Management

Possibly the most difficult problem associated with any production system is the scheduling, distribution and maintenance of input raw materials and output finished products. Ordering, storage, scheduliing, transportation and inventory control problems are all involved.

For complete assemblies, such as aerospace systems, the same difficulties are associated with spare parts and subsystem production. Obviously, more rapid production and delivery response to users' needs for spare parts could reduce inventory requirements.

While many aspects have been the subject of computerization efforts, more or less successful, only isolated phases have been examined, and no overall comprehensive system has been thoroughly approached.

Human Limitations

Current aerospace systems productions depends heavily on intermediate stages of human intervention, including design conceptualization, decision making, data communication, report documentation, etc., which, if computer assisted, can be made efficient. If not so aided, then these stages as well as other manned activities (such as materials and products handling) become manpower intensive. Such activities are usually relatively slow and economically inefficient when compared to the automated and/or computerized components of the operation. Moreover, direct human output cannot be significantly modified, yet automated stages are being continually and increasingly improved by orders of magnitude in speed, versatility and economy. Because of these constant changes, the roles, capacities and costs of human involvement need to be continuously re-examined in order to maximize man's unique creative features while assigning routine responsibilities to computerized functions.

Indirect Costs

The role of human limitations is perhaps most felt in the area of the indirect costs of manufacturing (5). While manufacturing technology has traditionally been applied with notable success - as in the case of NC machines - lately it has been recognized that this traditional approach has been pursuing an ever vanishing target. Largely because of the combined effects of shop floor automation and the ever increasing complexity of modern enterprise, the indirect costs of manufacturing amount to 60-70% of product cost. These costs include such factors as planning, scheduling, expediting, inventorying, energy management, engineering changes and responding to the latest set of legislated requirements. The effect of continuing to apply technology in the traditional way is to continue to increase the indirect burden.

Electronics and Computers

The increasingly rapid advances in electronics and the rapid developments in computer hardware and software are easily observed on all sides.

Large scale integrated circuits and newer memory storage principles, in just the last two to three years, have revolutionized computers and no end is in sight. Micro- and mini-computers with advanced memories and peripheral auxiliary equipment can now replace larger computer systems at small fractions of the cost for acquisition and operation. The new processors have less space and environmental control requirements, yet perform with greater versatility and faster rates. This new computer technology is quickly supplanting the obsolescent systems; equally important, it is opening new horizons in performance and handling problems not previously amenable to computer solutions. There are now small inexpensive memories capable of storing millions of data words, magnetic disks which allow random access to billions of such words, and parallel processors. These make the integrated management of large information handling and production oriented systems entirely feasible. In particular, the advent of the distributed data processing systems concept, with supporting hardware and software, now makes increasing computer capability available at local sites (6).

Competition from Abroad

In response to interest by Congress in increased productivity, competitiveness of the United States in world markets, price stability and economic growth, the United States Comptroller General issued an analytical report (7) in June of 1976. It noted that virtually everything produced in the United States is procured, in one form or another, by the Federal Government; the Department of Defense alone obtained items or services from more than 25,000 contractors. A major portion of the items procured were made by batch processes which are amenable to automation techniques to improve productivity. The report also stressed that the United States rate of increase in manufacturing productivity was among the lowest in the world, a factor reflected in the consistently declining United States balance of trade position since 1971 as increased imports of high technology products - once a major export of the United States - arrive from foreign countries.

The Comptroller General suggested that foreign competitors were moving ahead of the United States in applying manufacturing automation. The report took to task the national private sector for neglecting or being unaware of the situation, for taking actions not in the best interest of the United States' economy or for not moving fast enough to sustain the national socioeconomic way of life.

In support of these criticisms, a 1975 survey (4) shows that Japan had almost three times as many manufacturers of "robot" or automation machines as the United States - the ratio being 70 to 26 - and that the European Economic Community nations exceeded the United States with their 33. Moreover, the Japanese have been most innovative in using the "robots" in all types of production ranging from miniature electronics and watches to complete steel mills.

The more recent statistics (8) paint an increasingly stark picture. There are now about 35,000 industrial robots installed in the world. Japan has 30,000 in operation, Western Europe has 3,000 and the United States has about 2,000. Japan now has 120 robot manufacturers who turned out 7,000 units in 1978. (Basically, a robotic facility with 2 or 3 people easily surpasses the productivity of a conventional plant employing 50 workers.) Between January, 1975, and January, 1978, the Japanese were able to increase their productivity by 33 percent, while the annual rate of United States productivity growth during this same period was 2 percent. For 1978 the United States productivity grew by only 0.4 percent, the smallest increase in five years (8).

There is also increased pressure from the industrial output of less developed countries with their enormous labor advantage. This is translated into a highly competitive product. For example, Korea and Taiwan threaten the United States leadership in manmade fibers (8).

United States domination of the nuclear power industry has ended; Sweden, France, West Germany and Canada are now major forces in this business.

This is the kind of competition that United States manufacturing will be facing in the 1980s (9).

Integration of New Technology

New technology, including hardware, concepts and software, appears continually in the marketplace as a logical result of ongoing evolutionary processes in human thought, industry and in the striving for improvement. The majority of these technological improvements usually represent only small advances which can be implemented with relative ease by simple addition, replacement or modification of existing systems. Occasionally, some new documentation or training procedures may be needed. However, with revolutionary new ground breaking technological advancements, serious dislocations and readjustments appear.

For example, those who bring new automation into their plant find that the new capability creates shock waves all around it. A newly automated production unit, such as a Sheet Metal Fabrication Center, with ten, twenty or more times the throughput of the obsolescent facility replaced, has an impact on its operating environment. This impact must be recognized, understood and anticipated so that the new operation can be successfully integrated.

In the area of computer integrated manufacturing, the combination of advanced computer and new manufacturing technologies multiplies the problems associated with the care, feeding and efficient usage of the newly acquired capability by several orders of magnitude. Items which must be considered include proper raw material inventory and feed, split second scheduling of input and output, product transfer, maintenance and service, health and safety factors, compatible rapid quality control, material flow scheduling, personnel training and compatibility at the interface, other human factors including labor union support, alternative routing in case of serious operational difficulty, etc. Those decision makers who install such new hardware without arranging for integration with such items are destined to ultimately suffer drastic losses through the inevitable patchwork ad hoc quick fixes.

THE AIR FORCE'S ROLE

The goals of all phases of the military-industrial aerospace partnership are to streamline, optimize and economize production and inventory response. The state-of-the-art descriptions given above clearly spell out the need for increased computerization and integration of all aspects which are amenable to this treatment. It is evident that integrated and computer aided design and manufacturing capability will increase efficiency and responsiveness of industry to the needs of the public and, more critically, to the requirements of the United States Government and national security. It is also reasonable to recognize that the competition between manufacturers and the enormous startup costs and growing pains to develop such an integration project preclude the development being initiated by industry.

The Department of Defense, with its need for the latest and most efficiently produced technological hardware, is a logical initiator and manager of such efforts. Within the Department of Defense, the Air Force has had the most pertinent experience and capability by virtue of the pioneering work of its Materials Laboratory that resulted in the development of Numerical Controlled Machine Tools (NCMT), and the Automatically Programmed Tooling (APT) language in the 1950s and 1960s. The current ICAM Program is a logical extension of this earlier precedent setting NC program. The NC program was also a joint effort between the Materials Laboratory and the priate sector, with full mutual coordination between all interested parties.

ICAM PROGRAM CONTENT

TECHNOLOGY THRUSTS

In the initial Air Force study on manufacturing processes amenable to ICAM enhancement, 162 technical efforts in 10 clearly definable thrust areas were identified. These areas included the obvious shop floor systems (fabrication, assembly, test-inspect-evaluate, materials handling) and support activities (control and external functions design). Also recognized as important were the "smart" or intelligent sytems required for planning and Group Technology (GT), plus simulation, mathematical and Operations Research (OR) techniques. For the computer aided activities associated with manufacturing, a program "thrust" area was assigned to Data Base and Data Automation activities.

However, it soon became clear that if the systemizing and integrating goals of the ICAM Program were to be realized, there would have to be a validated overall guiding network or master skeleton. This would provide interfaces between the various thrust areas and bind them together as their development was programmed. It would also provide a way to "flesh out" the skeleton by assembling any program results back into an integrated whole. This defining and integrating framework was given the name "architecture of manufacturing", by analogy to the role played by architecture in defining and organizing the component elements in a building.

The ICAM Program logo (Figure 4) is a graphic representation of the thrust areas. The concentric pattern captures the transition from the inner thrust areas of concepts out to the shop floor.

Organization and Scope of Program

The ICAM Program development scheme consists of five basic activities (Figure 5):

    (1) Define manufacturing architecture;

    (2) Develop integration methodology;

    (3) Establish support systems;

    (4) Establish application systems;

    (5) Demonstrate application systems.

In essence, these five activities describe exactly what the ICAM Program does. Figure 5 also shows how the activities are related.

ARCHITECTURE OF MANUFACTURING

To validate the existence of a meaningful "architecture of manufacturing" for the aerospace industry, a coalition of aerospace companies was created in 1977 to study the manufacturing operations in the industry. More than 750 source documents and some 4000 specific factory activities and functions were examined and analyzed. These were incorporated into a collection of "factory view" models which described specific plants and factories and their modes of operation (20).

These specific factory views were then correlated into an overall "composite view" model which was adopted as the basic "architecture". The

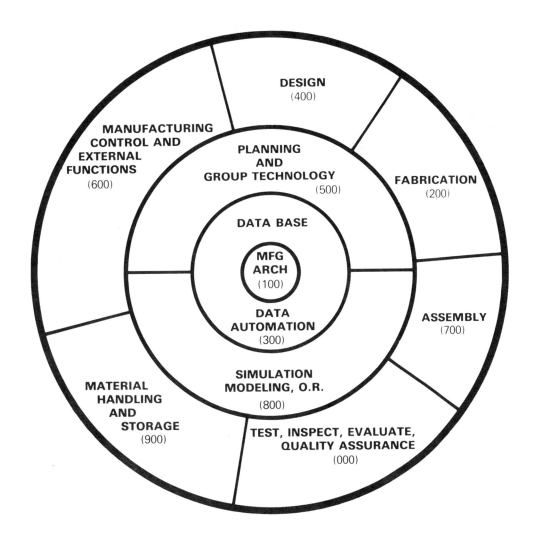

ICAM TECHNOLOGY THRUSTS

FIGURE 4

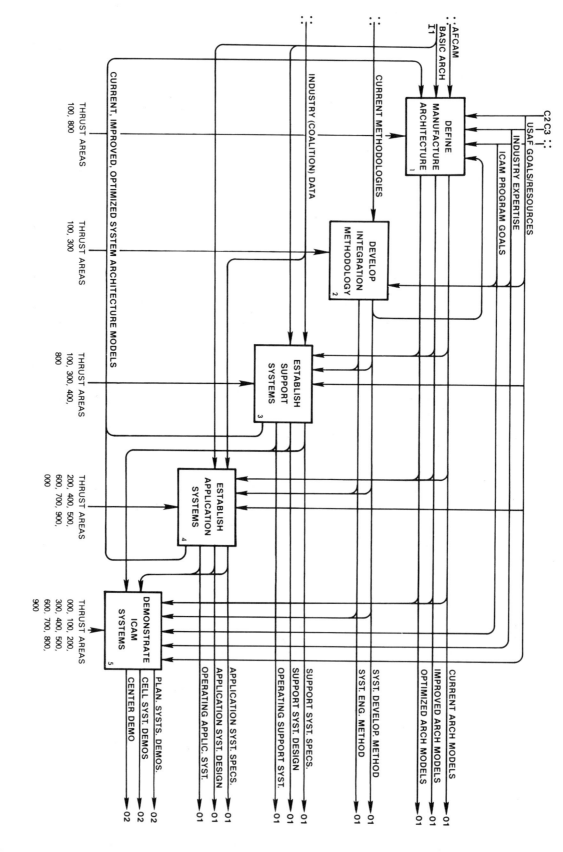

ICAM PROGRAM AO

ICAM IDEF$_0$ DIAGRAM

FIGURE 5

coalition established that this architecture was applicable not only to aerospace manufacturing in general, but also to all production industries.

This architecture of manufacturing can be presented in many forms. The hierarchical "tree" pattern (Figure 3) is the most useful comprehensive form. However, while this picture shows the functions of manufacturing and their relationships, it does not provide either the information content required for manufacturing decision making or allow for simulation to determine the probable effect of decisions. These aspects of architecture are discussed below under the heading "Integration Methodology". First, what is the purpose of an architecture:

(1) Provide a mechanism for top-down planning;

(2) Provide a mechanism for bottom-up implementation in a modular fashion.

Basically, the architecture answers the question; if one doesn't know where one is going, it doesn't matter what road one takes. Using the roadmap analogy, the architecture provides a clear and unambiguous description of both the possible destinations and the ways of reaching them for a particular purpose.

Once the overall picture has been decided upon, formal evolution into working subsystems recognizes operating stages of increasing responsibility, complexity and susceptibility to computer enhancement. As indicated in Figure 2, these are categorized, respectively, as process, station, cell, center and factory states, each having its own software and hardware needs and operating modes. Orderly development of ICAM requires the properly timed resolution and coordination of each stage as it relates to a particular scenario within the architecture.

Definition of the components of this implementation hierarchy is as follows:

(1) Process — A manufacturing process is a single operation or set of operations carried out by a person or machine not aided by an external hierarchy of program driven circuitry or computerized software. Processes are primarily controlled by a person or a station controller. The highest level of control for a process is a cell.

(2) Station — The station is the lowest level of automated control and is composed of sets of manufacturing processes under the control of software resident in or under the direction of the respective station. Stations control processes. Stations do not control other stations and stations are controlled by cell controller software.

(3) Cell — A cell is an automated control of two or more stations to include material handling and may include a single process external to any station control in the respective cell. A single station under cell control must be accompanied by a process not under station control. Cells are controlled by center software.

(4) Center — A center is the automated control of two or more cells. A center may include a single station external to any inclusive cell. A single cell under cell control must be accompanied by a single external station. Centers do not control other centers. Centers are controlled by factory controller software.

(5) Factory — The factory is the automated control of two or more centers. A factory may include a single cell external to any inclusive center. A single center under factory control must be accompanied by a single external cell. Factories do not control other factories. Factories are controlled by management personnel and policies.

First results of the ICAM Program will be integrated into the lower hierarchies of the "architecture of manufacturing", that is, at the process and the station levels (building in a "bottom-up" fashion). As validations are obtained through these demonstration efforts, production processes and stations responsive to ICAM modifications will be assembled and integrated into cell functions and so on up to the more complex center and factory levels. The lower levels will be advanced in performance primarily by hardware developments under ICAM, while the integration required at successively higher levels will depend increasingly on software.

Example: Use of Architecture

The use of the architecture can be illustrated by example. Suppose a manufacturing subsystem entitled "Manufacturing Control - Material Management" (MC-MM) is to be extracted - that is, defined by the architecture - so that it can be built as a module or integrated set of modules. The goals of the MC-MM are to:

(1) Improve schedule realization;

(2) Allow better control of resources - people, material, equipment;

(3) Improve shop floor material flow;

(4) Reduce cycle time;

(5) Reduce inventory at all levels.

Using the architecture as a basis (Figure 3), the first thing that is done is to relate shop floor control to the architecture from the bottom-up - that is, the shop floor. This is naturally in the produce product area (Note A6 of Figure 3). Next, in order to realize the other objectives, we look at the other applicable nodes. Figure 6 shows all that apply, while Figure 7 shows the meaning - that is, what interaction with these nodes enables a shop floor control system to do. It is easily seen that the goals of the MC-MM would be impossible to achieve without interaction with these

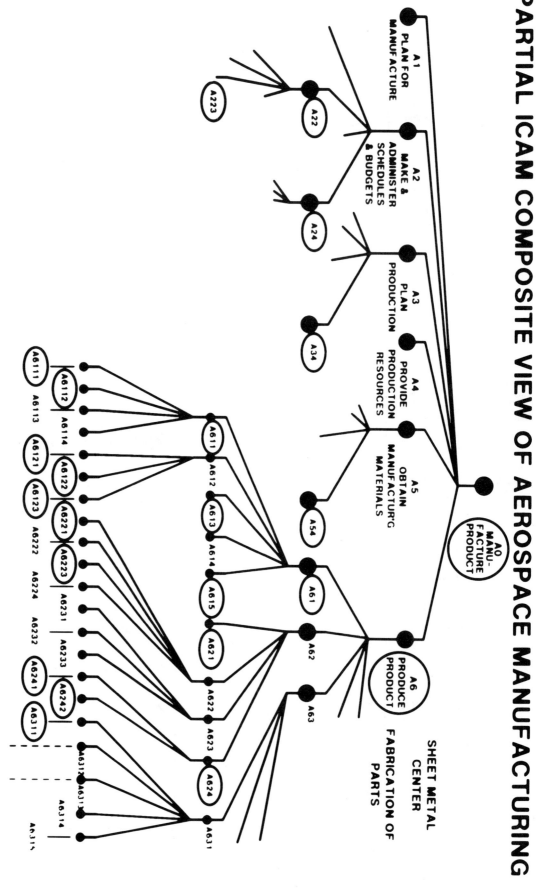

IMC-MM
PARTIAL ICAM COMPOSITE VIEW OF AEROSPACE MANUFACTURING

FIGURE 6

TO PHYSICAL PROCESSES

IMC–MM

RELATE SHOP FLOOR CONTROL TO MANUFACTURING ARCHITECTURE

A2 MAKE AND ADMINISTER SCHEDULES & BUDGETS

- DEVELOP MASTER SCHEDULES
- DEVELOP COORDINATING SCHEDULES
- MONITOR PERFORMANCE TO SCHEDULES & BUDGETS

A3 PLAN PRODUCTION

- DETERMINE DETAILED METHODS OF MANUFACTURING
- DEVELOP PRODUCTION INSTRUCTIONS
- VALIDATE AND RELEASE PLANNING

A5 OBTAIN MANUFACTURING MATERIALS

- CONTROL PROCUREMENT OF PRODUCTION MATERIALS (MRP)
- PROCURE (PURCHASING)
- MANAGE MATERIALS INVENTORY

A6 PRODUCE PRODUCT

- SHOP FLOOR CONTROL

FIGURE 7

functions of the architecture. The resulting system development is a vastly improved concept (Figure 8) with both realtime shop control and control at the factory level which reaches into much higher level activities such as Production and Process Planning, as well as scheduling through the shop. The significance of this is not fully appreciated until one begins to consider the links of the IMCMM to material handling systems and decision support systems as an integrated sheet metal center is actually being designed and built. Some of these links are shown in Figure 9. The procedure described here is actually currently underway within the ICAM Program (21). The meaning of these other terms will be discussed later.

Integration Methodologies

Having explained, by example, the use of the ICAM Architecture, it is clear that at the least the architecture is simply a formal representation of the structure and logical information content of manufacturing. From this structure, logical subsystems can be extracted, built and then integrated back into the structure, much like a jigsaw puzzle. Some of the current pieces will be discussed later.

In order to actually accomplish the integration task, a methodology (collection of tools) which provides a total representation of the architecture of manufacturing has been developed by the ICAM Program. Called IDEF (for ICAM Definition language), it is a graphic notation with its own rules of syntax, construction, validation, referencing, storage, search and retrieval.

IDEF exists in three mutually-supporting versions. They are: $IDEF_0$, for function modeling; $IDEF_1$, for information modeling; and $IDEF_2$, for dynamics modeling.

The specific intent of these forms is:

IMC-MM
IMPROVED CONTROL CONCEPT

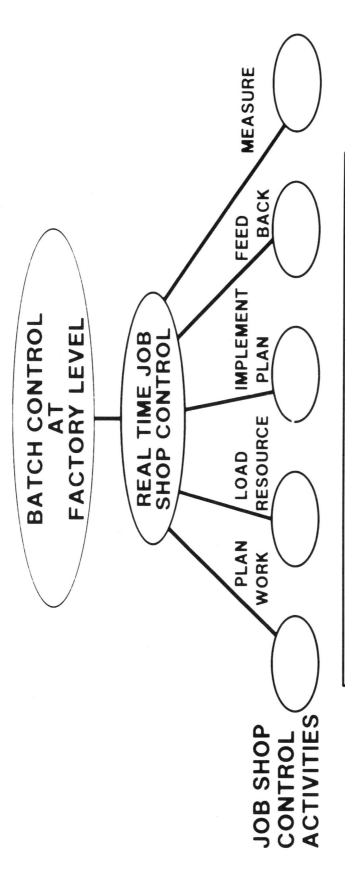

FIGURE 8

43

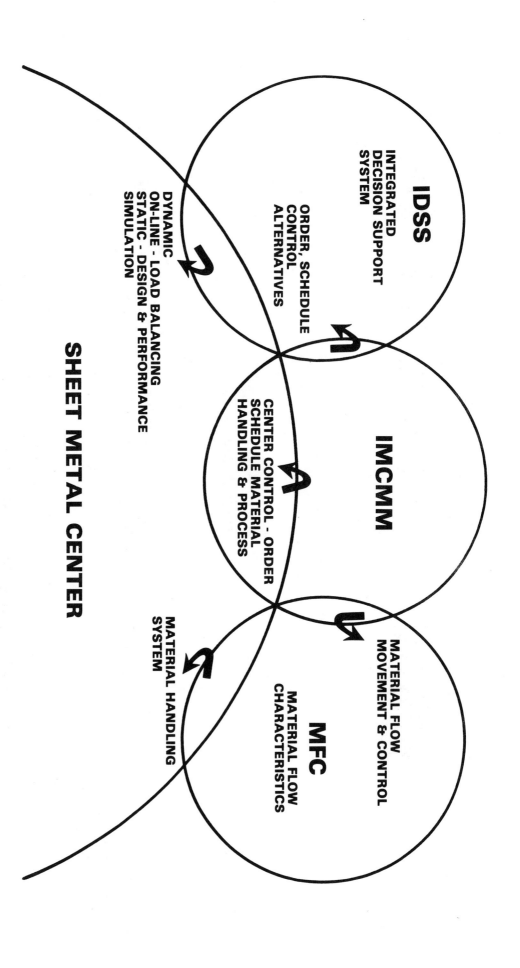

INTERACTION BETWEEN IMCMM AND OTHER FUNCTIONS

FIGURE 9

$IDEF_0$ Function Model answers the question: what are the activities that are performed and how are they related?

$IDEF_1$ Information Model answers the question: what information is required to perform the activities?

$IDEF_2$ Dynamics Model answers the question: how is the information used to perform the activities?

The Function Model is essentially a descriptive model which is used to conceptualize a problem or a system. Figure 5 is an $IDEF_0$ diagram of the ICAM Program.

Figure 10 is a computer produced $AUTOIDEF_0$ diagram. This activity might be part of the IMCMM Project discussed earlier. The activity labeled "Maintain Reparable Spares" is decomposed or broken down into four labeled activity boxes. The four boxes both identify and define the scope of the "parent" box activity. The boxes represent activities (shown as verbs), and the arrows show what is processed. Depending on which side of the box an arrow contacts, the arrow may be an input (left side), control or constraint (top), output (right side) or mechanism (bottom). Each of these boxes can be further decomposed into its own component boxes at the next lower hierarchical level (maximum of six boxes in a single diagram permits step-by-step grasp of the most complex functional arrangements). Identification and cross-referencing capability is maintained through the use of node and box numbers joined sequentially. At this time, $IDEF_1$ has been taught to several hundred people. ICAM projects are now actually described in the language itself. $AUTOIDEF_0$, enabling users to draw $IDEF_0$ diagrams via CRT and communicate with others is now available (on the CYBERNET computer time-sharing network).

$IDEF_1$ is intended to now fill in the skeleton of $IDEF_0$ to the extent

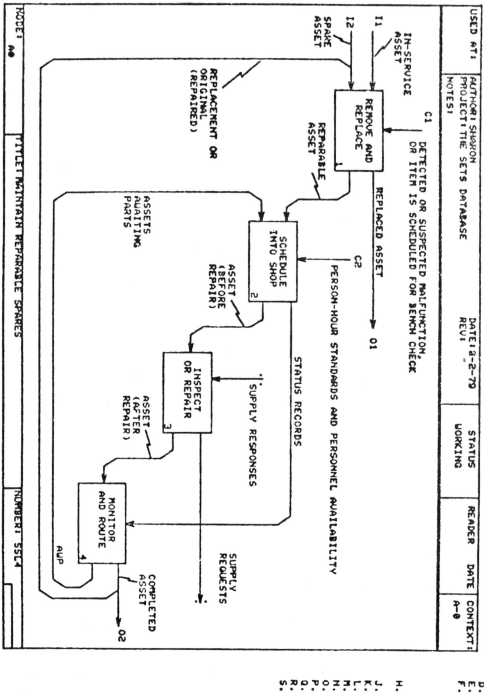

AUTOIDEF₀ DIAGRAM

FIGURE 10

required to actually design data bases to support performance of the function described, as well as design of the computer code itself. $IDEF_1$ takes the form of ERA models (Entity Relation Attribute). Figure 11 contains an attribute diagram example for the Purchase Spare Parts module of the spares module shown above.

$IDEF_2$ now allows the system designer or the user of built systems to perform simulations to check first the general validity of a model and, secondly, the expected performance of the system which it represents in a particular scenario. These models again take different forms for different purposes; however, in all cases they operate off of the same data base as the information model.

An example $IDEF_2$ model is shown in Figure 12. All three models taken together provide sufficient information to conceptualize, design and build integrated systems. In actual practice, this approach is labeled the ICAM System Development Methodology (SDM). This SDM progress from "AS IS" scenarioios of today, to "TO BE" factories of tomorrow is in the eight step-four phase sequence of:

Needs Analysis

Requirements Definition

Understand the Problem

Preliminary Design

Detail Design

Formulate and Justify Solution

Construction and Verification Testing

Integration and Validation Testing

Construct and Integrate Solution

Implementation and User Acceptance

Maintenance and Support

Implement and Maintain Solution

Also included in the SDM are internal program management tools such as con-

ATTRIBUTE DIAGRAM EXAMPLE

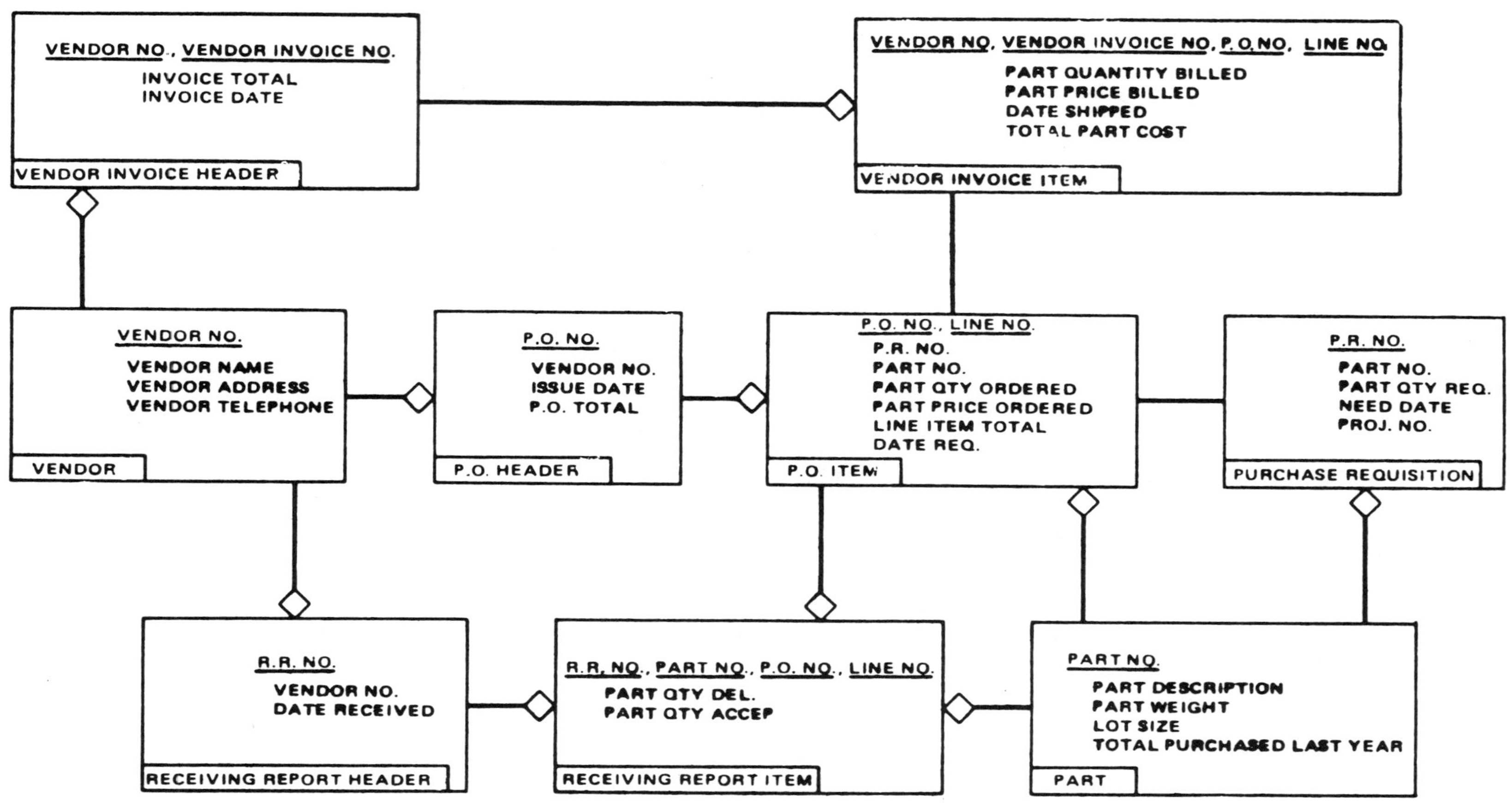

FIGURE 11

48

INSPECT AND ADJUST —
ENTITY FLOW DIAGRAM

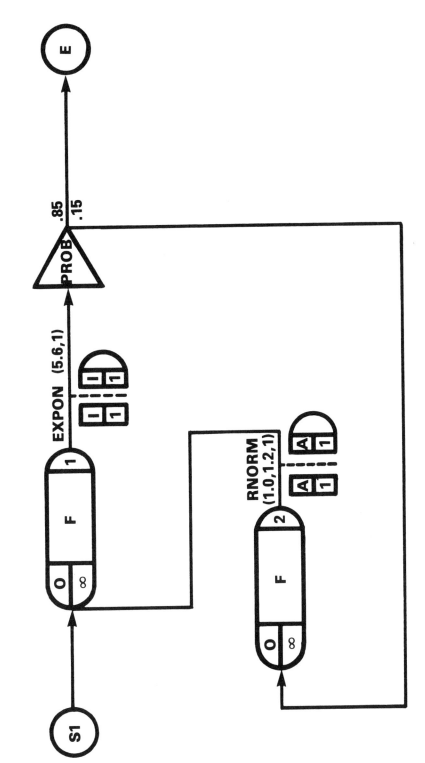

FIGURE 12

figuration control which enable the Air Force to manage all projects and aspects of the program.

Support Systems

While the architecture and integration methodologies of the ICAM Program serve the primary purpose of both its own integration and leading the way for industry, Support Systems are actual short term program spinoffs with immediate applicability. Included, for example, are Integrated Decision Support Systems, Group Technology Coding and Classification and a Manufacturing/Cost Design Guide.

The intent of the Integrated Decision Support System (IDSS) is to eliminate seat-of-the-pants decision making - that is, to use the computer as the tool of management. "What if" type of decisions are possible on a simple shop floor level - e.g., what if I buy a particular machine? - through the much more difficult question - what if my production run must be doubled?

The ICAM Group Technology Coding and Classification (GTCC) concept ranges from the use of geometric modeling, to define a particular part shape, through both its process planning and scheduling. Also included is the interaction with the IMCMM to perform dynamic routing through the shop.

Manufacturing Cost/Design Guide refers to a tool that the design engineer would use to help decide what materials and processes should be used to make a particular part based upon cost as well as performance. Of course, in the ICAM concept it is clear that both the MCDG and the GTCC would be part of IDSS. In fact, the user access to this total capability would be through another ICAM support system known as GUS (General Utilities System).

Applications Systems

These features of ICAM tend to either be more shop floor hardware related or to bridge the gap between the shop floor and higher levels of the architecture. The IMCMM is an example of the latter case. ICAM robotics is an example of the former as is a sheet metal formability project which has produced demonstrated algorithms able to predict the formability of a particular part on a particular machine and set up the machine to form the part correctly on the first try (19). This work also includes an advanced brake press which automatically compensates for springback.

The ICAM approach to robotics also illustrates another important concept of the Program.

(1) Look as far ahead as possible.

(2) Design an effort to start in that direction.

(3) Design an intermediate effort to learn from the start and move closer to the goal.

(4) Start 1-2-3 simultaneously repeating 2 and 3 as the goal gets closer.

Figure 13 shows how this is being done in robotics. A robot work station using today's technology was put in operation 12 months after contract start (16). A robotics cell is scheduled, in a second aerospace company, for 12 months later (22). Both of these projects are pointing the direction to the use of robots in a sheet metal assembly center.

ICAM Program Demonstrations

The ultimate demonstration of ICAM will be at the center level. Implementation of a sheet metal fabrication center is planned for the 1985 time period. Conceptual design of such a center has already been started. Figure 14 shows one of the candidate approaches. The roadmap of Figure 15 points the way toward this center.

Over the scheduled period, sheet metal fabrication and other manufac-

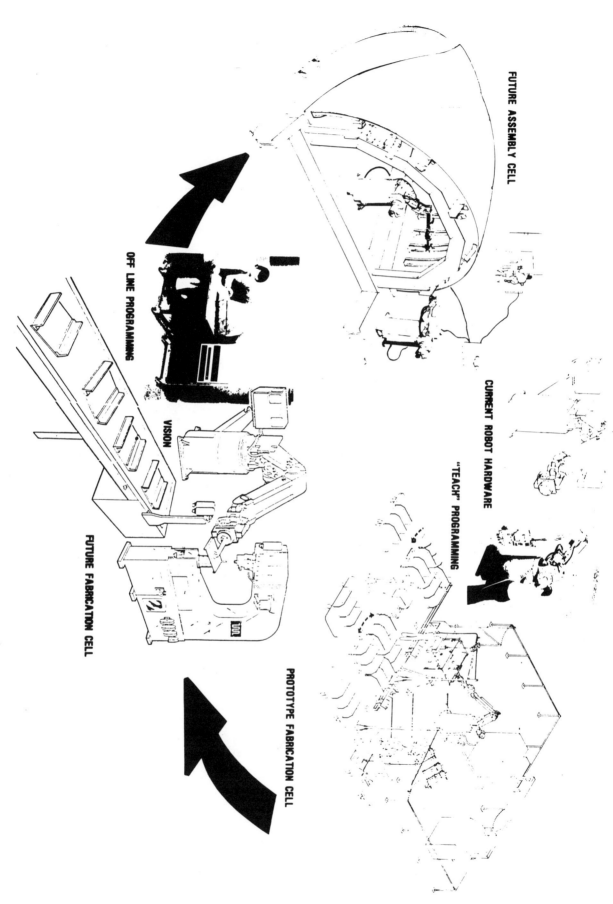

ICAM ROBOTICS PROJECTS

FUTURE ASSEMBLY CELL

CURRENT ROBOT HARDWARE

"TEACH" PROGRAMMING

OFF LINE PROGRAMMING

VISION

FUTURE FABRICATION CELL

PROTOTYPE FABRICATION CELL

FIGURE 13

52

ENABLING TECHNOLOGY FOR S/M FABRICATION (2105)

SHEET METAL CENTER "CIRCULAR" SYSTEM

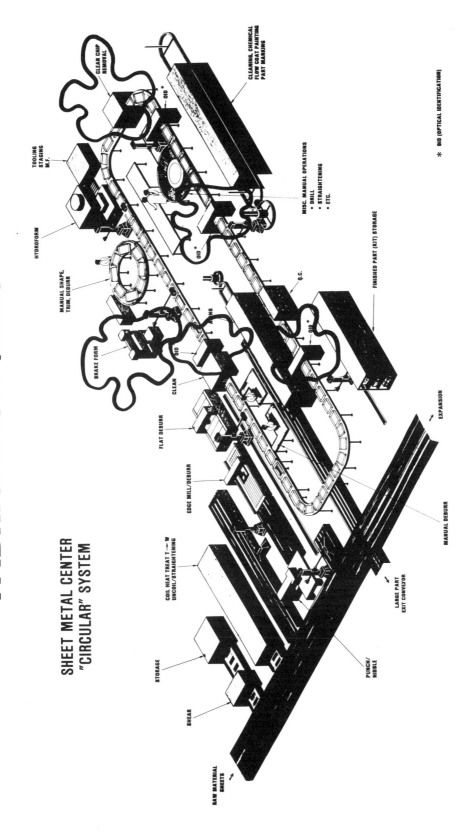

FIGURE 14

BASIC ICAM ROADMAP
FISCAL YEARS

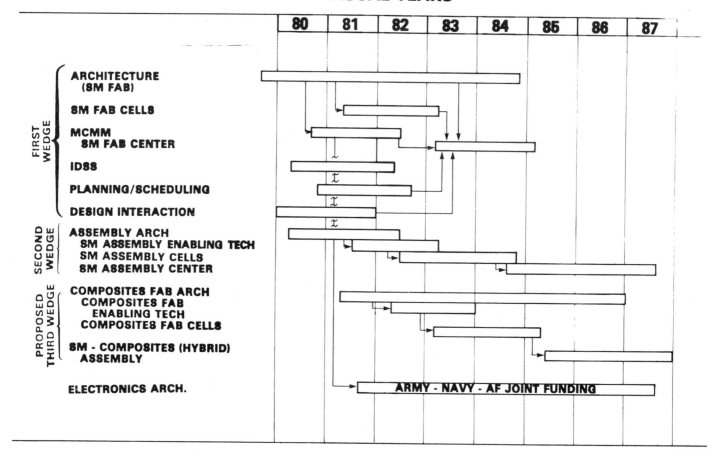

FIGURE 15

turing shop floor areas will be addressed as shown. A general assembly architecture will begin in FY80. From this assembly architecture will evolve a sheet metal subassembly center, composite fabrication projects and, toward the end of the ICAM Program, a hybrid center for assembly of composites to sheet metal. In the electronics area, it is also anticipated that the ICAM approach will be followed, but this will likely be a joint Army-Navy-Air Force CIM effort which uses the ICAM methodology.

The Payoff

The Air Force ICAM Program considers computer integrated manufacturing a continuously evolving "total technology." Some elements of it can be considered available today but need more logical and systematic application. Other elements may require substantial modification or even a complete change in approach.

For example, ICAM will allow planning ability permitting engineers not only to design a part optimally, but also to subject the part to performance evaluation, and to quickly plan its most economical fabrication with constraints of schedule, availability of raw materials and variability in materials and/or processes. Design and processing information will become available in standard data formats, deliverable promptly to management for "what if" simulation ranging from risk analysis to plan layout.

Deliverables of the program are useful individual products, but perhaps the major product will be the demonstration in production that ICAM, properly formatted and structured, synergistically raises efficiencies and can be harnessed to provide very substantial benefits at all levels of manufacturing management and operations.

Considering the ICAM Sheet Metal Center (Figure 14) as an example, the ICAM Program approach to evaluation of this center will include:

- independent/multiple work cells

- flexible routing

- automated handling, transfer, orientation & store

- accomodate work load & technology changes

- automated nesting & patterning

- automated tool change & set-up

- operation from central control

- freedom from lot size & frequency

and perhaps most importantly, a:

- system organization to permit

  * phased development & implementation

  * addition of new cells

  * accomodation of a range of user requirements

Performers

The ICAM Program is a learn-by-doing effort. Projects are conducted by various different contractors. While their near-term results are relatively independent, in the longer term they will all be integrated through (1) the architecture, (2) simulation, (3) the demonstration centers. The list of initial projects and contractors (Figure 16) gives an indication of some of the integration required. It is important to remember that each project shown has its own independent deliverables and that all of these deliverables must integrate into the whole of the program. The ICAM coalition contractor style - combined with the architecture - virtually insures that this integration will occur. Figure 17 shows Prime (P) - Subcontractor (S) relationships throughout the Program. Both technology transfer and integration are brought about by the Prime-Subcontractor role reversal which occurs throughout the Program.

Project	Project Title	Contractor
1102(1)	Architecture II. Function Model	Rockwell
1102(2)	Architecture II. Information Model	Hughes
1102(3)	Architecture II. Integration	SofTech
1102(4)	Architecture II. Tools	Boeing Computer Services
1102(5)	Architecture II. User Model	Higher Order Software
1102(6)	Architecture II. Design Interface	Northrop
1202	Alternate Architecture Displays	Boeing
1302	Hypothesis of New Standards	NBS
2103	Sheet Metal Center Concept Design	Boeing
2104	Sequential Forming of Sheet Metal Parts	MIT
4201	GUS Requirements Analysis	Boeing Computer Services
5202	Group Technology Characterization Coding for Sheet Metal	Vought
5204	Geometric Modeling for Process Planning	Aachen
5301	Sheet Metal Forming/Process Modeling	Battelle
6101	Manufacturing Control/Material Management	General Electric
6102	Job Shop Control	Salford
8201	ICAM Decision Support System Prototype	Hughes
8201A	ICAM Decision Support System	Higher Order Software
9104A	Robotic Station	General Dynamics
9104B	Robotic Cell	McDonnell Douglas
9104C	Robotics Applications for Assembly	Lockheed
9105	Robotics Standards	NBS
9301	Material Flow Characteristics	Research Triangle Inst.

FY 79 NEW PROJECT LISTING

1303	Human Factors for ICAM Implementation	Honeywell
5101A	Manufacturing Cost/Design Guide Data	Battelle
5101B	MC/DG Computerization	Grumman Aircraft

ICAM PROJECTS
FIGURE 16

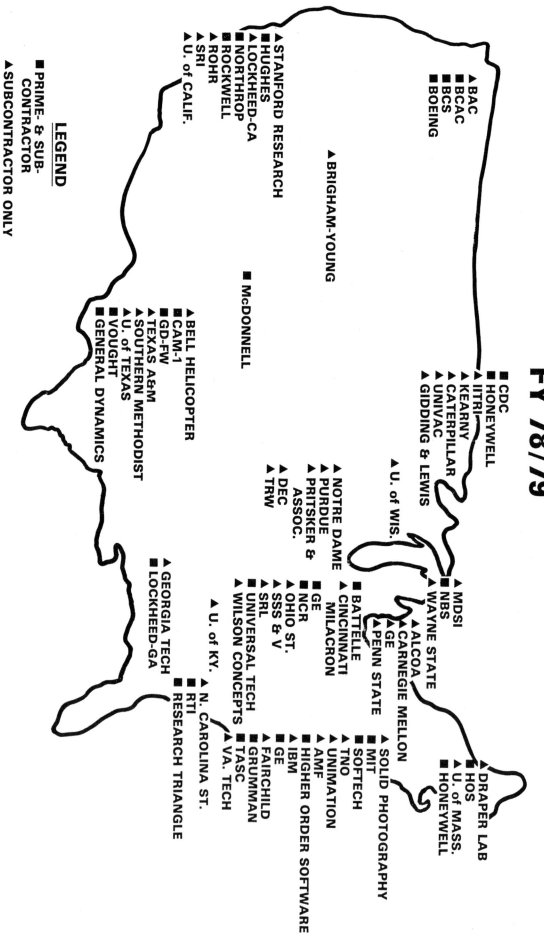

ICAM CONTRACTORS
FY 78/79

LEGEND

■ PRIME- & SUB-CONTRACTOR

■ PRIME- & SUB-
CONTRACTOR

▲ SUBCONTRACTOR ONLY

FIGURE 17

58

The mechanism by which ICAM is to be implemented rests heavily on involvement with the private sector. This sector is the destined user and must eventually supply the bulk of the funding as each industry and manufacturing establishment evolves its operation toward the methodology resulting from ICAM. The early participation and cooperation of the private sector with the Air Force is thus a vital aspect of the ICAM Program.

As in the case of other Air Force manufacturing technology projects, ICAM projects are being contracted out to the private sector. Emphasis is being placed on coalition efforts (cooperating groups of contractors or subcontractors) on the same project. This approach has proven attractive to industry, allows formulation of results in industry-oriented style and facilitates rapid transfer of results to users. As a further incentive and to provide additional communication, there are mechanisms for periodic review by the private sector for an Industry Fellows Program and Summer Faculty Program and for timely workshops and symposia.

In its ultimate integrated form, ICAM would allow production only barely within our ability to comprehend now, managerially and technically. Figure 18 shows the ICAM "Dream Chart" of the future manufacturing environment.

ICAM payoffs will be multi-dimensional and will occur in both "hard" technical areas and in more intangible ways as a result of changes in attitude and organizational thinking. While the latter is difficult to measure or predict in dollar terms and will vary from organization to organization, a positive result in terms of improved productivity is virtually assured. For example, efficiency will be improved simply by the replacement of the computer "application" concept of non-synchronized departmental functions in favor of a controlling data base concept. The demonstrated

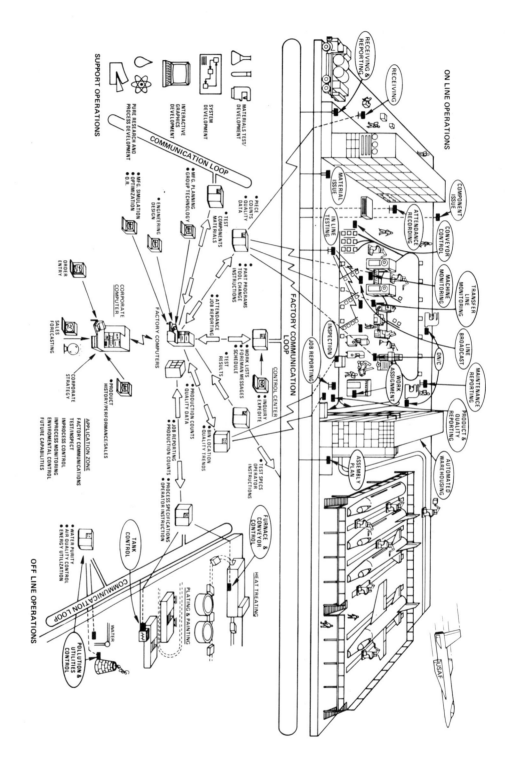

COMPUTER INTEGRATED MANUFACTURING

FIGURE 18

advantages of integration will thus bring about a change in management philosophy and an end to numerous inefficiencies.

Prediction is simpler in the "hard" areas and relatively easy to demonstrate in technical projects like robotics. One major aerospace corporation has estimated that their five-year internal ICAM project will result in a significant reduction in their overhead. The program for the DoD bulk buy of Numerical Controlled Machine Tools in 1956 required an investment of $40 million, but is providing a multi-billion-dollar payoff. Today's government ICAM investment should also provide a multi-billion-dollar payoff.

Modern surveys of relative productivity indicate that a factor on the order of 38 percent of improvement in productivity is due to new technology and that improved technology is by far the largest factor in productivity improvement.

ICAM is a major investment in new technology, not for the sake of the knowledge, but to insure that the resultant significant productivity improvement is placed on the agenda.

Meeting this goal requires a long-range aim. However, work done in other countries indicates that with the proper foundation, the U.S. can retain a manufacturing leadership role in the 1990's. The basic requirement today is commitment and cooperation for the systematic development of a logical approach to manufacturing automation and computer management.

REFERENCES

(1)   (a) "IPAD Prospectus", NASA Langley Research Center, Hampton, Virginia, February 10, 1975.

      (b) "IPAD Introductory Manual", NASA Contract NASI-14700 to Boeing Commercial Airplane Co., Seattle, Washington, November, 1977 Provisional Draft.

(2) By way of example, the number of specialized material data information centers alone is too great to describe exhaustively, but a representative few may be cited:

      (a) Thermophysical properties - Purdue University, Lafayette, Indiana

      (b) Radiological properties - Battelle Memorial Institute, Columbus, Ohio

      (c) X-Ray scatter - American Society for Testing Materials, Pittsburgh, Pennsylvania

      (d) Standard thermodynamic data - National Bureau of Standards, Washington, D.C.

      (e) Electromagnetic spectral data - Sadtler Labs, Philadelphia, Pennsylvania

      (f) Chemical properties - Chemical Abstracts, Columbus, Ohio

(3) "Manufacturing Technology: A Changing Challenge to Improve Productivity", Fred Haynes, GAO Report 3, June, 1976.

(4) "Robots in Metal Working", a review symposium in American Machinist, Vol. 119, No. 20, p. 87 (November, 1975).

(5) "Indirect Costs: A Productivity Issue for Manufacturing Technology", John C. Williams (IIT Research Institute), in Manufacturing Productivity Frontiers, Vol. 3, No. 4, p. 1-6, July, 1979.

(6) "Distributed Data Processing", Special Report/22 in Computerworld, CW Communications, Inc., Boston, Massachussetts, 30 July, 1979.

(7) "Manufacturing Technology - A Changing Challenge to Improve Productivity". Report to the Congress by the Comptroller General of the United States (Report LCD-75-436, 3 June, 1976).

(8) "Challenges to Manufacturing", a luncheon address presented at the

Computers in Manufacturing Conference, Chicago, Illinois, June 27, 1979, by Allan M. Christman.

(9) "Worldwide Computer-Aided Manufacturing Survey, 13 August - 10 September, 1977", Trip Report by Dennis E. Wisnosky, AFML/LTC, 1 December, 1977.

(10) "Air Force Computer Aided Manufacturing (AFCAM) Master Plan", AFML-TR-74-104, July, 1974.

(11) "Computer-Integrated Manufacturing", Joseph Harrington, Jr., Industrial Press, Inc., New York, New York, 1973, and Reprint, 1979.

(12) "Program Management Plan for ICAM", Manufacturing Technology Division, Air Force Materials Laboratory, Air Force Wright Aeronautical Laboratories, WPAFB, Ohio, 1 December, 1977.

(13) "Passing the Threshold into the Information Age - Perspective for Federal Action on Information", Giuliano, U. et al (Arthur D. Little, Inc.), Cambridge, Massachussetts, NSF, Washington, D.C., Division of Science Information, January, 1978. PB 281-720, PB 281-721.

(14) "Standards for Computer-Aided Manufacturing", National Bureau of Standards (NBS) (under AFML Contract MIPR FY 14577600369). Interim Reports NBSIR 76-1094 (R) dated June, 1976, October, 1976 and January, 1977. Final Report, AFML-TR-77-145, January, 1978.

(15) "The ICAM Program Report", issued periodically by AFML/LTC, WPAFB, Ohio 45433 (First issue, Vol. 1, No. 1, June, 1978).

(16) "ICAM Project 9104A Robotic Station", Contractor General Dynamics - Fort Worth, Texas, Air Force Project Manager Ms. Rosann Stach.

(17) ICAM Project 1102(4) Tools, SofTech, Inc., Waltham, Massachussetts, Subcontracted to Boeing Computer Services and Control Data Corp.

(18) F-16 Technology Modernization Program, Reference MTAG Keynote Address, October 22, 1979, General Alton D. Slay.

(19) ICAM Project 5301 "Sheet Metal Forming/Process Modeling", Battelle Columbus Laboratories, Michael Moscynski, Project Manager.

(20) "ICAM Architecture Task I", SofTech, Inc., Waltham, Massachussetts, Final Report AFML-TR-78-148.

(21) ICAM Project 6101 - MCMM, General Electric Corp., Schenectady, New York, ICAM Project Manger David Judson.

(22) ICAM Project 9104B "Robotic Cell", Coauthor McDonnell Douglas Corp., St. Louis, Missouri, AF Project Manager Michael Moscynski.

DENNIS E. WISNOSKY

Dennis E. Wisnosky was born in Washington, Pennsylvania. He received his B.S. degree in Physics and Mathematics from California State College (PA) in 1965. While working on his Masters degree in Electrical Engineering (University of Pittsburgh, 1968), he worked as a research associate at the Mellon Institute (now part of Carnegie Mellon University). Following this, he was Director of R&D for Bruker Scientific, Inc., Elmsford, New York where he served for a time in the West German Headquarters. From 1971 until 1975, Mr. Wisnosky was with the Air Force Materials Laboratory, serving as the Chief of Computer and Information Services, a function which he founded. From early 1976 to June, 1980, he served as Manager of the Air Force Program for Integrated Computer Aided Manufacturing (ICAM). He has been very active in community activities, has received two Air Force Outstanding Performance Ratings, has been in the Executive Development Program and has published widely in several different fields. He received the Bicentennial Manufacturing Achievement Award (1976) and the Manufacturing Achievement Award (1977) from the Society of Manufacturing Engineers. He earned his second Masters degree (in Management Science) from the University of Dayton in August of 1977.

Mr. Wisnosky is currently the Manager of the Manufacturing Organization and Automation Technology Center at International Harvester.

CHAPTER 3

HIERARCHICAL APPROACH TO A CAM SYSTEM

Hierarchical Approach To A CAM System

By Kazuto Togino
Director
Matsushita Research Institute Tokyo Inc.

This paper shows how the hierarchical approach formed by Mesarovic and others[1] can apply to the analysis and synthesis of actual CAM systems. Taking the actual system CAM-1, some intelligent machines and an Automatic Programming system for programmable Sequence controllers (APS system), the analysis and synthesis in terms of "strata" and "layers" is described. Analyzing the CAM-1 system, a decentralized computer aided manufacturing system, in which participants are involved not as an instrument but as a decision maker motivated, is mapped out to oneself as a multiechelon system. The CAM system would be not only a technical innovation, but also an organizational innovation.

1. INTRODUCTION

It is a matter of course that increasing the productivity in Japanese metalworking industries is an important problem for the Government from now on. However, there are many barriers to overcome which have never been experienced. The creation of technical innovation to overcome these barriers is a national and social need. The CAM system is the most important technical innovation and must be accelerated. It is to be noted that the CAM system is not only a technical innovation, but also an organizational innovation. I would like to say that the CAM system should be viewed from the angle of the organizational innovation rather than the technical innovation.

Mesarovic's hierarchical approach[1] gives us an important tool for the CAM system, but this approach has not been applied. In this paper, the actual system "CAM-1 system", which consists of a computer aided production planning system and a computer aided NC programming system, is analyzed in terms of "strata" and "layers". This paper also describes how the APS system (Automatic Programming system for programmable Sequence controller) is synthesized in terms of layers (levels of decision making). Since the APS system would become an essential subsystem as well as the APT system, the outline of the basic APT system is described.

Analyzing these systems, a decentralized computer aided manufacturing system would be mapped out to oneself as a multiechelon system. In the decentralized system, participants are involved not as instruments merely carrying out an assigned task in the most efficient manner, but as a decision maker solving subproblems.

2. STRATIFIED DESCRIPTION OF CAM SYSTEM

Mesarovic defines the strata as follows: One describes the system by a family of models in which each model is concerned with the behavior (i.e., input-output) of the system as viewed from a different level of abstraction. For each level, there is a set of relevant features and variables, laws and principles in terms of which system's behavior is described. For such a hierarchical description to be effective, it is necessary that the functioning on any level be as independent of the functioning on other levels as possible. We use the term "stratified system" or "stratified description" in this concept of hierarchy.

As an illustration, consider two examples of the CAM systems which need a stratified description. One is an intelligent machine, and the second is an integrated manufacturing system.

Stratified Description of an Intelligent Machine

Roscher told us by the following allegory that the roundabout method of production gives us higher productivity. "A fisherman can catch three fish a day with bare hands. When he makes a boat and a net, by sharing a part of his labor, he can catch thirty fish a day with the assistance of the boat and the net." Adopting Roscher's allegory to a numerically controlled machine shop in metalworking industries, the boat corresponds to a machine tool, the net to a numerical control tape and the fish to machined parts.

In order to increase the production, the machining process has been motorized and automated. The motorization and automation is modeled on three strata as shown in Fig. 1: the level of power (motorization in the machining process), the level of intelligence (computerization in the information processing) and the level of diagnosis (automating of the diagnostic function for maintenance). The top level is an essential function to the unmanned factory like Williamson's "System 24" in order to realize a high production rate. This function could shorten the down time, which is the time for detecting and repairing something wrong in intelligent machines. Fig. 1 does not illustrate a hierarchical model of automation; it illustrates how the roundabout method of production is adapted to the metal working industries.

For detailed illustration of the intelligence, consider the second level of Fig. 1 in reference to the preparation of production planning and NC tape for the NC machine shop. The operator is more productive with the assistance of programs (production schedule and NC tapes) than direct communication with individual NC machine tools. The roundabout method of production as seen in the production schedule and NC tapes shows two levels above the NC machine shop, as shown in Fig. 2.

Integrated Manufacturing System: CAM-1

The CAM-1 system has been developed by the Toshiba Machine Company, Ltd., a machine tool builder. The company is at present developing a more advanced CAM-N system. The system is for a job shop type of machine shop. The system is stratified as shown in Fig. 3.

The top stratum is a master plan stratum in which the production for two years to come is planned at the beginnning of the calendar month. The inputs are firm and forecasted orders, and the constraint is capacities allowed to be loaded. The master plan is mapped out by a simulation model called PPSS (Production Parts Simulation System).

The second stratum is a scheduling stratum. The following section illustrates how jobs are scheduled on a calendar day. The lowest stratum is a machine shop possessing 83 conventional machine tools and a DNC controlling 13 NC machines at the present time.

3. LAYERS: LEVELS OF DECISION COMPLEXITY

Mesarovic defines the layer as follows: In complex decision-making situations, the solution of any problem is sought in a hierarchical approach. Essentially, one defines a family of decision problems whose solution is attempted in a sequential manner, in the sense that the solution of any problem in the sequence determines and fixes some parameters in the subsequent problem, so that the latter is completely specified and its solution can be attempted; the solution of the original problem is achieved when all subproblems are solved. This arrangement is represented diagramatically in Fig. 4(a). The output of a decision unit represents a solution which depends upon a parameter fixed by the output of a decision unit on a higher level. Such a hierarchy is referred to as a hierarchy of decision layers.

Manufacturing process P has two inputs: a manipulated input m from a given set M (a set of alternative actions) and an input u from a given set U (a set of uncertainties). It has also an output y in a given set of outcomes Y. The existence of uncertainties makes the decision problem complex. The functional hierarchy in decision making as shown in Fig. 4 contains three layers: (1) the selection of strategies to be used in the solution process, (2) the reduction or elimination of uncertainties and (3) the search for a preferable or acceptable course of action under prespecified conditions.

Consider these two examples: one is the APS system, which is an automatic programming system for programmable sequence controllers of sequentially controlled transfer lines; the second is the scheduling process in the CAM-1 system.

Decision Hierarchy in Generation of Sequence Control Program

Programmable controllers (PC) are widely used as a soft-wired sequence controller with micro-computer in place of a hard-wired sequence controller with relays. Fig. 5 shows the main technological planning steps for the generation of a sequence control program of the transfer line from the part geometry. All these steps are necessary whether or not they are programmed automatically. These steps are similar to the technological planning steps for the generation of a numerical control program.

The sequence program to PC is generally in ladder diagrams and is manually loaded by the program loader. The ladder diagram is designed from the sequential motion of machines by skilled engineers in the engineering department. The APS system will assist the designer generating the ladder diagram from the sequential motion sheet (APS sheet). The APS sheet is helpful in standardizing the description of the sequential motion of machine units. Fig. 6 shows the outline of the APS system, in which the output is from a prototype APS system.

Decision Hierarchy in the CAM-1 System

The CAM-1 system assists operators in their production planning and NC programming. The machine shop possesses 83 conventional machine tools operated manually and 13 NC machine tools controlled by a DNC system.

As shown in Fig. 7, the system consists of two subsystems: one is the computer aided production planning system, and the second is the computer aided NC programming system.

1) Computer Aided Production Planning System

A decision-making hierarchy contains five layers in the computer aided production planning system. The task of the master plan layer in the fifth level is to allocate firm and forecasted orders (jobs) on the calendar month for two years. The planner, as a decision maker, makes the master plan and replan watching capacities available for the machines on PPSS (Production Parts Simulation System).

The task of the fourth level is to explode a job into parts. The task of the third level is to calculate the standard lead time of the parts associated with the job. Since the parts are sequentially processed by several machine tools, the lead time

of each machining process is calculated with the following e-
quation: LT (Lead Time) = + A/B, where = 2, 1 or 0, A is
the estimated machining time, B is the available time of machining process and unit of the time is one day.

In the second level, there are two tasks: one is to check
whether or not the parts are in time for the due date; the
second is to check whether or not the load for the machines is
available. A production planner as a decision maker gives a
parameter (d) of priority equation as follows: If the job is
in time, $\propto$ = 2 and d = 1.0. If the job is not in time, $\propto$ = 1
and d = 1.3; furthermore, if the job is not in time, $\propto$ = 0 and
d = 1.5. He also checks peak loads and shifts the date releasing the parts for smoothing loads in the machine shop.

The task of the first level is to make the daily schedule on
the calendar month. The allocation of the parts to the machine
shop (releasing) is set by the priority (P) of the parts, which
is calculated by the following equation:

$$P = (a*x + b*y + c*z) * d$$
x: parameter for minimizing tardiness $(0 \leq x \leq 9)$
y: parameter for increasing the productivity
   of the machine shop; the shorter processing
   time is the larger value $(0 \leq y \leq 9)$
z: parameter for minimizing the total time on
   the floor; the value is in proportion to the
   number of machining process $(0 \leq z \leq 9)$
a, b, c: weight $(1 \leq a, b, c \leq 8, a+b+c = 10$

2) Computer Aided NC Programming System

The right side of Fig. 7 shows four layers of decision making
in the computer aided NC programming system; tool selection,
determination of cutting condition, cutter path generation and
post-processing and NC tape selection. In the NC tape selection level, the DNC system selects the NC tape of the parts to
be machined.

4. MULTIECHELON SYSTEMS: ORGANIZATIONAL HIERARCHIES

In order that the manufacturing system is flexible and adaptive
to uncertainties in an economical environment, the structure of
a manufacturing system must be dynamic. In order that participants be motivated, they must not be "instruments" merely carrying out an assigned task in a most efficient manner.

A modern manufacturing process, in general, involved uncertainties regarding the consequences of implementing various alternative actions. These uncertainties make the decision-making
process complicated. In order to solve the complex problem,
we decompose the problem into subproblems. This means that the
overall goal is decomposed into subgoals. The subgoals, in

general, conflict with each other. For example, a conflict is found out between minimization of inprocess inventories and the minimization of idle-time of machines.

Mesarovic[1] defines the echelon as follows: It is necessary that: (1) the system consists of a family of interacting sub-systems which are recognized explicitly, (2) some of the sub-systems be defined as decision (making) units and (3) the decision units be arranged hierarchically, in the sense that some of them are influenced or controlled by other decision units. A diagram of a system of this type is given in Fig. 8.

A level in such a system is called an echelon. These systems will be referred to also as multiechelon, multilevel and multi-goal because various decision units comprising the system have, in general, conflicting goals. This conflict appears as the result of the evolution and composition of the system. This conflict is necessary for efficient operation of the overall system.

The decision units in Fig. 8 could be computer algorithms or operators as instruments if there were no uncertainties. In the modern manufacturing system, the participant is viewed as a decision maker; he recognizes levels of satisfaction and discrepencies between the actual and operational goal and feed-back to the decision maker at his upper level. He also coordinates decision makers at his next lower level.

In such a multiechelon CAM system, participants as decision makers are assisted by their personal computers, and their efforts satisfying their subgoals are consistent with the overall goal.

5. CONCLUSIONS

The CAM system is not a real system, but a concept. Therefore, the number of CAM systems could be equal to the number of developers of the CAM system. It is recommendable that the basic guide of the CAM system is based on the hierarchical approach in terms of strata, layers and echelons.

This paper analyzes and evaluates the existing CAM systems and a subsystem of the CAM system being developed from this point of view. It also points out that the future CAM system must be designed so as to motivate participants; they are not instrumental, but intellectual.

In order that the CAM system be adaptive to the ever-changing social environment, the system must be metabolic. If the CAM system is developed on the basis of the above hierarchical approach, it would evolve into a desirable system. Such evolution is called "orthogenesis". The CAM system is not only a technical innovation, but also an organizational innovation.

REFERENCES

1 M.D. Mesarovic, D. Macko and Y. Takahara: Theory of Hierarchical, Multilevel Systems, vol. 68, Mathematics in science
  and engineering, Academic Press, 1970.

2 K. Togino: CAM System in Unmanned Factories, Proc. Intl.
  Conf. on Production Engineering, Tokyo, 1974.

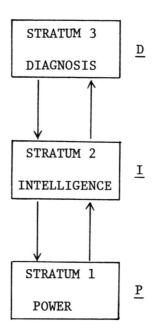

A THREE STRATA DIAGRAM
OF AN AUTOMATED MACHINE

FIG. 1

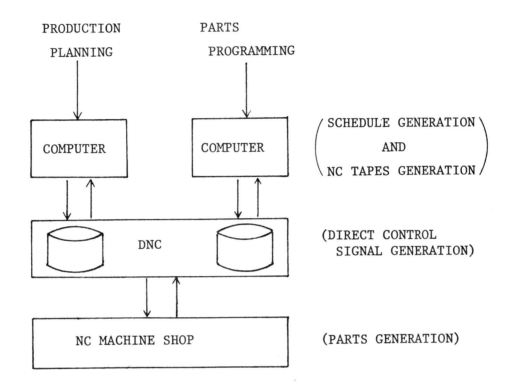

A THREE STRATA DIAGRAM
OF A PARTS GENERATING MACHINE

FIG. 2

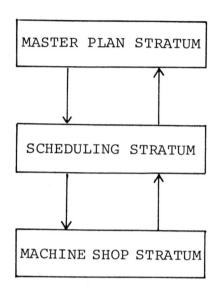

A THREE STRATA DIAGRAM OF CAM-1 SYSTEM

FIG. 3

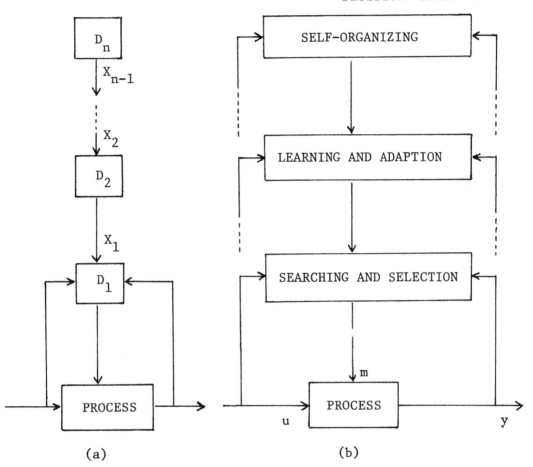

(a)

(b)

MULTILAYER HIERARCHY OF A DECISION MAKING SYSTEM
AND A FUNCTIONAL THREE-LAYER DIAGRAM OF DECISION HIERARCHY

FIG. 4

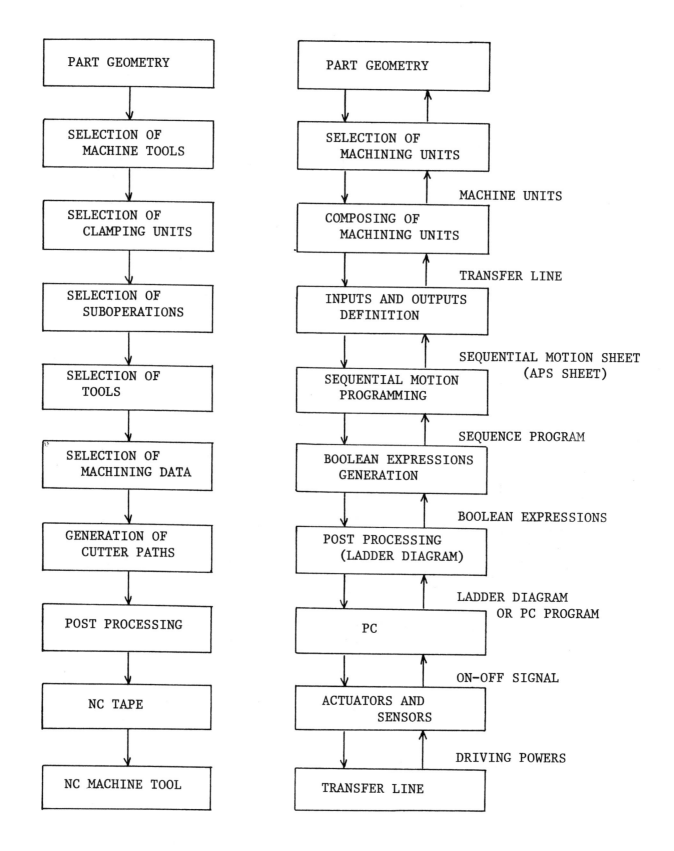

DECISION MAKING HIERARCHY OF PLANNING PROCESS OF A TRANSFER LINE
COMPARED TO NC PROGRAMMING PROCESS

FIG. 5

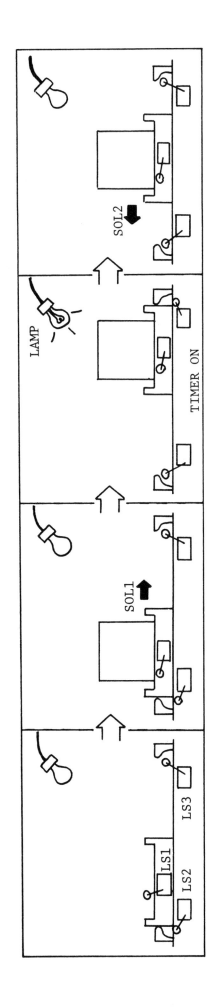

SEQUENTIAL MOTION OF A UNIT

FIG. 6 (a)

81

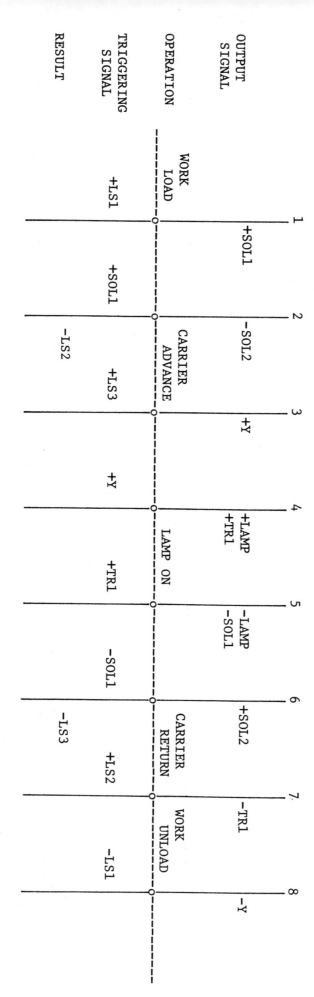

SEQUENTIAL MOTION CHART

FIG. 6 (b)

```
SPNAME/ APS EXAMPLE MACHINE
CYCLE/ CAR1
INPUT/ (LS1=0,'WORK DETECT') , (LS2=1,'BACKWARD EXTREMETY') , $
       (LS3=0,'FORWARD EXTREMETY') ,
                    ⋮

OUTPUT/ (SOL1=0,'FORWARD SOLENOID') ,                              $
                 ⋮

RUN=SET(AUTO=1,STRT=1,LS1=0,LS2=1,LS3=0)
RUN=RST(PB1=1)
MODE/ AUTO (RUN=1)
OPER/1
SOL1=SET(LS1=1,LS2=1,Y=0)
OPER/2
SOL2=RST(SOL1=1)
RESULT/ LS2=0
OPER/3
Y=SET(LS3=1)
OPER/4
LAMP=SET(Y=1,LS3=1)
TR1=SET(Y=1,LS3=1)
OPER/5
LAMP=RST(TR1=1)
SOL1=RST(TR1=1)
OPER/6
SOL2=SET(SOL1=0)
RESULT/ LS3=0
OPER/7
TR1=RST(LS2=1)
QPER/8
Y=RST(LS1=0)
MODE/ MAN (MAN=1)
SOL1=SET(PB2=1)
SOL2=SET(PB3=1)
LAMP=SET(PB4=1)
END/ CAR1
FINI/
```

INPUT DATA (SEQUENCE PROGRAM)

FIG. 6 (c)

```
RUN=(/PB1)*(AUTO*STRT*/LS1*LS2*/LS3+RUN)
Y=RUN*(LS1)*(LS3+Y)
TR1=RUN*(/LS2)*(Y*LS3+TR1)
SOL1=RUN*(/TR1)*(LS1*LS2*/Y+SOL1)+MAN*PB2
SOL2=RUN*(/SOL1)*(/SOL1+SOL2)+MAN*PB3
LAMP=RUN*(/TR1)*(Y*LS3+LAMP)+MAN*PB4
```

OUTPUT-1 (BOOLEAN EQUATION)

FIG. 6 (d)

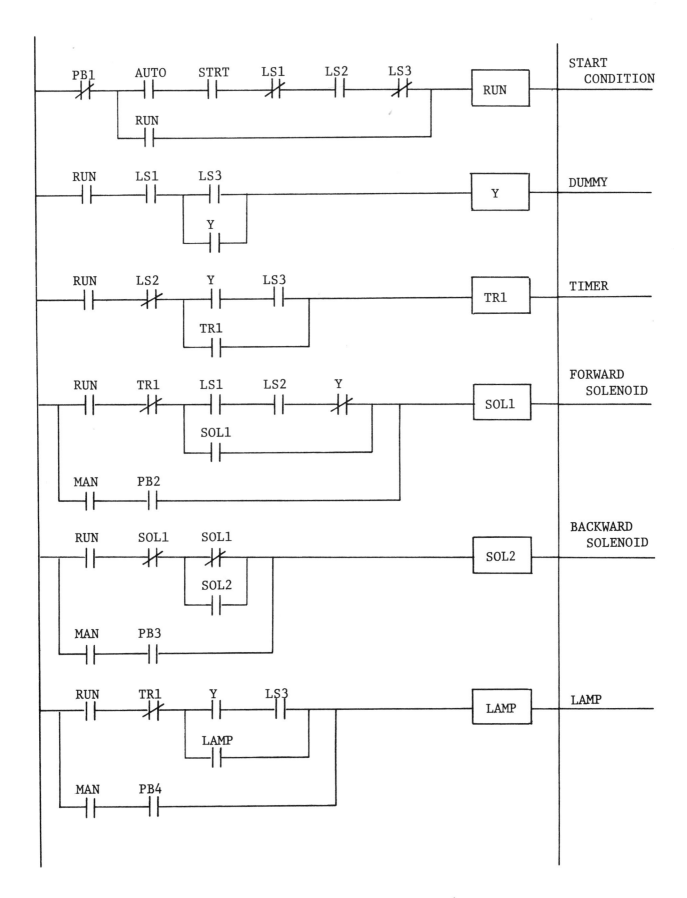

OUTPUT-2 (LADDER DIAGRAM)

FIG. 6 (e)

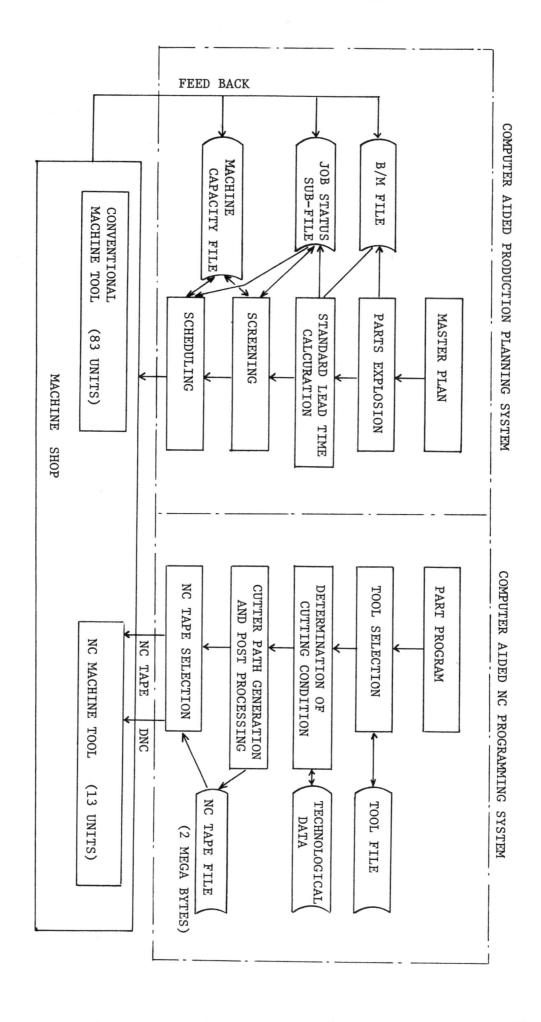

DECISION HIERARCHY IN CAM-1 SYSTEM

FIG. 7

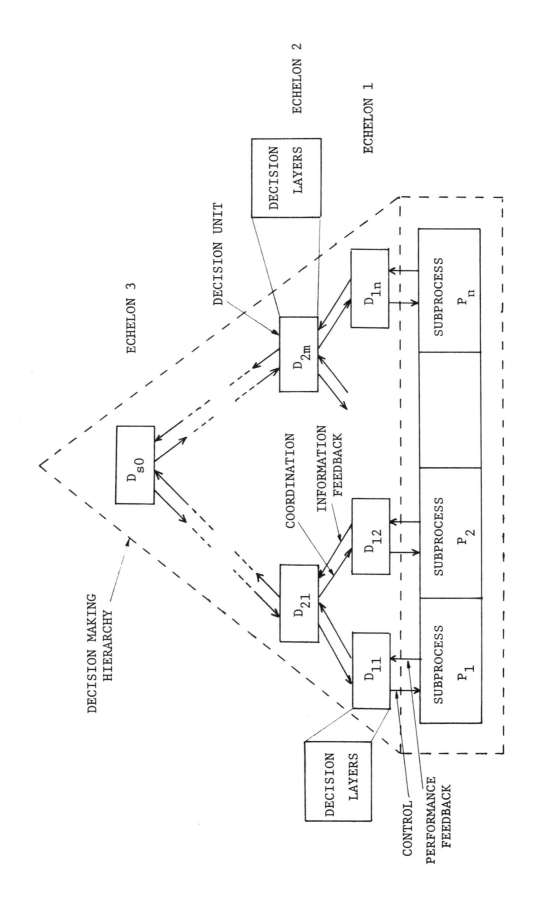

MULTIECHELON SYSTEM

FIG. 8

87

CHAPTER 4

COMPUTER GRAPHICS

Computer Graphics Benefits For Manufacturing Tasks That Rely Directly On The Engineering Design Data Base

By Aaron Feder
and Ken Victor
Northrop Corporation
Aircraft Division

Accurate, complete and timely engineering design data is mandatory for manufacturing tasks, such as numerical control, tool design and quality control inspection, etc. Computer graphics saves considerable time and money by passing design data to the manufacturing organization for usage on the CRT. Engineering/manufacturing coordination is thus provided, duplication of work is avoided and manufacturing functions efficiently done on-line by the computer are performed. Northrop uses either the 2-dimensional CADAM or the 3-dimensional CADD, depending on various criteria for cost effectiveness. Specific examples are presented of the productivity thus attained for design and fabrication of the F-18 vertical tail, inlet ramp structure and hydraulic tube routing. Problem areas are defined.

INTRODUCTION

For the past ten years, computer graphics usage has been slowly developing in the aircraft industry with limited success for engineering designs, tooling drawings, quality control inspection, generating cutter path data for numerically controlled machines, and for creating a common geometry data base. Northrop, in the last year, has taken advantage of computer graphics technology to decrease costs in performing the above mentioned tasks. Northrop uses a Lockheed-Northrup developed Computer Aided Design And Manufacturing (CADAM) system and a McDonnell Douglas developed Computer Aided Design Drafting (CADD) system. Northrop did not elect to use the CADD companion programs, such as GNC, CAQA, CALL, etc. No attempt was made to compare the total capability of the two systems; only the way Northrop uses them is described herein.

CADD serves most cost-effectively at Northrop as a complex three-dimensional (3-D) design problem solver, to create layouts, and for premockup design visualization; while CADAM serves best as a detailed production drafting tool. Thus, the simpler CADAM is used for two-dimensional (2-D) drafting, dimensioning, notes, schematics and details. CADD is used to study, visualize and lay out complex parts, such as landing gear installation and motion confirmation and definition of geometry clearance problems - none of which could be accomplished in a reasonable time nor with sufficient accuracy on the two-dimensional drafting board.

An automated tie between CADD and CADAM allows 3-D data to be extracted from the CADD data base and converted into a CADAM drawing. Thus, CADD is used for its upstream function (layouts/studies); the resulting 3-D geometry data is converted to a 2-D geometry format, which is then transmitted onto CADAM for use in making detailed drawings or numerically controlled cutter paths.

Figure 1 describes the best uses for each of the systems.

CADAM AND CADD EACH HAVE THEIR PLACE

FOR IMPROVED PRODUCTIVITY

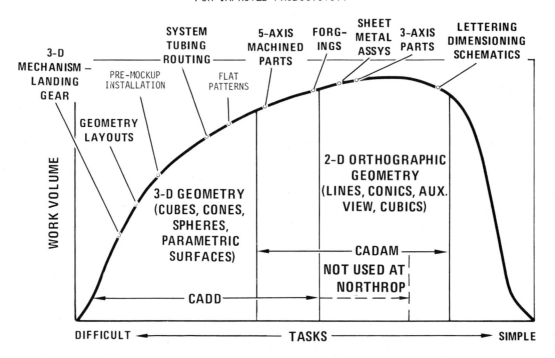

FIGURE 1

If the designer and his manager are clever, then the "family tree concept", depicted in Figure 2, is used. Thus, not only are productivity benefits obtained from making detailed drawings, but these benefits are multiplied if the layout of that section is also done by computer graphics using loft and analysis inputs. Then - by erasing, adding various auxiliary views on the CRT, adding notes, details, call-outs, fastener patterns, moving entities around, etc. - assembly drawings are completed based on the geometry data base. In a similar way, details and machine parts drawings use the layout geometry as a time saving start.

If you are especially clever, detailed drawings are then passed on to manufacturing where tool design uses the engineering geometry for: template design, for tooling hole coordination, and as a time saving start for accurate holding and tooling fixtures, etc. Numerical control programs the 3- or 5-axis machine cutter path directly on the CRT, superimposed on an edited and modified engineering drawing. The developed cutter path is replayed and the cutting parameters are verified and most errors are easily found.

Quality Control directly compares dimensions on the CRT anywhere on the drawing with that actually measured on the produced part, without having to measure the drawing with a scale or do manual trigonometric analysis.

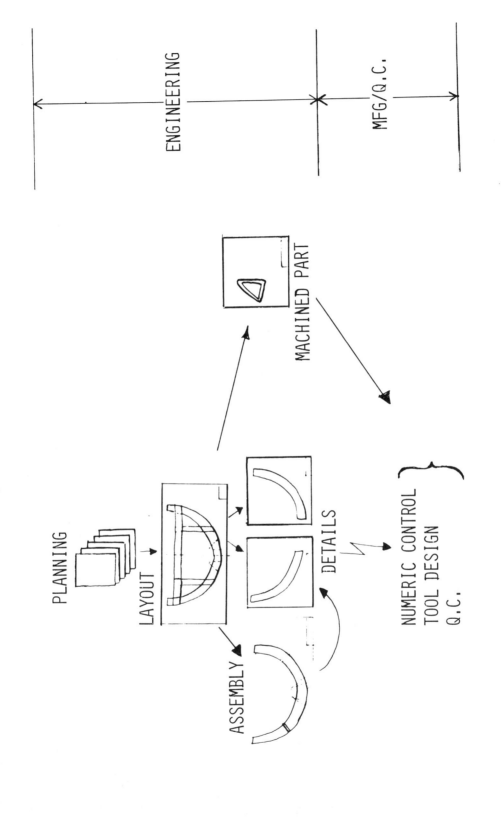

"FAMILY TREE" CONCEPT SAVES WORK

PLANNING

LAYOUT

ASSEMBLY

DETAILS

NUMERIC CONTROL
TOOL DESIGN
Q.C.

MACHINED PART

ENGINEERING

MFG/Q.C.

FIGURE 2

93

B. MANUFACTURING BENEFITS FROM COMPUTER GRAPHICS

Three representative examples are given herein defining the productivity benefits obtained when manufacturing uses data created by engineering on the CRT terminal and stored in the computer for common use.

1. Automated Hydraulic Tubing Design and Production

In the past, Northrop aircraft tubing has been "mocked up", manually bent and fitted to the proper clearance on the mockup and then the drawing made "after the fact" to reflect the valid mockup design - all time consuming and error prone. Using the automatic CADD tube forming method, first, CADD users design the tube assuring proper clearance (Figure 3). The parts listing and tube descriptive information and geometry data (Figure 4) are stored in the computer. Manufacturing accesses this data to understand the production requirement. Then, an automatic tube bending machine (Figure 5) driven by the computer stored geometry data forms the tube (Figure 6) to the correct dimensions. This tube is then installed in the mockup (Figure 7), any discrepancies noted and appropriate changes made on CADD with the iteration process repeated as required.

FIGURE 3

TUBE CONSTRUCTED ON CRT

..........................APPLICATIONS..

-1001   1   75J690001   P   FISA   CUMISUP

....................DRAWING NOTES...

1 THIS DRAWING APPROVED BY:

2 FABRICATE, ASSEMBLE AND PRESSURE TEST
   TO 12000 PSI PER PS 14010.

3 BEND RADIUS TO BE 1.62 IN. + -.015, -.015 TO
   TUBE CL.

4 APPLY IDENT TAPES PER PS 16001 WITH
   DIRECTIONAL ARROWS FOR FLOW IN AT - A -
   END.

5 TUBE END A PREPARED PER PS 17145. USE
   CONNECTOR ST7M202T08 DYNATUBE MALE
   CONNECTOR.

6 TUBE END B PREPARED PER PS 17146. USE
   CONNECTOR ST7M183T08 PERMASUAGE TEE.

7 SEE RAX FOR DISPLAY

8 TUBE LENGTH 31.103

9 MODELS AND EFFECTIVITIES SHOWN ARE FOR
   INITIAL RELEASE. SEE NEXT ASSEMBLY FOR
   UPDATED MODEL AND EFFECTIVITY INFORMATION.

10 FINISH PER 74A900000.

11 MARKING PER PS 16001.

COORDINATE DATA	POINT	X/B.L.	Y/F.S.	Z/W.L.
END A	1	37.62	508.00	90.44
	2	37.62	509.87	90.44
	3	38.14	515.00	88.99
	4	38.14	524.45	88.99
	5	33.42	528.72	88.99
	6	28.60	533.55	86.07
	7	28.60	534.37	86.07
END B				

...............................DEVELOPMENT PARTS LIST............................

1	-1001		DP TUBE	MN	.500 OD X .026 X 31.10
					3 AL-2.5V TITANIUM SPEC MMS 1205, COND. CWSR 105
1	ST7M202T08	5	DYNATUBE MALE CONNECTOR CONNECTOR END A
1	ST7M183T08	5	PERMASWAGE TEE CONNECTOR END B
AR	ST9M389H123	9	TAPE

FIGURE 4
DESCRIPTIVE DATA FOR EACH TUBE

FIGURE 5
TUBE PRODUCED BY AUTOMATED BENDING MACHINE

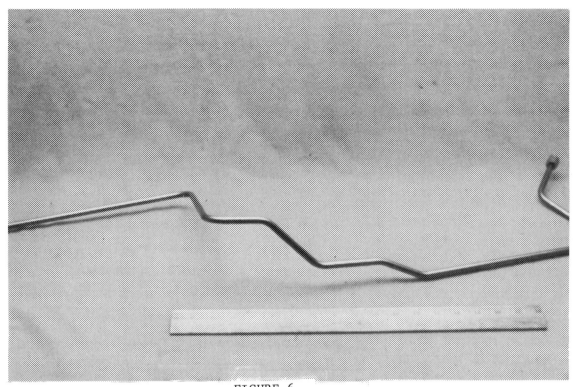

FIGURE 6
PICTURE OF BENT TUBE

FIGURE 7
COMPUTER PRODUCED TUBES ARE ACCURATELY
INSTALLED IN DEVELOPMENT FIXTURE

Direct benefits of this program are saving many thousands of hours for the hundreds of tubes in the aircraft in the following way: -by designing the tube on CADD, accurate geometry is developed eliminating clearance errors; -by eliminating "hand written" tube descriptive data and their manual dissemination and checking and by standardizing the parts list, approximately 15 hours per tube are saved on the mockup and many errors are eliminated; -by establishing an engineering data base and designing the tubes accurately initially, there are fewer changes to tubes and much quicker response to those changes that do occur; -by automating geometry input to the tube bending machine, hundreds of hours of teletype coding is eliminated; -by eliminating hand bending of tubes on the mockup, many hours are eliminated.

The current automated method of tube forming is depicted in Figure 8. A productivity ratio of about 4.5/1 has been measured for this automated method compared to the previous "manual fit and form" approach.

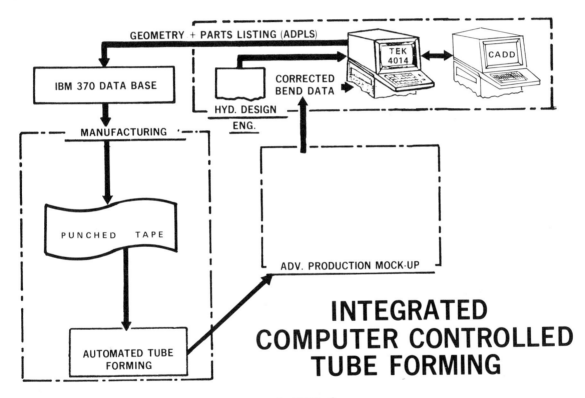

FIGURE 8

When accurate tube designs have been verified, premockup spatial information is obtained by superimposing the landing gear mechanism, and tire and hydraulic tubing in 3-D (Figure 9). Neither the tubing design nor its spatial relationship relative to the landing gear can be determined accurately on the 2-D drafting board. Thus, not only does CADD provide knowledge of the validity of this geometric installation prior to mockup conformation, but accurate data is also available to designers responsible for the structure and subsystems that go into that part of the airplane.

LANDING GEAR (STOWED)
PLUS HYDRAULIC TUBING
(CADD)

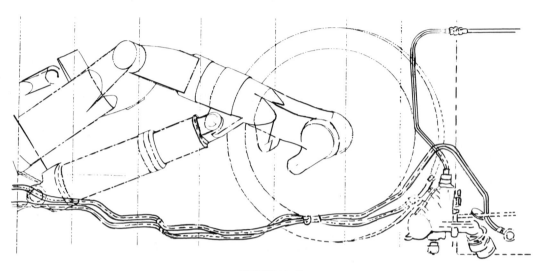

FIGURE 9

Now the CADD data is transferred to CADAM where structure, fittings and details are added and an installation drawing is made (Figure 10) to accurately define, for example, the wheel-well aircraft section through which the tubing must be routed. (Note: Installation drawings could have been completed in CADD).

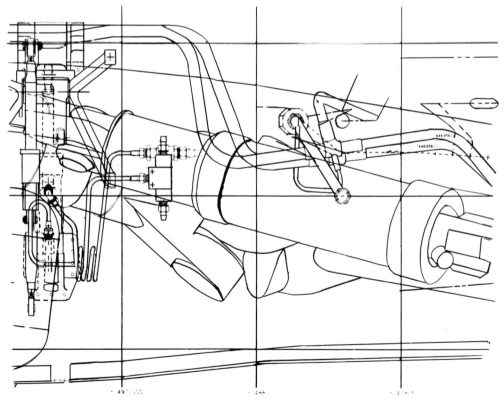

FIGURE 10
CADAM WHEEL-WELL INSTALLATION DRAWING (COMBINATION CADD + CADAM DRAWING)

2. F-18 AIRCRAFT VERTICAL TAIL DESIGN AND PRODUCTION

An integrated design, development and manufacturing function for the F-18 vertical tail is now being done using CADD and CADAM. The one feature that makes this component especially suitable for computer graphics is the fact that the main structural box (Figure 11) skin is made of graphite/epoxy laminate (many plys of cloth bonded together) cut by a numerically controlled machine. Thus, the individual varying length plys end at different locations as they are laid-up on the vertical tail to obtain the accurately tapered skin thicknesses.

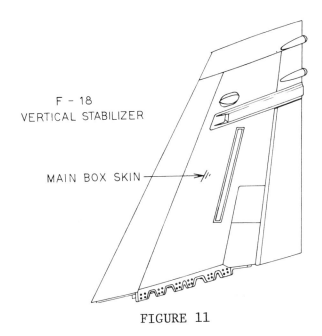

F - 18
VERTICAL STABILIZER

MAIN BOX SKIN

FIGURE 11

Eight engineering and manufacturing functions are involved in this task-- all integrated by use of CADD and CADAM:

- Loft data
- 3-dimensional design
- Stress analysis
- Detailed design
- Tooling
- N.C. programming
- Manufacturing
- Quality assurance

Data among these activities is passed downstream using the computerized data bases. Thus, all use the same accurate data; geometric constructions are done only once, downstream organizations do not have to do work over again; and time and money are saved because each organization does their work faster on the CRT.

LOFT

First, using loft data, callable from the CADD terminal, the designer creates a 3-D skeleton model of the vertical tail (Figure 12) showing the air foil shapes and all the basic geometry data, including section cuts and accurate locations of spars and ribs and their intersection with the tail surface.

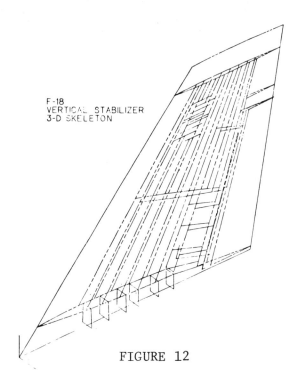

F-18
VERTICAL STABILIZER
3-D SKELETON

FIGURE 12

STRESS

Stress analysts start with this CADD design model, modify it on the CRT to create the structural finite element model, then make a NASTRAN computer run to obtain stress, loads and deflection results - all displayed on the CRT.

DESIGN

From the stress analysis results and aerodynamic and design considerations, the number of plys, ply patterns and ply orientation are obtained. The designer determines each individual ply pattern and the overall ply installation design.

From here the CADD system does a number of things:

1) Flat patterns of the individual plys are developed accurately representing the three-dimensional geometry

2) Tooling holes are coordinated and incorporated in all of the drawings, right on the CRT

3) Section cuts are made automatically, not only for tooling, but also for substructure definition

Now the data is transferred to CADAM.

The side view of the completed panel is shown in Figure 13. The "inner heavy line" (darkened for clarity) is the end of ply 12 which we will discuss below. Each of the 66 ply shapes that make up the skin are shown on this view. Note that data needed by manufacturing, such as cutouts, trim lines, tool holes and the titanium attach beam to the fuselage is accurately stored in the data base and shown on the drawing, thus achieving an early coordination between engineering and tool design.

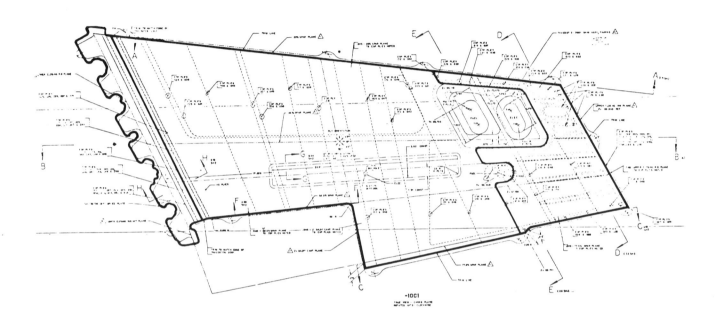

FIGURE 13
SIDE VIEW OF COMPLETED PANEL

Ply 12, in the accurate flat pattern form (engineering drawing) is shown in Figure 14. Notice the tool holes, excess trim, definition of ply orientation, as well as accurate locations for tubing access doors and electrical conduits have already been coordinated and are in the data base.

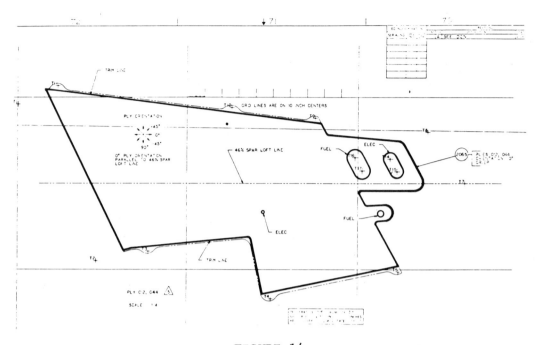

FIGURE 14

FLAT PATTERN DRAWING OF PLY 12

TOOLING

The bonding fixture is drawn on CADAM with tool holes and the panel and ply geometry shape obtained accurately from the data base. Figure 15 shows a finished skin panel lifted out of the bonding fixture. Note that the data base includes tool point locations, cutouts and accurate location of "headers" - all obtained from CADD data.

GRAPHITE/EPOXY SKIN PANEL
BOND FIXTURE

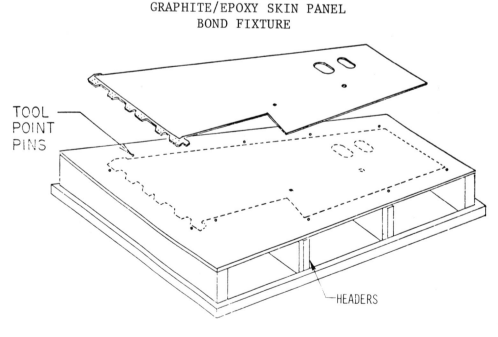

FIGURE 15

The CADAM generated bonding fixture (tool design drawing) is shown in Figure 16. Again, note the tool points, the loft profile trim (drawn on the bottom) and the panel skin geometry - all transferred from the CADD engineering drawing and available to the tool designer on the CRT prior to his starting the drawing.

Now, numerical control programming is ready to do their work of cutting the individual plys.

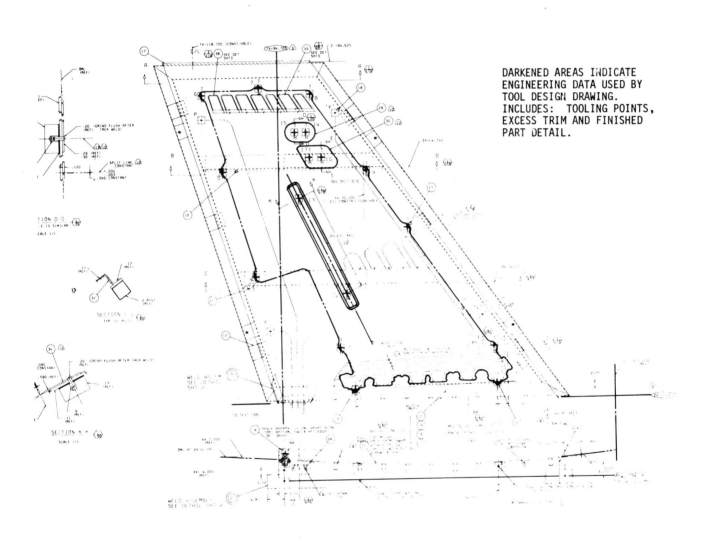

DARKENED AREAS INDICATE ENGINEERING DATA USED BY TOOL DESIGN DRAWING. INCLUDES: TOOLING POINTS, EXCESS TRIM AND FINISHED PART DETAIL.

FIGURE 16

BONDING FIXTURE DETAIL (DRAWN ON CADAM)

NUMERICAL CONTROL

Numerical control edits the CADAM ply geometry from Engineering and develops the optimized cutter path for each ply (Figure 17 for ply 12) using CADAM. Pigtail loops have been added and are required because the cutter cannot make 90° corners so instead the cutter runs along the loop. Note again that accurate coordinated tooling holes are obtained from the data base. If the cutter path were not developed on the CRT, then very time consuming and error prone measuring and redrawing of geometry and coding of IBM cards would be required.

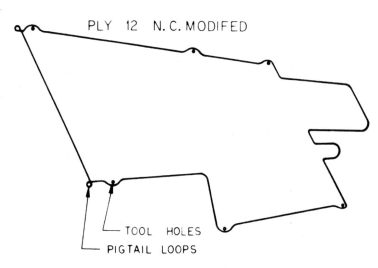

PLY 12 N.C. MODIFED

TOOL HOLES
PIGTAIL LOOPS

FIGURE 17
N.C. NESTED PLIES ON CADAM MINIMIZES SCRAPPAGE

Figure 18 shows nearly optimized CADAM nesting of some of the plys so as to minimize scrappage of the graphite epoxy sheet stock.

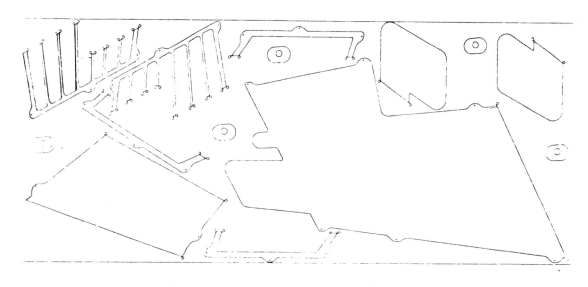

FIGURE 18

MANUFACTURING

Figure 19 shows ply 12 being put into the bonding fixture by Manufacturing. Note that other plys are already in the fixture.

In the old way, this lay-up procedure would have used 3" tape instead of larger ply shapes. Now using plys (most about 100" by 60"), with tooling holes defined, <u>the lay-up time has been reduced from about 2½ days (3 shifts, each day) to less than one 8 hour shift.</u>

Finally, Quality Control will inspect the completed panel.

FULL PLY 12 BEING LAYED UP
INTO BOND FIXTURE

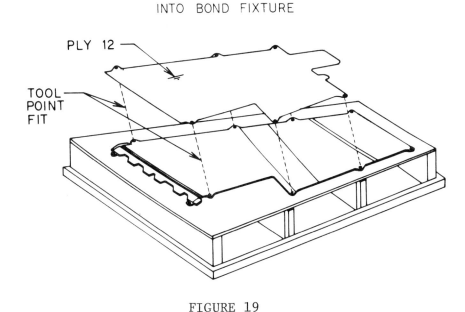

FIGURE 19

QUALITY CONTROL INSPECTION

CADAM generated locations of a set of points that define the outer skin shape are shown in Figure 20. These points, displayed on the CRT, are then compared with measured dimensions to very accurately and quickly check the finished part.

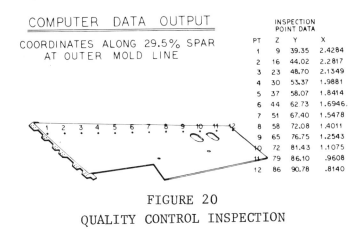

COMPUTER DATA OUTPUT

COORDINATES ALONG 29.5% SPAR
AT OUTER MOLD LINE

INSPECTION
POINT DATA

PT	Z	Y	X
1	9	39.35	2.4284
2	16	44.02	2.2817
3	23	48.70	2.1349
4	30	53.37	1.9881
5	37	58.07	1.8414
6	44	62.73	1.6946.
7	51	67.40	1.5478
8	58	72.08	1.4011
9	65	76.75	1.2543
10	72	81.43	1.1075
11	79	86.10	.9608
12	86	90.78	.8140

FIGURE 20
QUALITY CONTROL INSPECTION

HIGHLIGHTS

Quantitative productivity benefits were not measured, except for ply lay-up. However, similar tasks for other components indicate about a 9/1 productivity ratio improvement over previous "manual" methods. In addition, non-quantifiable benefits were obtained and are discussed below.

The highlight of this effort has been for all functions involved in designing and producing the F-18 vertical tail to work together using the data bases. Not only is coordination emphasized, and accuracy maximized, but also a single method of passing data is provided, eliminating duplication of work and minimizing errors and use of obsolete data. Additional benefits occur because each activity does their specific job faster through computer graphics and because of inter-relation benefits described herein.

3. CADD ELIMINATES 5-AXIS MACHINING USE FOR SHAPING HONEYCOMB

The problem being solved here is that 5-axis machine time is very costly and is in very short supply at Northrop. Thus, cutting of compound curvature surfaces for flexible honeycomb parts by 5-axis machines is to be avoided whenever possible. The solution is to deform the flexible part stock against a specially contoured tool, so that the part's compound surface (to be cut) becomes flat, and can be machined by a simple Marwin Router ("salami slicer"). Both sides of the part are machined this way. The flexible part is then "flexed" back into the required compound surface shape.

CADD made this application possible because of the following capabilities: 1) triangulated flat pattern software allows an accurate flat layout of an equivalent compound surface, 2) accurate 3-D method of geometry construction, and 3) double precision accuracy.

Roughly, the 5-axis machine is 1.7 times more costly per hour and the Marwin Router 2.5 times faster. Thus, cost savings of a factor of over 4 result from using the Router, in addition to intangible benefits of releasing the 5-axis machine for more complex work.

Figure 21 identifies the part in question - an F-18 engine inlet air ramp structure.

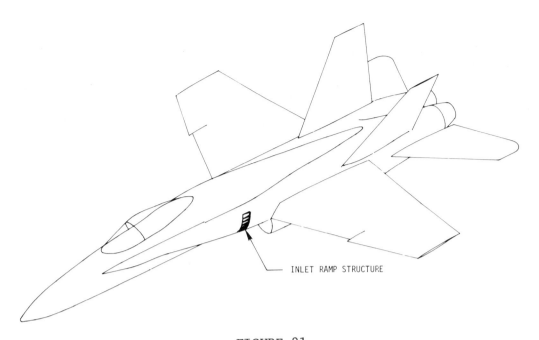

FIGURE 21

F-18 INLET AIR RAMP STRUCTURE

Figure 22 shows the finished contoured aluminum honeycomb shape done on CADD with section cuts in 3-D space. Curves A and B are drawn as 3-dimensional cubic equations from the control points at each cross-section.

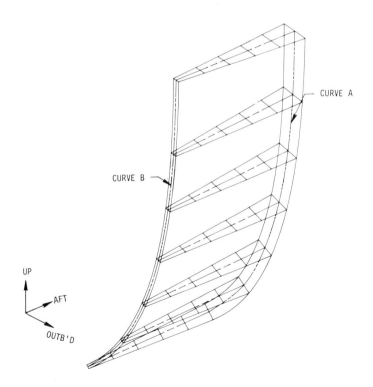

FIGURE 22
INLET RAMP STRUCTURE
(COUNTOURED ALUMINUM HONEYCOMB CORE)

Figure 23 shows the unwrapped flat pattern using the CADD triangulated program. Section cuts and curves A and B from Figure 22 were translated and rotated to proper locations in Figure 23 using analytical geometry performed by the computer. The computer thus insured correct flattened geometry. Uncut raw stock was placed around the finished 3-D layout of the unwrapped flat pattern (as shown in Location 1).

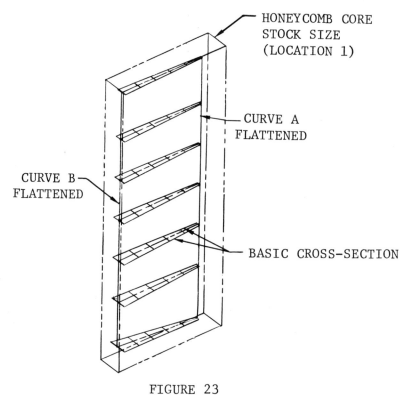

FIGURE 23
UNROLLED FLAT PATTERN DEVELOPED ON FLATTENED CURVES A AND B

A flat cutting plane was established parallel to the base of the cutting machine (Figure 24). The basic cross-section (shown as phantom lines depicting the compound surfaces) was individually bent on CADD so that the upper surface met this flat cutting plane. The resulting deflection of the basic stock shape was such that it coincided with the contoured cutting table top. Then the "salami slicer" cuts along the flat cutting plane but the results of cutting this plane are the same as if the contoured dimensions of the upper surface were cut by a 5-axis machine. This procedure must be repeated to cut the inboard surface.

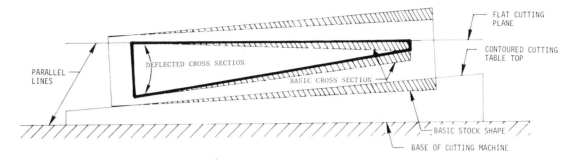

FIGURE 24

EACH BASIC CROSS-SECTION (AS SHOWN IN FIGURE 23)
IS DEFLECTED AS SHOWN HERE TO MEET CUTTING PLANE

The finished model is fully defined in CADD and shown in Figure 25, complete with 0,0 set point. Computer data representing the top of the table was converted from CADD surface data to X, Y, Z point data, which was given to the numerical control programmer, who converted that data to APT data for part programming. This was required because we did not have the CADD/GNC program operational.

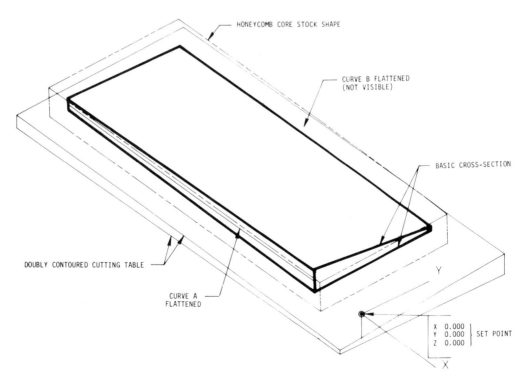

FIGURE 25

CONTOURED CUTTING TABLE

Figure 26 shows the three-view basic data used for the tool design
detailed drawing. Section cuts detail accurately how much pre-deflection
is necessary. Basic data consists of three views of the table and several
cross-sections, of which four are shown.

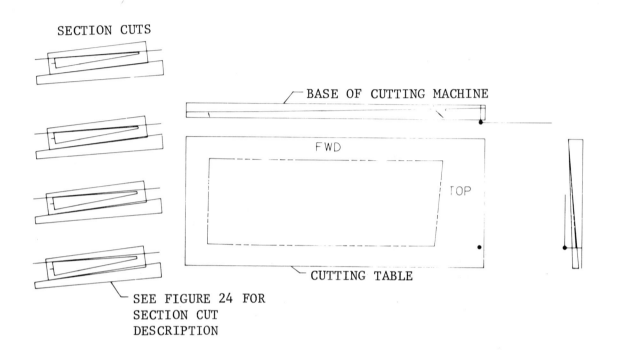

FIGURE 26
BASIC DATA FOR TOOLING DRAWING

The beauty of this method is that only one 5-axis machined cut is required
to make the tooling table surface because thereafter, a simple "salami
slicer" is used in place of the 5-axis machine to cut the parts surfaces
by accurately pre-deflecting the part to achieve the equivalent of the
contoured surface. This process shows benefits of clever CADD usage in
engineering so as to reduce manufacturing costs over and above benefits
obtained by use of a common data base explained in the first two examples.
Obviously, this process can also apply to wing leading and trailing edges.

C. PROBLEM AREAS

We were learning how to productively use these new tools, thus we encountered many problems, which fell into five categories:

1) Planning and Coordination

In using CADD/CADAM, planning and coordination items listed below are all in addition to those performed for the conventional "manual" work. Thus, extra time not available during a hectic development program is necessary to make efficient use of computer graphics. This "extra time" is required of especially "harried" managers/leadmen, who additionally have to take time to understand the necessary job, sometimes different than when the job was "manual"; as well as understanding the advantages, limitations and developments required for computer graphics. Since only about 15-20% of F-18 drawings were done on computer graphics by Northrop with our limited number of CRTs, effective planning required the following:

- Overall game plan
- Best drawing choice in engineering for manufacturing usage (requires early manufacturing coordination)
- Changed geometry format that is presented to manufacturing
- Efficient procedures and discipline in carrying out the procedures
- Efficient and complete data base usable by both Engineering and Manufacturing
- Good operators
- Efficient CRT scheduling
- Sufficient planning prior to going to CRT
- Efficient work at CRT

2) Computer and system "downtime" was abnormally high; response of computer to user commands was sometimes too slow to allow efficient system usage. Recently, computer system changes have helped alleviate this problem.

3) When a designer has finished his drawing on the board, he is really finished. The designer's work on the CRT is useless, under our present administrative system, unless "hardcopy" drawings are produced for check purposes and for dissemination. Our present methods for obtaining "hardcopy" has various time consuming manual steps and also contains various bugs. Thus, it took too long, sometimes, to go from the CRT to completed, released mylar drawings.

4) Some designers and managers, especially "old timers" concentrated on things perceived to be wrong and did not accept new procedures dictated by computer graphics, largely on an emotional basis and on "unfortunate" unsatisfactory isolated experiences.

5) Additional capability is required to eliminate time consuming "go-around" methods and frustrations in construction modes.

D. CONCLUSIONS

1. The combined engineering-manufacturing projects described herein have shown that productivity and product quality are increased if a common data base is used, from which the many disciplines involved obtain geometry data for use in their function. Furthermore, reduction of work occurs because each technology builds upon the upstream geometric data produced, rather than starting from "scratch" or duplicating work already done. Computer data makes possible an accurate part production and more accurate assembly of parts. A prime "fallout" of computer graphics has been that each user must understand the other technologies involved and coordinate with them at greater depth throughout the program in order to perform his task on the CRT.

2. More complex, current aircraft require computerized 3-dimensional geometry layout capability because of the increased complexity in mechanism design (such as landing gears), more complex spatial allocation (such as tubing routed through dense subsystems and structure installations), and low drag, high lift configurations (containing compound curvature of surfaces).

3. The computer has made it possible for Engineering to very accurately produce drawings such that Manufacturing benefits in two ways: a) confidence in the dimensional accuracy so that manufacturing does not have to measure and redraw, and b) the capability for triangulated flat patterns to very accurately represent compound surfaces.

4. The introduction of Computer Graphics to the production design environment has exposed many hardware, software, administrative and organizational problems which are limiting factors to productivity, and which are continually subject to partial corrective actions.

5. Computer graphics is an emerging technology. Not since the invention of the computer itself has the designer and manufacturing engineer been given as powerful a tool to do his work. The methods and concepts in this paper are suggested to assist the Computer Graphic Technology to "emerge" at a more rapid pace. Obviously, we have just scratched the surface of the potential benefits attainable.

CHAPTER 5

INTEGRATING CAD AND CAM

Integrating CAD And CAM—Future Directions

By Dr. Edwin N. Nilson
Pratt & Whitney Aircraft

While most aerospace companies have moved into computer-aided design via the implementation of interactive drafting along a broad front, Pratt & Whitney Aircraft took a very different approach. This was to establish a complete interactive design/design analysis system for each of selected projects extending from preliminary design through the complete part description in an integrated data base. For these, drawings, where still required, are produced automatically. A similar approach is now being employed in extending this concept into manufacturing, carrying selected parts all the way through production. Interactive tool design, N/C programming, and, in the future, process planning, are carried out against the Engineering design data base where detailed part descriptions are available.

This distinctive approach of integrating CAD/CAM for selected projects has some significant advantages over concentrating upon the general application of interactive drafting, N/C programming, and now process planning. We were able to show dramatic lead-time and cost reductions quickly; the approach is rapidly accepted by management and by rank-and-file; it can be applied as widely as feasible and does not entail blanket application; the power of the integrated design/manufacturing data base is effectively displayed.

INTRODUCTION

The interactive computer-aided design system at Pratt & Whitney Aircraft-Commercial Products Division has been given wide recognition both inside and outside the aerospace industry as being at the forefront of CAD technology. This system is now being extended without interruption into several areas of Manufacturing--tool design, process planning, tool making, numerical control programming--representing a substantial development of interactive CAM.

The development of the P&WA interactive design process has differed markedly from the approach being employed in most other aerospace companies. The application is complete in the sense that it extends from preliminary design through fabrication of a part; it is modular in the sense that it can be used on one component or on several; it is heavily design-analysis oriented rather than design/drafting.

Its computing structure is most closely approximated by that being implemented by Boeing for the NASA IPAD project, a fact which has received NASA attention since early 1974.

The computing facility is almost unique among the computing facilities of high technology industries in this country: the computers are under direct Engineering control. Its personnel are strongly dedicated to the effective implementation of first CAD and now (interactive) CAD/CAM. The selection of equipment expresses recognition of the fact that combining heavy batch and heavy interactive work on a single computer is not practical: two separate but closely linked large-scale computers handle these two functions in parallel fashion.

New devices and techniques have been used for the communication of design information within Engineering and between Engineering and Manufacturing. The computer software supporting CAD/CAM is the result of extensive human engineering designed to make the interface between engineer and computer as simple as possible.

The time-sharing system employed on the interactive computer has been extensively modified by Engineering personnel to form one of the most effective and efficient systems yet devised, and the computing equipment employed is probably the best ever designed for this type of application.

The computing organization, itself, under Engineering but equally dedicated to implementing and integrating interactive CAM, is free to establish goals and directions. This organization is playing a major role in bringing Engineering and Manufacturing together in an interactive CAD/CAM system. Moreover, it is a line organization within Engineering.

Contrary to the possible interpretation of the title, that we intend here to forecast future directions for CAD/CAM in industry as a whole, our purpose is restricted to discussing the special characteristics of the P&WA system just enumerated, indicating some of their implications with respect to CAD/CAM generally, considering some of their relationships to present developments in CAD/CAM technology, and describing some of the important CAD/CAM developments expected to take place in P&WA in the next several years.

The use of minicomputers linked to the interactive host computer represents a significant application of distributed computing. Satellite interactive design and drafting facilities, inspection devices, N/C machine control (effectively DNC) share time on the host with engineers on some 85 to 90 other terminals.

DESIGN ANALYSIS APPROACH TO CAD AT P&WA

Pratt & Whitney Aircraft Engineering established its interactive design system one engine component at a time. The objective in each instance has been to start with preliminary design, to have the part description and properties gradually evolve, and to terminate the design phase of the process with a complete numerical description of the part, including all tolerances. Associated aerodynamics, heat transfer, stress and vibrational analyses in conjunction with the analysis of part life, durability and other properties are carried out as the design progresses.

The description of the part of component, together with the associated analytical properties, is built up in the integrated data base. This data base serves as the principal communication medium among engineering groups participating in the design. This integrated data base concept is illustrated in Figure 1. The final part description is made available to Manufacturing to continue the interactive process--in process planning, tool design, N/C programming.

A single canonical part description is selected with a view to serving both Manufacturing and Engineering: Engineering carries out its design/design analysis based upon this description, and Manufacturing employs it for process planning, tool design, etc.

Already the numerical description of all airfoils in the computer data base has replaced the drawing as the "official document" and is "signed off" as such. All part description for Manufacturing and for vendors supplying airfoils is in terms of this numerical description. If drawings of airfoils are desired, they are automatically produced on Calcomp or Xynetics plotter; but they are becoming redundant.

In developing these interactive design systems, we started with the turbines because the turbine was the pacing item in design and fabrication. We hoped to reduce the lead time, about 47 weeks, by one-half. The computing structure, which will be considered in a subsequent section, was applicable as well to compressors and the compressor system was made interactive within six months after the first phase of the turbine system. All remaining major design systems which were heavily analytical were made interactive in rapid succession.

The computer structure of the design process, itself, as distinguished from the modules for design analysis which always continue to evolve, is quite stable. Not infrequently a new part is designed as a variant of an earlier one. This stability of the design and design analytical processes are of paramount importance in the computerization.

A similar type of stability exists in Manufacturing which permits the direct extension of the interactive CAD system into CAM. We shall return to this in the next section.

EXTENSION INTO MANUFACTURING

It should be understood that we are not concerned here with the broad application of computing technology to manufacturing processes. The use of the acronym CAM in this very general sense is widespread. We are concerned here with those manufacturing processes where the application of computing is interactive. In particular, we are concerned here with the use of interactive computing by process planning, tool design, and N/C programming with the Engineering data base.

It is the integrated data base that becomes the primary medium for communicating designs from Engineering to Manufacturing, just as it served as a communication device between design groups. Moreover, this data base is augmented as it is employed in Manufacturing. Information required by the manufacturing engineer such as machinability of material, coefficients of expansion, feed and speed rates for N/C machines, and so on, are made available in the data base. In forging compressor blades, for example, a

CAD/CAM

COMPUTER-AIDED DESIGN/COMPUTER-AIDED MANUFACTURE

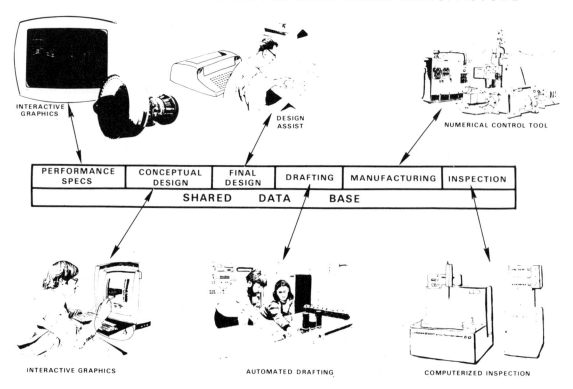

Figure 1

Figure 2

flash is produced which must be subsequently removed by machining. The airfoil which is described by Design must be extended to include this flash: indeed, the direction prescribed for the flash has a direct influence on the spring back or spring forward of the piece after forging. This extended airfoil is required in the data base for the toolmaker making the forging dies. Computing tools such as N/C programming languages, N/C program computers, and N/C post processors are, of course, already in the computer or in the process of inclusion.

It may be required to drill upwards of 1000 cooling holes in a hollow turbine blade or vane. (cf. Figure 2). The location and direction of each hole centerline and the hole radius are all rigidly prescribed by Design (Design Analysis). It is simply not feasible to process or even communicate such large amounts of data by human intervention. The hole information is in the design data base, is communicated directly to minicomputer controlling the (laser) hole drilling device.

Use of the integrated data base as a means of communication has literally introduced a new dimension into Engineering/Manufacturing communication. The engineering drawing, with its traditional three orthographic and one isometric projections, constitutes a device employed by the designer/ draftsman to portray a three-dimensional mental image on paper (two-dimensional). Manufacturing engineers are immediately confronted with the necessity of transforming the 2D drawing back into a 3-D mental image. This sometimes formidable problem is obviated when the part description is available in the computer data base. We have introduced an interactive 3-D graphics facility which, in effect, circumvents the 3D → 2D → 3D conversion. The designer or manufacturing engineer can continuously rotate, translate, zoom to get a feeling for the part geometry. Automatic perspective and clipping fore and aft as well as on the sides of the figure enhance the communication. Incidentally, if a particular view on the 3D scope is required as a reminder, merely pressing a button produces a Calcomp drawing.

Fully as important is the fact that the part description in the data base is the complete surface description rather than the equivalent of the draftsman's stick drawing. Thus, as many sections as may be desired are readily available. The stick drawing does not contain this information.

A striking example is afforded by our handling of airfoils. The draftsman would in the past create engineering master drawings of a few airfoil sections along the span. Neither he nor the manufacturing engineer knew what form the airfoil surface took between these sections. Manufacturing was expected to employ an "acceptable method of fairing" between sections, which actually meant that between prescribed sections, the airfoil was not definitely defined. Inspection could have no implications except at the prescribed sections. Figure 3 displays the contrast: defining part surfaces generally and airfoil surfaces, in particular, will produce sections of arbitrary orientation as required and make total inspection meaningful. We shall return to this example later when we discuss the closing of the interactive CAD/CAM loop with interactive inspection.

Figure 4 illustrates the changing form of communication from design to manufacture: the figure on the left describes the airfoil only by a reference to the computer data base. The forging die on the right was

AIRFOIL DATA

Engineering master drawings

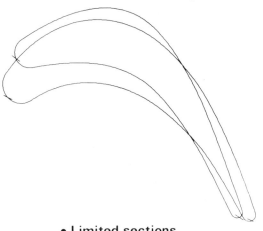

Computer data base

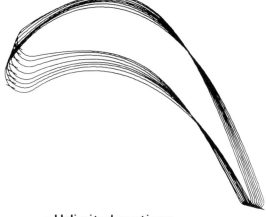

- Limited sections
- Hand fairing & scaling

- Unlimited sections
- Computer fairing
- Complete specifications

Figure 3

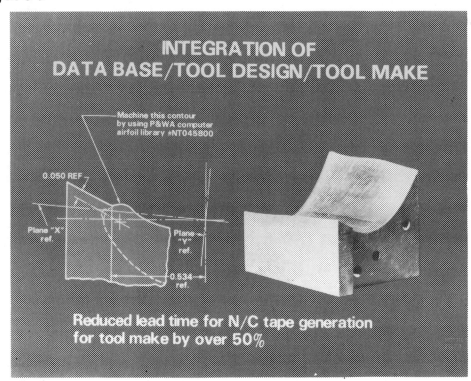

INTEGRATION OF DATA BASE/TOOL DESIGN/TOOL MAKE

Machine this contour by using P&WA computer airfoil library #NT045800

0.050 REF

Plane "X" ref.

Plane "Y" ref.

0.534 ref.

Reduced lead time for N/C tape generation for tool make by over 50%

Figure 4

constructed by N/C for which the N/C machining program was created interactively against the airfoil description in the integrated data base.

Figure 5 displays a drawing by Tool Design for a jig to hold a turbine
blade during the machining of its root. The blade is held in place by five
contact points. Engineering Design traditionally supplied airfoil
dimensions with respect to the stacking line which may be partly inside the
blade. Upon receipt of drawing, Tool Design had immediately to redraw,
using a tooling ball (lower left) as reference. This conversion is now done
directly from the design data base, requiring 10 minutes instead of 4 hours.

Figure 6 displays a die plane projection for forging dies for fan blades.
Determining this die plane formerly took a tool designer up to 2 weeks to
determine. It is now determined in 10 to 15 seconds on the 3-D graphics
system.

In Figure 7 there appears a 3-D cam used by one of our vendors in machining
fan blades. The cam, which was previously constructed by cut-and-try is
now machined N/C by working backward from a numerical description of the
airfoil which we supply. The construction of the cam now takes 3 days
instead of the 16 weeks required previously.

Just as in Engineering, a certain stability exists in Manufacturing
procedures. Completely new process plans, for example, are rare: most
are a variation of earlier process plans. In many situations the section
of a set of parametric values is sufficient to define a complete process
or tool design. Making tool design, process planning, and N/C programming
interactive enables the manufacturing engineer quickly to make the required
change. A fundamental point arises out of all this: the computing
structure which supports interactive design will support equally
effectively the technical processes of manufacture which can employ
interactive graphics or interactive computing. I have discussed this issue
with several members of the Boeing IPAD team, especially those conceived
with the Design/Engineering interface, and they concur with my position.

FEATURES OF THE P&WA CAD/CAM SYSTEM

The essential elements in our interactive CAD/CAM system appear in Figure 8:
the shared data base which has appropriate controls as to "read only" and
"read/write" and is properly separated into transient and permanent files,
on-line and archival; the program library of engineering application
programs (primarily for design analysis) which, incidentally, are in a
constant state of change--refinement, extension, replacement; and, finally,
the executive control structure which enables the engineer to select his
deck (or decks), call in pertinent data from the data base, operate on it,
and transfer the new results to the data base. Actually, the data
bookkeeping function is automatic.

The real significance of Figure 8 is that the user works at a graphics
(or typewriter) terminal having, as far as he perceives, a major computer
under his sole control. Except during a few periods of very heavy loading,
he is completely oblivious that 84 others are time-sharing the computer with
him. Upwards of 500 major interactive computer programs are available in
the library. If several individuals at different terminals must interact

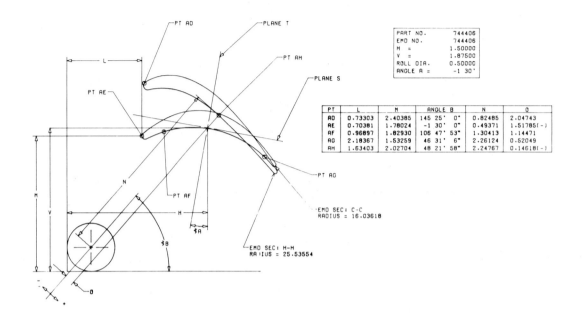

PART NO.	744406
EMD NO.	744406
H =	1.50000
V =	1.87500
ROLL DIA.	0.50000
ANGLE A =	-1 30'

PT	L	M	ANGLE B	N	O
AD	0.73303	2.40385	145 25' 0"	0.82485	2.04743
AE	0.70381	1.78024	-1 30' 0"	0.49371	1.51785(-)
AF	0.96897	1.82930	106 47' 53"	1.30413	1.14471
AG	2.18367	1.53259	46 31' 6"	2.26124	0.52049
AH	1.63403	2.02704	48 21' 58"	2.24767	0.14618(-)

Figure 5

FAN BLADE FORGING DIE LINE

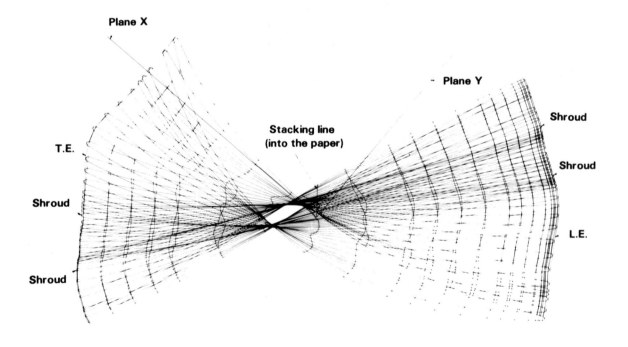

Figure 6

Figure 7

INTERACTIVE DESIGN SYSTEM OPERATION

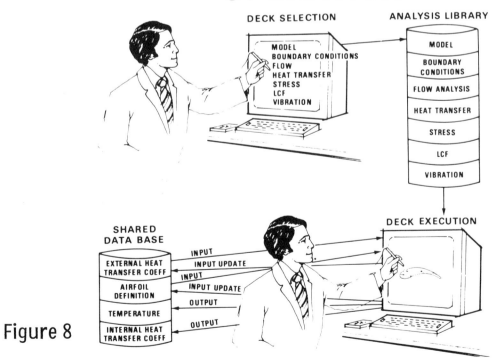

Figure 8

during a particular design phase, they do just that. Moving an interactive job from one scope to another, incidentally, is easier than transferring a telephone call from one phone to another! The whole system has been made simple for the engineer to use--many hours of human engineering went into this task.

There are in Engineering in P&WA-Commercial Products Division two IBM 370/168 computers which furnish support to this CAD/CAM system in Engineering and Manufacturing. (An XDS Sigma 8 and a Honeywell 516 are dedicated to Automatic Data Retrieval and Reduction for engine and component test stands and do not play any role here. Another major computing facility in the Manufacturing Division provides information systems support to that organization but does not come into the interactive CAD/CAM picture.)

One 168 is dedicated 12 to 15 hours a day to interactive computing. The second 168 is closely linked to the first and provides "batch" support: any deck requiring more than 2 CPU seconds is transferred to the batch machine, is worked there, and the results transferred back to interactive user. (A major role for the second computer is providing information systems support to Engineering as well as the batch technical support.)

On the interactive machine are hung some 85-90 interactive terminals: 3 IBM 2250 light-pen scopes, 35-40 Tektronix 4010 and 4014 storage tube scopes, 23 Hazeltine or T.C.I. alphanumeric scopes, and 24 typewriter terminals. The Evans and Sutherland 3-D graphics system is supported locally by a PDP 11 lined to the interactive 168, and a Computer Vision 3-D interactive drafting system supported by a Nova is similarly linked.

A PDP 11 similarly supports an inspection device for airfoils by means of which measurements of airfoils are very rapidly taken and transferred to the interactive (host) computer for bucking against the design data base. In 1977 there will be a prototype of DNC in the Engineering Experimental Shop when another mini attached to the same host will support a center-drive NC lathe and the laser hole drilling device mentioned previously.

Thus, there is not only the time sharing among scope and typewriter terminals but the simultaneous support of an increasing number of mini-computers in a distributed computing arrangement.

The shift in Engineering Design to interactive computing has been substantiated. Half of all design computing is now interactive, and nearly all the technical batch is loaded interactively. Some 30% or more of our engineers work interactively at one time or another.

CAD/CAM ENVIRONMENT AT P&WA

The Engineering/Manufacturing environment that has fostered CAD/CAM and permitted it to reach its present advanced state is, itself, of considerable significance.

First and foremost, the computing organization and the computers, themselves, are all in Engineering. This means in this case, not only that priorities are set within the department, but also that engineering programmers and computing machine systems people are dedicated to making interactive CAD/CAM a success. Thus, for example, when the otherwise highly effective time-sharing system VM/CMS turned out not to include a graphics capability, our systems people modified the computer operating system to include graphics. They have since made other changes to tune the system to the needs of engineers.

The human engineering that went into simplifying the man/computer interface for the engineer was closely related to this philosophy: the systems programmer and the applications programmer sat down with the engineer at the scope to determine precisely what was necessary to make the man/computer interface comfortable and convenient. This teamwork was a natural extension of the engineer/programmer team concept employed for a decade at P&WA in developing computer programs for Design.

All of this has taken place during a period when most major aerospace companies moved to consolidate corporate computing facilities, frequently in a separate division. A particular engineering organization was only one of this facility's customers, and response to engineering's needs has been generally less than satisfactory.

A concomitant facet is the freedom accorded the computing organization in setting its own objectives and in carrying out its responsibilities. It was this freedom of action which led to establishing close ties with tool making and tool design and to promote in Manufacturing the introduction of interactive computing and graphics. This, in turn, led to an informal CAD/CAM committee which is pursuing the goal of making three processes interactive (or automated where appropriate): the forging of compressor blades with screw press, the N/C machining of compressor disks, the casting of hollow turbine blades. These projects when completed will represent integrated interactive CAD/CAM processes starting back in design analysis and continuing through fabrication.

These efforts have now laid the foundation for establishing a formal CAD/CAM Committee for the P&WA Group-Commercial Products Division, Manufacturing Division and Government Products Division--which will work for the advancement and completion of interactive CAD/CAM.

In quite a different direction, there is in P&WA-CPD Engineering an excellent balance of interactive and batch scientific computing and inquiry/response and batch information systems work. This load is accommodated well by the two IBM 370/168's, one of which is dedicated to interactive work for 12 hours per day and to batch the rest of the 24-hour period. Inasmuch as there is really no way to accommodate heavy interactive computing and heavy batch concurrently on a single computer, this balance in our computing facility has been a critical factor in our success.

The modular approach used in P&WA in developing CAD systems has been instrumental in eliminating the necessity to cost-justify every new system. The first system reduced turbine design/fabrication lead time by nearly one-half. The compressor system which followed six months later established significant lead time reductions (6 to 1) and computing cost reductions (3 to 2) for a specific design task. No further cost-justification was necessary, and we continue to complete one CAD system after the other.

RELATIONSHIP TO CAD/CAM TECHNOLOGY

Some of the practical differences between the P&WA interactive CAD/CAM system and interactive CAD/CAM technology generally as well as philosophical differences are illustrated fairly well by Figure 9.

It is conventional to concentrate near the Engineering/Manufacturing interface by introducing interactive drafting in Engineering and NC programming which it feeds in Manufacturing. Some more progressive systems are introducing CAM-I's CAPP (Computer-Aided Process Planning) into such a facility. CAM-I's CAPP, itself, presuffixes a specific geometric modeling system with which existing drafting systems must interface.

Several problems surface immediately: (1) the CAM-I geometric modeling is process-planning oriented and there is a conflict with the needs of design. Similarly, with group technology: most existing systems are design oriented, with the retrieval of drawings, a primary application, while Manufacturing's interests call for classification with respect to machining processes. And even these problems would not be of great concern were it not for introduction and implementation across the board.

In the P&WA modules approach, a specific design system (e.g., turbines) is carried right across the picture, from preliminary design through fabrication. The geometric modeling for turbines, being limited in scope, is readily chosen to satisfy both Engineering and Manufacturing. Process planning is not making major excursions, is relatively stable, and therefore does not require a broad, general process planning approach. Variations from one design to the next can be handled by interactive adjustment. The same picture is true for the next CAD system, and the next, and the next.

P&WA in its approach, without introducing any process planning, geometric modeling, group technology of broad generality or, indeed, without waiting until useful tools in these disciplines are developed, can capture now, not only the cost and lead time reductions in CAD and CAM individually, but also the order of magnitude larger rewards in the CAD/CAM interface.

There is implicit here, actually, a criticism of the broad general approach: it does not exploit sufficiently the standardization and stability of design and manufacturing processes where these conditions are present.

ADVANTAGES/PAYOFFS OF THE P&WA SYSTEM

The modular nature of the application of the P&WA approach has many advantages:

1. Each module is, in fact, a prototype of the complete system.

2. Once the computing structure for the first module is completed, the applications to remaining segments of the design system are straightforward.

3. Existing and generally available computer software nearly suffices for the construction of the first module.

4. Lead time and cost reductions realized from the initial application pave the way for further application.

5. No new technology needs to be applied suddenly across the board.

6. At each stage we have a working system: there is no long delay in beginning to realize the benefits of CAD/CAM and no surprises.

7. After gaining the acceptance by a few engineers on the first module, we find the remaining engineers not wanting to be left behind and pushing to get part of the action.

There is a fundamental concern in first implementing interactive drafting rather than design analysis. I realize that the proponents of this course of action argue that once an interactive drawing is established, one can move upstream into design analysis.

Our experience has been that many existing drafting practices must be modified significantly as the interactive design analysis takes form. In a substantial percentage of cases, formal drafting will disappear as we have suggested above and as we will discuss in the concluding section. Once interactive drafting is firmly established, the modifications required to make total system interactive are going to be difficult to accomplish. By solidly entrenching old design practices in the new interactive drafting technology, we have created a new major obstacle.

It should be realized that a complete interactive design analysis/design structure is, in fact, a living documentation of the design process with automatic update. Moreover, as the computerized system evolves to this point of completeness, a detailed analysis of the design process takes place which probably would not otherwise take place. Redundancies and inconsistencies are eliminated, weaknesses are detected and remedied, and the design system, itself, evolves out of its sterotype as the computerization progresses. We have found, for example, that "seat-of-the-pants" engineering decision making was quickly replaced in many instances by quantified judgment.

Finally, there is the fundamental advantage that the part description generated in design analysis must be the surface description of the part, not the stick drawing generated in drafting. This complete surface description permits not only the designer/design analyst to do complete analysis, but provides the manufacturing engineer with as much information about the geometry of the part as he wants. This is particularly important in tool design and NC programming. The availability of 3D graphics hardware to combine with this complete surface description, as referred to above, to provide an effective means of circumventing the 3D → 2D → 3D problem.

FUTURE DEVELOPMENTS IN CAD/CAM

Near Term

All major interactive design processes are well on the way to completion. In most cases there are, however, a few gaps which remain in the mechanical design area, mostly of the "finishing touch" type.

CAD/CAM – INTERACTIVE

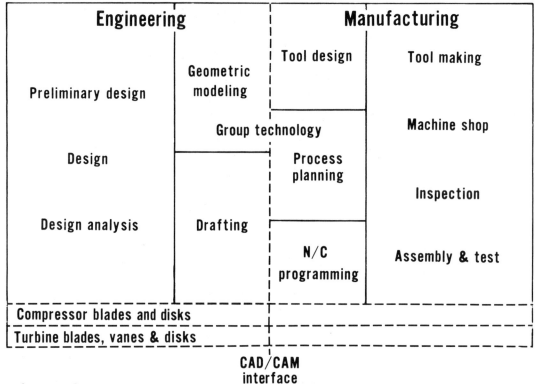

Engineering		Manufacturing	
Preliminary design	Geometric modeling	Tool design	Tool making
Design	Group technology		Machine shop
		Process planning	
Design analysis	Drafting		Inspection
		N/C programming	Assembly & test
Compressor blades and disks			
Turbine blades, vanes & disks			

CAD/CAM interface

Figure 9

CUTTER PATH AND N/C TAPE GENERATION BY INTERACTIVE GRAPHICS

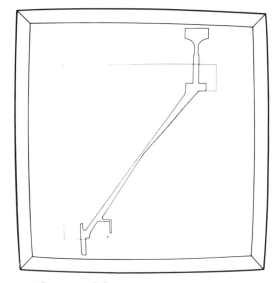
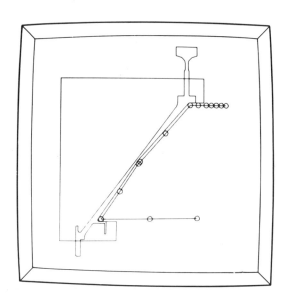

Figure 10

Figure 11

COMPUTER-AIDED DESIGN/COMPUTER-AIDED MANUFACTURE

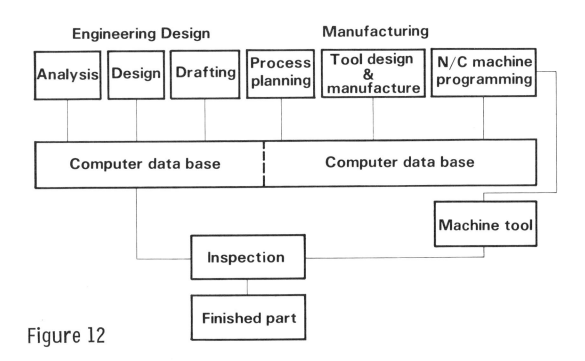

Figure 12

The application of interactive computing in design up to this point, however, has been in the order of Design priority--to produce most quickly those systems which are of primary benefit to Design. There are a number of parts not yet covered--they do not involve heavy design analysis--which are of particular interest to Manufacturing. We are now setting up an official joint CAD/CAM Committee (replacing an unofficial arrangement which has existed for some time) which will establish joint Engineering/Manufacturing priorities so as to capture full advantage of CAD/CAM as quickly as possible.

The principle has been established and accepted by both Divisions that all interactive technical computing for Manufacturing Engineering which impinges upon the Engineering Design data base should be carried out via time-sharing with Engineering interactive computer, and Engineering Computing is pledged to impartial support of both Divisions.

Specific programs in interactive CAM are well underway, starting with the part description and working all the way through production to the extent that this is feasible:

° Hollow turbine blades which are cast will be carried through the final forming of the waxes to be used in investment casting.

° Screw press forging dies for forging compressor blades are NC machined by NC programs constructed against the Design data base.

° Compressor disks will be turned without drawings. (see Figure 10). We will go from the disk description in the Engineering data base to the N/C program for a center-drive lathe. The N/C source code, itself, will be produced automatically. (We are currently doing precisely this for compressor disk templates.

Interactive and automatic inspection devices like ADAM (Automatic Digital Airfoil Measurement)--see Figure 11--and RADOC (Rapid Digital Optical Contouring) will complete the cycle--see Figure 12--by bucking the dimensions of the finished part against the Design data base. ADAM is already in full operation, supported by a PDP 11 minicomputer directly linked to the interactive computer as host. Recorded measurements up to 2000 in number receive preliminary processing in the mini and then are transmitted to the host for comparison. A large (JT9D) fan blade is "completely" digitized in 10 minutes with 2 minutes required for set up.

Interactive graphics is extending throughout Tool Design, Numerical Control Programming, and Tool Making at a rapid rate, and over the next 3 to 5 years, these areas promise to be nearly as highly computerized as Engineering Design. Tool Design is currently negotiating for an interactive drafting facility which will be directly lined to the Engineering interactive computer.

A prototype DNC installation is currently being introduced into Manufacturing which will be fed from the end of the Engineering Design process. Similarly, we are building a quasi-DNC setup in the Experimental Shop within Engineering. This consists of a cart on which are mounted a computer automation minicomputer, a Tektronix 4010 scope, two floppy disks, and a modem for four-wire linking to the Engineering interactive computer. This cart will move between the laser drilling device mentioned above and an N/C lathe.

The central role in all this played by the interactive Engineering computer is a signpost indicating the way in which the supporting interactive computing facility is headed. We plan to replace our 168 by the new 3033, as soon as VM is supported--probably spring of 1978. But it is evident that as soon as effective and efficient software is available for full blown distributive computing, we shall move in that direction.

Far Term

By the end of five years, we expect to have a mature interactive CAD/CAM system. Much of the present drafting effort will have disappeared. In those areas which remain, drafting will be completely interactive. But this drafting will go far beyond creating stick drawings and dimensioning with tolerances. For those parts which have little design analysis or for other reasons receive their initial precise definition in drafting, complete surface descriptions will be employed, with automatic sectioning capabilities, hidden line removal, shading, etc.

Three-dimensional scope communication between Design and Manufacturing will be commonplace. All N/C programming will be interactive and a significant part of it automatic. Tool design will come more and more to resemble part design in Engineering, incorporating a significant amount of design analysis.

The extent of our acceptance of CAD/CAM technologies, now in their early phases of development, is not clear. We shall certainly stay close to these as they develop and be involved in such efforts as CAM-I and I-CAM. We will continue to participate in the IPAD Industry Technical Advisory Board (ITAB).

We have, in fact, in the process of implementation the CMPP (Computer Monitored Process Planning) system devised by United Technologies Research Center which CAM-I recognizes as being at the forefront of the process planning technology. Initially this will involve interactive process planning for turned parts.

Advanced Numerical Control developments, the evolving of a geometric modeling technology, the effective introduction of group technology we will watch very closely, participating where this is appropriate and carrying on our own projects in-house. But I firmly believe that a fully matured (as best as can be visualized from this point) interactive CAD/CAM system will be in full operation in P&WA long before these advanced disciplines are ready for use.

CHAPTER 6

DESIGNING, OPERATING AND SELLING

On Designing, Operating And Selling Integrated Manufacturing Systems

By Dr. J. Hatvany
Computer and Automation Institute (Hungary)

and

A. Tari
Csepel Machine Tool Factory
Csepel Iron and Steel Works (Hungary)

Integrated manufacturing systems, comprising groups of computer-controlled machine tools, automatic workpiece transport, on-line computer scheduling, advanced process planning, a shared data-base and possibly a link to CAD, have passed beyond the experimental stage.

What problems arise when these systems are removed from the domain of the research and development teams that first designed them? How can they be integrated into the workaday operational routine of an engineering factory? How can tenders be prepared for delivering further systems, without involving research people of the highest qualifications each time? How can new systems be designed, delivered and installed to customers without incurring exorbitant overheads?

INTRODUCTION

Most countries whose national economy is largely dependent on their mechanical engineering industries, have in recent years found it necessary to launch major government-backed schemes for the development of integrated manufacturing systems [1, 2,3,4,5,6]. This course has been dictated mainly by the difficulties of recruiting and maintaining an adequate, skilled labour force, and by the greatly enhanced quality, flexibility and resilience requirements of the present-day market. These arguments are further enhanced in the case of an export-oriented machine-tool industry, where the economy not only wishes to *use* such systems, but also to *export* them.

In Hungary the State Office for Technical Development and other relevant organizations appreciated this need at a relatively early stage and in the period of 1975-80 launched five pilot projects. Of these one - located in Budapest Technical University and jointly run by a number of research organizations - is an experimental plant, at present comprising 3 lathes, 3 machining centres and 2 robots under

Presented at the PROLOMAT Conference, May 1979
Reprinted from Advanced Manufacturing Technology, P. Blake, Editor
North-Holland Publishing Company,© IFIP 1980

computer control, with a link to an interactive graphic CAD facility. The other four are production facilities installed in factories, of which Table I contains the main data.

* Including automatic part-changers

Name of factory	Type of component	Machine* tools	Control computer	Remarks
Csepel Machine Tool	Boxes and lids	5 maching centres	TPA/70	Incl. CAD facility
SZIM Machine Tool	Boxes and lids	4	R10	
EVIG Electric Motors	Motor housing	4	TPA/70	
HAFE Gears	Boxes and lids	3	TPA/70	

MAIN DATA OF FOUR PILOT CAM FACILITIES
TABLE I

Some units of these systems have been in operation for two years now and all four complete facilities will be entering into three-shift production within the next 20 months.

According to our initial intentions, the four pilot installations were to have led to a consolidation of the technologies of designing and making CAM systems, so that by the end of the above period, we should be able to design, produce and deliver further systems as a matter of routine. All experimentation was to have been confined to the experimental system at the University, specially earmarked for this purpose. This, however, was not to be the case. Both computer and machine-tool technology advanced far too fast to permit simple reproduction of even two year-old systems, and local requirements - related to the plant's products, environment and management methods - varied far more than was foreseen.

THE FACTORY ENVIRONMENT

In this Section we shall discuss some of the major problem areas which we have encountered in transferring integrated manufacturing systems from the research and development domain into a real-world factory environment.

These are
- the selection of personnel
- the level of performance required
- the training of operating personnel and the operating instructions to be supplied to them
- the balancing of automation and operator confidence requirements
- interfacing with the rest of the factory.

Personnel. One of the first, non-trivial tasks in the installation of a computerized manufacturing system in a factory is to recruit the right type of personnel for the acceptance, operation, maintenance and enhancement of the system. These have on the one hand to be people who are adequately versed in computers control technology, software techniques, electronics. Such professionals are generally biased towards research and development work, the better their qualifications, the more is their motivation creatively oriented. On the other hand they should be people whose prime objective is production in a disciplined, orderly, efficient machinery. This requires a mentality that strives for well-established manufacturing processes and evinces a conservative attitude towards even necessary and beneficial change.

While real-life people are, of course, generally not gradeable into such extremal categories, our experiences hitherto have indicated that this can be a serious problem. It is of great importance when the time comes to sever a novel system's links to the research and development which engendered it, and to ensure the primacy of production over all other considerations. At the same time experience has shown that it is not practicable to entrust computerized manufacturing systems to people who are wholly dependent on outside expertise even for minor adjustments.

Performance. Research and development departments and many computer and control system manufacturers tend to equate a high-potential system with a high-performance one. In their view a flexible system, well furnished with development tools, permits the customer to adapt to whatever concrete requirements he has. Most manufacturers, however, hold a different view - they require, especially at the outset, a polished, fully turn-key facility, that will perform as a production unit from the first moment.

In order to meet such requirements, very close preliminary teamwork is required between system designers and the customer's production engineers. This must begin with the selection of a representative set of parts to be produced on the system, followed by an analysis of alternative technologies for their manufacture.

Only once these have been exhaustively evaluated by simulation of various configurations, and process planning schemes, can the system, including tooling, tool-wear monitoring, workpiece transport, emergency re-routing arrangements, dimensional checking, etc. be so specified as to achieve economically sound performance levels.

Training and instructions. Bearing in mind the size and heterogeneity (electronic, electrical, mechanical, hydraulic, etc.) of an integrated manufacturing system, moreover the fact that its component parts are closely independent, user manuals, operating instructions and other training aids compiled along traditional lines tend to be very voluminous. While it is undoubtedly necessary to supply these as well, the relatively high rate of labour fluctuation in our factories renders operator and maintenance personnel training on this basis rather expensive. Our experience suggests that the presence of computers in the system permits a very profitable use of tutorial techniques, by means of which the system can itself - in an optional tutorial mode - teach its operators how to handle it. In order to achieve this, a multi-level handbook structure must be set up, whose lowest level is available for interrogation during system operation and in conjunction with diagnostic programs for shop-floor level trouble-shooting and maintenance.

Confidence. The designer and supplier of a flexible manufacturing system must conduct a continuous balancing act between two, contradictory sets of requirements. On the one hand, there will be those who require the system to perform in a wholly automatic manner, excluding any possibility of human interference, and thus ensuring that the manufacturing process will take place in exactly the planned mode and with the planned parameters (feed-rates, tool values, etc.). According to this philosophy, any departure from the previously scheduled and planned procedures and values is a failure and should be treated as such. The proponents of the opposing view require safeguards and manual operation alternatives at every conceivable location. In their opinion a costly investment in machine tools can not be exposed to the risk of idling on account of a computer or control system failure, moreover it is unrealistic to expect that castings, tool diameters, etc. will always be within the pre-programmed tolerance limits. They therefore require facilities for manually overriding the system whenever the operators see fit.

Experience has taught us to steer a very careful course between the two philosophies. It has often been stated that the main benefit from introducing a computer into the workshop is the increased control it gives to management over technology and scheduling. This benefit must not be lost, by making it easy to use the system in an anarchical fashion. At the same time care must be taken to prevent a loss of confidence in the system by production personnel, due to cumbersome procedures for making necessary adjustments or eliminating the consequences of partial system failures. Here too, a multi-mode system of operation can be very useful, where - as confidence in the system is established - there can be a progressive transition towards increasingly automatic operation. This can well be combined with a monitoring arrangement which reports reversions to lower modes to supervisors.

Interfaces. One of the hardest system introduction tasks in a plant is to match the system interfaces to the extant operating modes and organization of the rest of the factory. An integrated manufacturing system is far more exigent in this respect than the traditional workshop. It requires raw materials (or semi-manufactured parts) to be delivered according to precise time schedules and strictly within quality and dimensional tolerance limits. Tooling must be available in the planned quantity and quality at all times. There must always be a full complement of trained operating personnel for each of the three shifts. The system must be able to accept and issue the documents (work-sheets, bills of delivery, production status reports, etc.) which are used in the rest of the factory. All these interfaces must first be studied in detail by joint teams of the factory and system supplier personnel and then be set down in jointly agreed procedures. Although the introduction of a computerized manufacturing system may, in fact, require that a number of the previous practices and procedures of the factory be revised (indeed, this may be a major benefit of its introduction), these revisions must be determined and carried out before the system is installed. The reverse procedure will lead to lengthy arguments and to disillusionment with the whole idea of computer-based manufacturing.

Such, then, are some of the major problems of introducing integrated manufacturing systems into a factory environment. Some, as we have seen, are organizational (e.g. personnel selection), but most also have direct consequences in system design.

SYSTEM DESIGN

In Hungary at present the design of each integrated manufacturing system has been a research and development exercise, involving the active, personal participation of top-flight R & D personnel. In order to permit tenders for the delivery of systems to be prepared as a piece of routine engineering activity and to prevent the (necessarily) unique nature of each system from involving very high design and installation costs, it is necessary to:
- establish an appropriate organization,
- set out a standardized design procedure,

- develop appropriate sets of design tools
- lay down standard acceptance procedures.

Organization. In order to design, market and deliver turnkey, integrated manufacturing systems as a commercially viable exercise, it is necessary to establish a consortium-type organization comprising the machine tool, the computer and the control system manufacturer, and a team of production engineering, organizational and business experts. These must be linked together by a systems analysis and synthesis group, which will coordinate the entire activity and develop a unitary methods framework for its operation and documentation.

Such organizations have so far nowhere fully emerged. In the United States there are large machine-tool companies that have developed their own computer subsidiaries, there are systems houses which assemble ad hoc consortia and there are even users, who have established their own automation divisions. In Japan, there are large, diversified corporations which can assemble all the necessary potential from their own subsidiaries. But in Europe - and also for the majority of medium-sized US businesses - the requisite organizational form has been very slow to develop. The solution for the smaller countries may well lie in constituting multi-national, multi-disciplinary consortia.

Design procedure. For system design to become routine engineering, accepted design procedures have to be established. These must start with the clarification of the customer's requirements and the supplier's possibilities.

The first step must be a thorough, joint technological assessment with the user's production engineers, of the manufacturing task which the system will be expected to satisfy, and of the technology to be used. This step necessarily involves the selection and analysis of a representative set of products, as previously mentioned.

The next step is an economic analysis of the pay-off the system is expected to yield. In our view, no satisfactory method at present exists for accurately assessing the economic benefits (especially the so-called secondary ones, like lead-time reduction) which accrue from the introduction of a manufacturing system. Nevertheless, this is a point that must in future be clarified and agreed right at the outset, for otherwise subsequent friction over the cost-effectiveness of proposed or requested enhancements, etc. is inevitable. If there is an agreed basic assumption on profitability criteria, all later decisions can be based on them.

A further, early step in the procedure is an unequivocal clarification of what the customer expects the user to guarantee. Should it be the value of throughput per unit of time? Or the degree of utilization of the machines in the system? These can have widely differing consequences, and unless they are jointly established at the outset, can lead to endless disagreements and waste of resources on both sides.

It is only after these steps have been taken that the more traditional design procedure can follow.

Tools. The only way drastically to reduce design costs is, as far as possible, to automate them. The main component parts of the CAD system for the design of integrated manufacturing systems which we are hoping increasingly to use are:
- a module library
- an interactive system design technique
- simulation
- computer-aided documentation.

The module library should, ideally, be an international effort along the lines previously recommended at PROLAMAT :7], based on an agreed set of interface and functional content description standards. However, even if compiled on a narrower national (e.g. I-CAM) or corporate basis, a computer database containing in readily accessible, standard form the description of all system modules so far developed, is a very great aid to design.

The core of a computer-aided system for manufacturing system design, must in our view be an interactive, computer-based implementation of a mature, well-documented system design procedure, such as SADT (Structured Analysis and Design Technique, developed by SOFTECH Inc., Boston, Mass.) [8]. For our CAD system we have developed a graphically interactive version of such a technique, which automatically generates not only the requisite documentation, but also the computer input to subsequent analysis and simulation programs, such as ISDOS, SIMULA and GPSS [9].

Simulation of the operation of the system under both normal and failure-mode conditions, for normal and for extremal part mixes will give the designer a 'handsome' experience of system behaviour, that could otherwise only be gained by very expensive (both in money and confidence) experimentation. The adaption of a unitary, computer-based design technique will render this phase almost automatic.

Finally the biggest advantage of using computer tools for system design is the help these techniques can give towards the generation of documentation. The design of an integrated manufacturing system is necessarily a team activity. Through the introduction into the design office of a set of interactive work-stations with editing and figure-drawing facilities, all accessing, updating and building a common data-base, the two - hitherto sequential - phases of design and documentation can be dovetailed into each other.

Acceptance. Since an integrated system is - by definition - more than the sum of its independent modules, it is essential at the outset to design the system in such a way, that its sub-systems and modules should be separately testable. Where necessary, this may involve the need to design separate programs or hardware simulators, but it is nevertheless vital that the acceptance criteria and procedures for each module and sub-system be clearly established and documented in the design phase. It is only thus that unnecessary and costly recriminations can be avoided in the commissioning etage and that the whole commissioning and acceptance procedure can be adequately planned. (No departure from this piecewise commissioning plan should later be permitted, as this is a sure way, towards rocketing installation overheads.)

These appear to be some of the main steps required to reduce the presently very high tendering, design and installation costs of manufacturing systems. However, the supplier will also carry much of the subsequent responsibility for system maintenance.

MAINTENANCE

The maintenance of a manufacturing system containing computers, electronic controls, communication links, etc. in a very closely intertwined fashion is a frightening prospect for many would-be customers. The only way we see towards selling them such a system is to offer facilities by means of which the user's own - not very highly trained or equipped - personnel can them-selves avert most failure conditions. The means to doing this, are:
- computer-aided fault location
- multi-level software facilities.

Diagnostics. For a computer-based manufacturing system to be attractive to a customer who is a relative novice to shop-floor electronics, it must demonstrably have very full diagnostic facilities. These should be on four levels. One, the basic level, being run automatically at pre-determined times, should check the fundamental operability of the system. (E.g. a check of the DNC data-link by sending out a message to each controller and reading it back, as an integral part of the "Switch-On" procedure.) The second level is one where the operator specifically requests a check of a particular facility. The third, should be the trouble-shooting facility that helps factory maintenance personnel locate a fault (e.g. a faulty circuit board) and exchange it. Finally, the fourth level is one for the supplier's maintenance personnel to run in case of major failures. Implementing such a full range of diagnostics is no simple matter - they have to be designed both into the software and hardware (e.g. status registers) of the system.

However, their pay-off rate is very favourable indeed.

Multi-level software. By full analogy with the above considerations, we have also designed software to be available at several levels. The lowest level is that accessible to the operator, who may generally only change numerical values or sequences in a currently running program, but whithout access to that program's library version. At the second level the factory's production engineering personnel can permanently change production-related programs (e.g. to include new machine tools, new machine data, etc.). The highest level - at which the system software itself can be accessed and changed - is reserved to personnel of the supplier [10]. In each case the appropriate levels are protected by passwords and similar devices.

SUMMARY

Can the problems which arise when integrated manufacturing systems emerge from the R & D environment, be satisfactorily met? Can these systems be tendered, designed, delivered at reasonable cost? These questions are of practical concern to us in Hungary. The above paper - not a "scientific" one, in the usual sense - attempts to share our thoughts and experiences on these problems with the reader.

REFERENCES

1. Yoshikawa, H.: Unmanned machine shop project in Japan. In "Advances in computer-aided manufacture", Ed. D. McPherson, North-Holland, 1977. pp. 3-20.
2. Zimmerman, M.: ICAM: Revolution in manufacturing. Machine Design, Vo. 49, No. 1. /1977/
3. Knörnschild, M., Kessner, H.: CONCEMA - computer control of machine tools. In "Advances in computer-aided manufacture", ed. D. McPherson, North-Holland, 1977, pp. 241-248.
4. Stute, G., Bauer, E., Wilhelm, R.: Workflow layout of a flexible manufacturing system. Ibid. pp. 257-277.
5. "Automated Small Batch Production Technical Study", NEL, Glasgow, 1978.
6. Proc. of the CMEA Conference and exhibition on NC technology", DOM Technicky, CSVTS, Bratislava, 1978.
7. Hatvany, J.: The distribution of functions in manufacturing systems. In "Advances in computer-aided manufacture" Ed. D. McPherson, North-Holland, 1977, pp. 23-27.
8. Ross, D.T.: Structured analysis: a language for communicating ideas. IEEE Trans. on Software Engineering, Vol. 3, No. 1, pp. 16-34 /1977/
9. Bernus, P.: Plan for a computer-aided systems design facility. Internal Memo /in Hungarian/. Computer and Automation Institute, Budapest, 1977.
10. Hoffmann, P., Nagy, S.S., Vaskovics, Gy.: DNC enhancements increasing user autonomy in system modification and error control. In "Advances in computer-aided manufacture", Ed. D. McPherson, North-Holland, 1977. pp. 249-256.

CHAPTER 7

ROBOTS AND CAM

Source: Numerical Control Society, Tenth Annual Meeting and Technical Conference Proceedings

The Industrial Robot
In Computer Aided Manufacturing

By George E. Munson, Jr.
Unimation Inc.

INTRODUCTION

Any discussion of how best to combine and apply proven technologies in our manufacturing process must include an awareness of the prime objectives. There are only two - increased productivity and reduced costs.

While this might be a distasteful thought to some (purists), it is reality. The strength of our economic base and the enhancement and enrichment of our lives flow from this well-head.

This paper is not intended to develop an "industrial philosophy of life"; but its purpose is ill served if recognition is not given to certain constraints that have inhibited productivity growth, jeopardized our competitiveness in world markets and adversely affected our manufacturing cost structures.

What is in question here is how best we can combine and apply our developed technologies in a cost effective manner towards an ever increasing degree of total automation in the manufacturing process itself. This will involve discarding many "traditional" approaches while cautiously avoiding engineering monuments that lead to oblivion.

Some of the constraints which require reevaluation are:

Economic justification - All important, traditional techniques are liable not to take into consideration indirect but cost effective benefits of automation.

Labor resistance - Usually results from poor communications between labor and management and the lack of meaningful retraining programs.

Facility restrictions - Insufficient space and outmoded building designs (e.g., high rise storage).

Awareness of available technology - Proven equipment selection is seriously hampered by poor technology information transfer.

Unsatisfactory installations - For whatever reasons, poor performance is a deterrent to technology application.

Purchase of equipment vs. technology - E.G., one estimate says that 92% of capital spending is for newer models of existing technology vs. 8% for new technology equipment. Also, "islands of automation" are created - usually a quick fix with major problem area untouched and early obsolescence pre-ordained.

Resistance to change - Needs no elaboration.

While by no means an exhaustive list, these are certainly serious deterrents to our economic growth. Especially when we consider that many foreign industries and governments have long since become "enlightened" in effectively applying new technolgies. And they have done so with the long and not short term benefits in mind.

THE COMPUTER

Computer technology is perhaps as advanced as any technology available to American industry. Yet, the degree to which this technology is used in manufacturing applications is minimal, relative to the potential. Some of the reasons for this have already been given.

Resistance to change is perhaps the foremost deterrent to computer application (as with any new technology). Far too many manufacturing and process control managers are reluctant to give up the flexibility of human control because of alleged peculiarities in "their" manufacturing processes. The fact is, efforts to automate often reveal a lack of understanding and control of what is really going on in the existing process.

Nevertheless, computers are finding their way into our manufacturing systems. Giving the manufacturing managers their due, this is in spite of rapidly changing and sometimes confusing advances in computer hardware and software. Hopefully, work sponsored by such groups and agencies as the NSF, NSF/RANN grantees and CAM-I will do much to sort out and coordinate CAM systems and procedures.

THE INDUSTRIAL ROBOT

The industrial robot was conceived and designed for flexibility and nonobsolescence. In its conception, recognition was given to several factors:

1. Hard or special purpose automation assumes fixed product design for a long period to justify the investment. In other words, automating a process could only be justified if the life cycle or volume of the product was sufficient to yield an acceptable return on the investment within a very limited life span after which the automation is scrapped.

2. Tedious and hazardous jobs would be increasingly more difficult to fill as the available labor force became more reluctant to perform such tasks.

3. Truly flexible automation must be adaptable to a multitude of advances in manufacturing techniques including compatibility with advanced NC machine tools, group technology principles and computer aided and directed manufacturing systems.

Such design criteria define the major attributes of an industrial robot. It must have enough degrees of freedom (axes of motion) to perform in the human environment; it must have an easily programmable control system of adequate memory capacity; and it must be easily integrated into the process of which it forms a part.

Such criteria suggest a high degree of sophistication. Sophistication, however, is not synonymous with complexity as is so often thought. In fact, the opposite case is what makes the true industrial robot such a viable and flexible manufacturing tool.

THE UNIMATE INDUSTRIAL ROBOT

Unlike European and especially Japanese developments, robot technology in the United States has not been broadly exploited in the market place except by one firm, Unimation, Inc. Therefore, the following discussions will use the Unimate industrial robot as a model (Fig. 1).

The Unimate is a hydraulically powered, completely self-contained robot including solid state electronically controlled servos and a programmable read only memory (PROM). It is available with various degrees of freedom up to 8 and various size memories, currently up to 8K.

In the jargon of the computer field, it employs a dedicated minicomputer to control and direct its functions (Fig. 2). In a real sense it is a CNC machine. It also includes the functional elements of a soft-wired programmable controller. And it is readily adaptable to communicating with and/or taking directions from an executive computer within the framework of a CAM system.

Its dexterity is exemplified by the diversity of jobs it is currently performing in forging, glass handling, press loading, machine tool loading, spot welding, MIG welding, die casting,

palletizing, investment casting and a multitude of other material handling and transfer operations.

THE ROBOT AND
COMPUTER AIDED MANUFACTURING

Until very recently, robot applications have not been in a CAM environment. Except for large scale automotive installations and in specific types of jobs such as die casting, most applications can be classified as "islands of automation." Worse still, the robot has been applied to archaic machinery which demands truly anthropomorphic attributes which the robot was never designed to emulate.

The roboticist can only take heart that, if he has done his job well, his machine is ready, willing and able to perform in a truly integrated automated manufacturing system. In the meantime, he must be content with filling needs effectively in "islands of automation," knowing his robot will not be obsoleted by new technology applications.

In the case of the Unimate, the extent to which it has met present needs and is ready to meet future needs is illustrated by three contrasting examples:

Example 1

The complexities in producing high quality die casting are found primarily in the hydraulics of forcing molten metal at high velocities into complex mold cavities. However, removing the casting from the die cast machine, cooling, trimming and transferring them to fin-

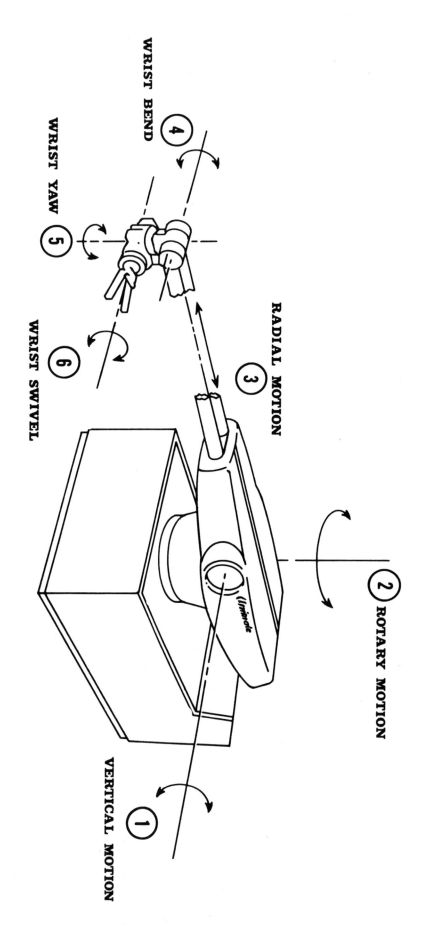

Six Program-Controlled Articulations of Unimate Industrial Robot:

WRIST BEND ④

WRIST YAW ⑤

WRIST SWIVEL ⑥

RADIAL MOTION ③

ROTARY MOTION ②

VERTICAL MOTION ①

Figure 1
Unimate Industrial Robot

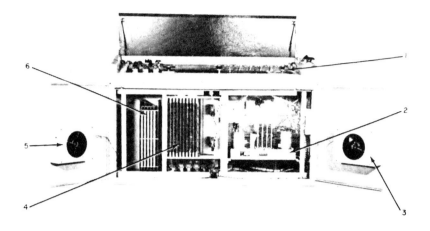

1. Control Panel
2. Power Supply
3. Fan
4. Electronic Card File
5. Fan
6. Memory

Figure 2

Unimate Control Console Assembly

ishing operations involve substantial costs which have been dramatically reduced through the use of robots having a high degree of manipulative dexterity (Fig. 3). Installation of the robot and interfacing it with the machinery involved is quite simple. I/O functions which are standard in the robot facilitate its use as a programmable controller as well as a transfer device. The robot's flexible memory provides low cost techniques for alternate actions to be taken as determined by external decisions. All faculties of the robot are employed to advantage in a relatively simple but highly productive system.

Example 2

A foundry operation involves successive complex work piece manipulations at several sequential stations. Several process parameters are sensed, decisions are made and actions are called for. One robot is employed at each station

(Fig. 4). A family of work pieces are processed randomly through the system. A central process computer controls the entire operation by integrating information between the process parameters and the robot. The robot is capable of storing in its (local) memory eight programs which are randomly selected by the computer as dictated by the work piece and related process requirements. In addition, the computer has on file numerous additional robot programs to provide for the entire family of work pieces. When and as required, appropriate programs are transferred from the computer to the robot's local memory where they remain for as long as required. The robot programs are originally generated in the conventional manner of actually leading the robot through the required motions, point-to-point. This is a representative robot/CAM system. The robot is identical to that used in example 1 except for the addition of a

Figure 3
Unimate Unloads Die Cast Machine and Feeds Trim Press

Figure 4
Unimate in Investment Casting Foundry

simple, low cost computer interface.

Example 3

NC machine tools have made possible the manufacture of complex, close tolerance production parts that would be extremely difficult to make with manual machines. The advent of CNC has added even greater flexibility to NC equipment. Application of the principles of group technology will do much to increase machine tool utilization and will form a more sophisticated basis for machine selection and purchase.

The high costs of material handling, machine loading and unloading and in-process inventory are still present, however. It is in this area of concern that the sophisticated industrial robot will play an important role.

An example of a highly integrated DNC system (and, incidently, an example of Japanese aggressiveness) is operating in Fujitsu Fanuc, Ltd., Tokyo, Japan.

A total of 18 NC machines (Figs. 5 and 6) including 11 lathes are employed in the machining of a large variety of pulse motor parts. The system performs 454 operations to manufacture 151 different types of parts and it is tended by only seven operators. Fujitsu estimates that conventional machining would require 50 operators for the same work load.

Eight of the lathes are loaded and unloaded by a single Unimate traveling on an overhead rail and positioning system (Fig. 7). The Unimate is equipped with a unique hand (end effector) capable of handling the various shapes, sizes and weights of parts.

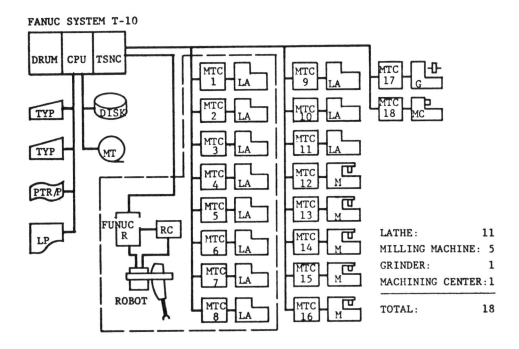

Figure 5
Robot-DNC System

Figure 6
Robot Mounted on Overhead Conveyor Serviced 8 NC Lathes

Features of the hand (Fig. 8) are:

1. Three fingers which open and close centripetally to clamp the work piece;

2. Rotation (of the work piece) by an electric pulse motor. This function is required for orienting irregular shaped parts relative to the lathe chuck;

3. Detection of opening and closing of the fingers. By comparing the actual position of the fingers to where they should be when the work piece is clamped, presence, absence or improper clamping of the part is determined;

4. Longitudinal, controlled motion of the hand to insert the work piece into the chuck.

This system includes the DNC (Fanuc System T-10), FANUC R, the robot and the lathes (Fig. 9). The magnetic disk memory in the DNC system stores the NC command data and robot command data for all work pieces to be machined. Fanuc R is a special interface which sends and receives the robot command data required to operate the robot and its hand.

154

The Industrial Robot in Computer Aided Manufacturing

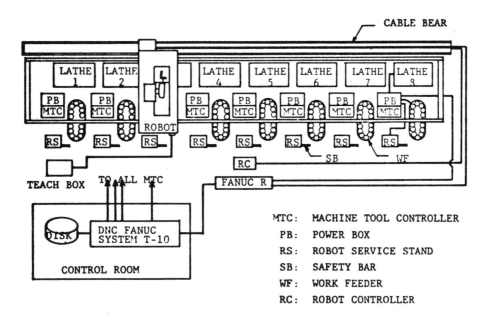

MTC: MACHINE TOOL CONTROLLER
PB: POWER BOX
RS: ROBOT SERVICE STAND
SB: SAFETY BAR
WF: WORK FEEDER
RC: ROBOT CONTROLLER

Figure 7
Plan View of Robot Travelling Above Lathes

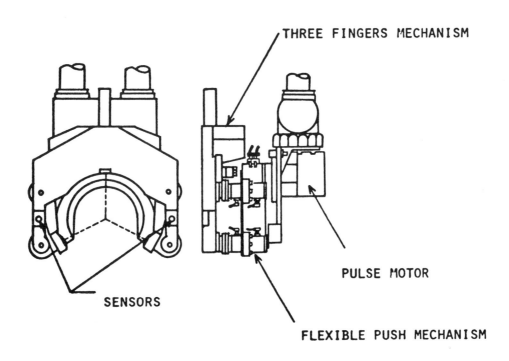

Figure 8
Special Multi-function Robot Hand

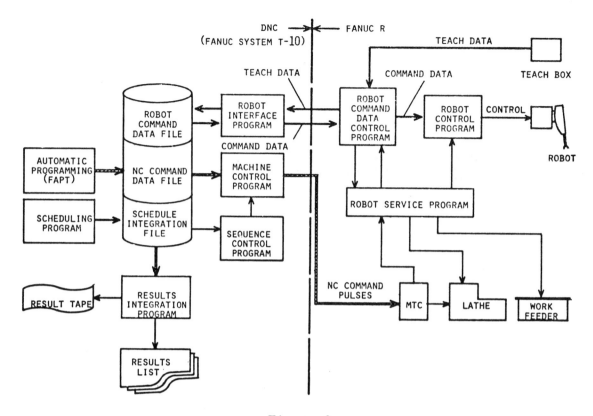

Figure 9
Function of Robot-DNC System Software

As in example 2, the robot command data file is loaded initially by manual, point-to-point teaching of the robot and transferring the data from the Unimate's memory to the data file. In playback, the DNC, then, supplies the appropriate robot service program as required by the lathe demanding service and the work piece involved.

A single operator monitors the system operation. He supplies work pieces to the work feeders, samples fabricated parts for testing, adusts tools, etc. Fujitsu says that four operators per shift would be required to tend the eight lathes if the robot was not employed. By American (traditional) standards, it is questionable whether the system could be cost justified. However, when all direct and indirect costs are considered

(multi-shift) operation, minimum in-process inventory, no personnel breaks, etc.), increased productivity and reduced costs are probably quite attractive.

THE ROBOT AND THE COMPUTER

The foregoing examples illustrate the ease with which the industrial robot is integrated into CAM systems. Exactly how best to interface the robot with the computer can be controversial and therefore bears consideration. Again the Unimate industrial robot is used as the model.

There are four basic approaches to be considered:

1. <u>Interaction with a process control computer</u>. This is the simplest approach and, in fact, is already commonly applied (and there-

fore is not discussed further). It involves interfacing with the Unimate through already available communication channels such as OPERATE EXTERNAL, WAIT EXTERNAL, MEMORY ACCESS CONTROL, RANDOM PROGRAM SELECTION, ALTERNATE PROGRAM SELECTION, etc. so that the Unimate and the equipment with which it works are synchronized in real time. Obviously a computer, per se, is not always needed since a simple programmable controller or even limit switches will often be adequate.

2. Computer control of the Unimate memory address. The Unimate is a point-to-point machine, and each position in space consumes one program step in the memory. The normal mode of operation is for the Unimate to advance through each of its taught program steps sequentially as all stored commands in each step are satisfied. In other words, addressing the memory is a controlled function within the Unimate.

However, it is possible to address all steps in the memory externally. In the case of a variable combination of robot actions which are to be a function of external data, a computer could be used to select the next action by proper addressing to the robot memory. Thus, all the necessary Unimate motions would be recorded in its memory using the standard teach mode. In playback, the external computer directs the sequence through which the robot

is to proceed.

3. Mass storage of the programs in the computer. In this case, the Unimate does not have its own memory. Teaching programs is done in the usual manner, but storage is in a central computer. It is possible for the central computer to store programs for many robots. The care needed to insure that each Unimate has access to the computer (memory) when it requires new information, plus the cost of interface circuitry and adequate computer memory capacity, may make such an approach cumbersome and uneconomical.

4. Direct computer control of the Unimate. This assumes that the computer is to generate all control and memory functions for the robot. In other words, it must duplicate that which has already been designed - the Unimate electronic system. Such a substitution is unlikely to be economically sound.

INPUT-OUTPUT INTERFACE
WITH UNIMATE

Definition

1. The basic unit of information in the Unimate is a 16 bit binary word. Fifteen bits are information carrying and the sixteenth is used for odd parity checking.

2. A complete Unimate program step (or byte) is made up of eight 16 bit words, or a total of 128 binary bits.

3. Of the eight 16 bit words, six are used to control the six motion axes of the Uni-

mate, while the remaining two are devoted to auxiliary or ancillary information such as OPERATE EXTERNAL, WAIT FOR EXTERNAL, CLAMP, WELD, TIME DELAY, etc.

4. In Unimation's lexicon, the eight 16 bit words are spoken of as "groups". The group assignments are:

Group 1: Auxiliary commands
Group 2: Auxiliary commands
Group 3: Swivel servo
Group 4: Out-in (radial motion) servo
Group 5: Yaw servo (wrist)
Group 6: Down-up (shoulder motion) servo
Group 7: Bend servo (wrist)
Group 8: Rotary (waist motion) servo

5. The system is a time-shared one which is normally run by a four kilohertz clock. This provides a scan time for each group of 250 microseconds and an update rate of 500 hertz. For particular interface requirements, provision is available to suppress this rate or to enforce asynchronous control of it.

Teach Mode Input-Output

1. The present position/condition code for any group is available as a 16 bit binary number.

2. Simultaneously, the present command code in the memory for that group is available.

3. The present memory address is available as a 10 bit binary number. A new address may be externally selected.

4. The groups are identified by eight individual output lines. They may be selected by external control.

5. The memory may be altered or modified by a 16 bit parallel input to the Unimate.

Repeat Mode Input-Output

1. The present position/condition code for each group and the memory content for that group are simultaneously presented as two 16 bit parallel words.

2. The rate is governed by the internal clock; therefore, the eight groups are sequentially presented for 250 microseconds each and updated at 500 hertz.

3. The memory content may be changed or modified, but the incoming information must be synchronized with the internal clock.

4. The eight individual group identification lines are available and may be used for synchronization.

Example 1: Computer Control of the Unimate Memory Address

Consider a grouping of metal cutting machines, each having an array of automatically changed tools. The grouping permits efficient processing of a range of similar but slightly different parts in the most economical way. Loading, unloading and transferring is best done by the versatile robot. Now, rather than program the robot with individual programs for each possible part, necessitating a large memory file, let us take advantage of the things already available in the computer. It already has information identifying the parts, the number of each kind to be processed and the sequence in which the process is to take place. Using record-playback we "teach" the robot the location of every point in space involved in selecting the part, loading and unloading it from each of the machines, presenting it to inspection equipment and dispatching it from the system on pallets, registering the address of each point or the beginning of each simple sequence with the computer. The computer can now feed the robot with the address corresponding to actions that must be taken in completely passing any given part through the system, using information it already has.

The Unimate input-output:

1. A single line from the Unimate presents a request for address information.

2. A maximum of 10 bit normal straight binary address information should be presented in parallel to the Unimate (1024 step memory).

3. A single line from the Unimate acknowledges receipt of the address; OR the present Unimate memory address is available as a 10 bit parallel straight binary word.

4. The 10 bit parallel binary address information is available during programming of the Unimate for entry into the computer.

Example 2: Mass Storage of the Programs in the Computer

Where it is desirable to have no local memory in the Unimate, provision can be made to interface with an external computer for this purpose.

In this case, however, particular attention must be paid to the timing in terms of the external computer's availability. During programming (or teaching) of the Unimate, when the record button is pressed, all 128 bits of information can be stored in a scratch pad memory which can then be unloaded to the external computer when access is available. The timing can be controlled by the external computer.

When the robot is in operation in the repeat mode, however, the situation can be more complex. The Unimate operates asynchronously and therefore will require new command information at irregular intervals. In the worst case, a new 128 bit word may be required as often as every 100 milliseconds.

Whether the information transmittal is serial or 16 bit parallel it certainly can be accomplished in less than 100 milliseconds (in fact, 16 milliseconds should suffice). The Unimate would have two 128 bit scratchpads, one being loaded while the other is being used. If, however, the computer cannot react on demand because of higher priority interrupts, then the scratchpad buffering in the Unimate must be increased accordingly. The additional buffering would be determined by dividing the maximum access time to the external computer by 100 milliseconds.

Now, any difficulties of this nature could be overcome by retaining enough solid state memory locally in the Unimate to contain all the program steps of one Unimate cycle (typically ranging from 16 to 64 steps, or 2K to 8K of memory). This could be loaded from the external memory to the Unimate prior to the initiation of each cycle. Should the external computer not be available, or should a priority interrupt occur, the Unimate would simply wait until it could obtain service.

While the idea of mass storage in an external computer may seem attractive, we must recognize that so many megabits of mass storage must be paid for. It is unlikely that any robot user who has a computer system also has unused memory capacity. Consider how much more economical it would be to simply provide a mass memory for the Unimates without involving the computer. A disk file of large capacity typically has a maximum access time of eight milliseconds. This means that up to 16 Unimates could share a common mass memory with only a single scratch pad in each Unimate and NO access time problems. A program for one Unimate could be modified or corrected while the others continued in operation.

Example 3: Direct Computer Control of a Unimate

When we talk about direct computer control of a Unimate, we do not mean interaction with a process control computer for a system, since this is the normal process occurring today in Unimate applications. We must mean, therefore, substitution of a standard (?) computer for the electronic system of a Unimate.

The computer must have additional memory to the extent it would have been available in the Unimate (anywhere from 1K x 16 to 8K x 16). The computer must have the computational ability to perform the arithmetic of er-ror determination. It must have complex programs allowing it to handle real time decision making and promulgation of auxiliary and ancillary signals.

Since the present Unimate electronic system is a pre-programmed, dedicated minicomputer with built-in I-O, the economic substitution of a programmable minicomputer seems very unlikely.

SUMMARY

Advances in computer technology have opened the doors to computer aided design, computer aided manufacturing, computer data base management and enhancement of group technology principles. Combining these technologies with conventional and NC machine tools and the sophisticated general purpose industrial robot, will yield higher manufacturing productivity, reduce costs and pave the way to the totally automated factory.

Robot R & D is being directed towards greater flexibility and dexterity, inclusion of adaptive controls, eye sight, tactile sensing, etc. However, today's industrial robot already has the versatility and adaptability to operate effectively in CAM systems.

The challenge is to combine and apply our available technologies now.

CHAPTER 8

ECONOMIC CONSIDERATIONS

Originally presented in 1972, rewritten for CAD/CAM: Meeting Today's Productivity Challenge

Economic Considerations Of CAD/CAM

By Kenneth C. Bonine
Data Systems Specialist
Western Data Systems Center
General Dynamics Corporation

Computer-aided design and computer-aided manufacturing are practical realities within the present state-of-the-art of interactive computing and data management. However, implementation of this new methodology depends upon justification of cost effectiveness over current design and manufacturing methodology and practice. Some of the features of the management and working environment are presented to provide context and perspective for evaluating the economic considerations. Examples are given to provide a quantitative basis for deriving dollar values for resources, time, manpower and hardware involved.

INTRODUCTION

The terms computer-aided design (CAD) and computer-aided manufacturing (CAM) are still subject to varied interpretation due to the multidimensional nature of the component words and the applications of the terms themselves. A working definition is thus in order for this paper.

The use of the electronic computer as a tool to assist in the design and manufacturing processes is an accepted way of business life. Efficient use of the computer as a tool has often been assumed but seldom has it had to be proven. One of the main factors complicating this situation is the necessity of having a certain amount of computing power simply to compete in some industries. The other major item is the definition and understanding of the relationship between the computer and the user in both the engineering and business aspects of problem solving.

The problem-solving loop of Figure 1 is the "real system" to be optimized for cost effective use. The three entities shown (users, operators, and computer hardware/soft ware) are usually controlled through three or more chains of command. The separate channels of authority and projectization have allowed the entities to be decoupled for accounting purposes. The result has been that, historically, cost effectiveness has been computed for and within the separate areas with little understanding of the actual overall cost effectiveness of the system.

The advent of interactive computing with the user actually in the loop in real time has served to shed more light on the relationship of the user to the machine. Activities such as those mentioned by Barry Boehm in his article "Keeping the Upper Hand in the Man-Computer Relationship" (Ref. 1) have focused more attention on some of the details of this relationship.

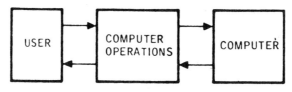

Figure 1. User/computer system loops.

It is this "person in the loop" dialogue with the computer that is the key to computer-aided design and manufacturing. The following definition from the CAD/CAM Conference in Davenport, Iowa (Ref. 2), clearly states the key principles.

"CAD is the application of computers to design where the designer converses directly with the computer by using a graphic or nongraphic console in such a manner that his problem-solving processes are highly responsive and essentially uninterrupted."

The proper emphasis is in computer ASSISTED design and computer ASSISTED manufacturing. For the purposes of the discussion:

CAD/CAM is not

1) A turnkey graphic computer system
2) A software program or aggregate or system of programs
3) A department or group so named

CAD/CAM is the integration of the following five elements into the process for specifying, designing, fabricating, and testing a product.

1) A PHILOSOPHY of using the computer to do the computational and rote parts, assisting the person who is the creative, innovative partner in the process in a responsive, on-line fashion.

2) The PEOPLE who are the key resource to be optimized. They are the ones who create the designs, devise and implement the manufacturing processes and make the key decisions.

3) The PROCEDURES which define the organized and necessary flow and verification of data. They also delineate the way in which control is effected and the appropriate decision making organization.

4) The PROGRAMS – The software (system utility routines, specific application programs) that is used to effect the analysis, geometry definition, tool path, etc.

5) The PROCESSORS – The computers, peripherals (terminals, printers, plotters, etc.) and communication equipment needed to interconnect them to each other and to any machine tool or other device used in the total process of creating, building, and testing a product.

While this is not a very succinct or pithy definition of CAD/CAM, it contains the essential elements and conveys the notion that it is a multidimensional process that is closely coupled. This is the sense in which the term CAD/CAM will be used in this paper, and with the understanding that the terms "design" and "manufacturing" are taken in the broadest sense to include all the activity engaged in by engineering, material, and manufacturing to create and produce a product.

The relationships between the user and the computer facility will be explored with a view toward determining the necessary environment for efficient use of the computer as a partner in CAD/CAM. Both the tangible and not-so-tangible factors of cost effectiveness will be discussed and some examples of quantifiable results will be shown.

ENVIRONMENT

To obtain a clear understanding of the user/computer environment, several things must be put in perspective. First, while the computer does represent the end product of a technology, to the end user it is simply a tool. Second, as a tool, the computer (and programming, per se) have no intrinsic value. Only insofar as it is an effective tool in helping the user solve his problems does the computer (or programming) have any value whatsoever to him.

Computer-User-Program Relationship*

The computer facility has become a most important tool of the engineering, manufacturing, financial, and management functions of many companies. Simultaneously, it has grown to be a very large item in the budget. Yet choosing, among all the varied configurations of the myriad available computing systems, the one that best satisfies the given needs at the lowest cost is a process fraught with guesswork, intuition, and compromise.

Determining an optimum system is so important to the company in terms of potential gains in engineering output, management efficiency, and in substantial cost savings, that a rational, scientific basis for making such a determination would be invaluable. At present, no such basis exists for a facility of the scale to be found in a company the size of a major aerospace firm.

The difficulty lies in determining the relationships among the set of problems to be solved, the people who are to solve them, and the machines with which they are provided. In the past, many studies have focused on such machine dependent parameters as add-times, throughput, instruction set and central memory size. It seems apparent, though that the interactions in the total problem-solving system must be considered to obtain a rational basis for specifying a part of that system.

Figure 2 shows that there are five mutually interacting modules, each having a unique set of describing characteristics. If we consider the problem set, the solution set, and the users as fixed and the channels and computers variable, the usual question arises: "What characteristics of channels and computers are required to solve the problem set at a *minimum cost for the entire system?*" Since the problem set itself is dynamically changing, with new problems entering and completed solutions leaving, a more practical definition of the goal is to find the channel and computers that minimize the system cost for a required rate of problem solution.

---

*Part of this section is derived from the excellent report by R.A. Phillips and R. Berman of North American Rockwell (Ref. 3).

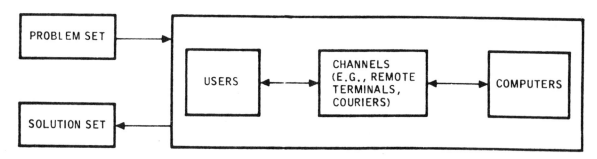

Figure 2. Problem-solving system.

Choosing an optimum computer system that includes the user is indeed a very significant and widespread problem that is beginning to receive the attention it deserves.

While consideration heretofore has largely been concentrated on the machine-cost side of the picture, user costs are growing to dominant importance. Sackman (Ref. 4) warns that reducing human costs "probably has the greatest long-range payoff in a market characterized by decreasing computer costs and rising personnel and software costs." This prediction has become fact today. In addition, the tremendous rate of increase in capability coupled with reduction in size and cost of minicomputers has made the business of defining an optimum (in the sense of computer performance) configuration in one mainframe almost obsolete. Distributed network configurations allow more flexibility in meeting user requirements. The computational power can be distributed allowing each node in a system to be less complicated, more responsive, more user oriented (Ref. 5).

New criteria for what is needed are involved with the user in the loop and interactive, such as:

1) Response time — absolute and variability
2) Tutorial vs. operational
3) Scheduled vs. open terminal access
4) Modification and control of data "on the fly"
5) Reliability

Although the literature contains some useful information and enlightening insights in the area of the value of interactivity, nowhere does there appear an approach that offers a solution to any degree of generality. Along with the importance of the problem, the difficulty of constructing such an approach is stressed repeatedly. Calingaert (Ref. 6) provides perhaps the best exposition of the difficulties and possible methods of evaluating system performance. He stresses that "the performance of a system or a component can be discussed only in the context of a specific application or set of applications . . . *Performance as an independent entity does not exist.*" (emphasis added) and that "the evaluation of information handling system performance lies somewhere between an art and a science". Messrs. Phillips and Berman discuss a number of specific problems encountered in trying to develop a methodology to optimize system interactivity for a given environment. The results of some experiments are given and the initial conclusions. The ability to solve the problem is improved by aforementioned cost trends and the current need to optimize the human resource/process more than the computer hardware and software. Criteria for cost saving, ROI, etc. for a process can be established easier, with more certainty than hardware/software performance parameters which only bear on a portion of the process for a specific application.

While cost effectiveness considerations in CAD/CAM must take into account the whole of a complex, highly coupled system, the component parts of the system may be handled in a very straightforward way as we shall see later under the economics discussion.

If this system is not well understood by the analytical people who have been using these computers for more than ten years in engineering and design, one can understand the caution of manufacturing people about being caught up in this "computer-aided" business. However, it is with due respect to their pragmatism to note that they have usually maintained the upper hand. The computer (controller) being a properly subordinated box to *the tool* − the machine tool − actually doing the work. A similar, practical perspective should be the goal of this computer-user-problem system in order to properly assess the cost effectiveness in a given environment.

Organization

Most companies usually follow the dichotomy of a business organization, and a technical organization. Both organizations use the computer to assist in doing their work and very often have separate computers for this purpose. The computer facility may be controlled by one organization or the other − or both or neither. Some companies have the computer facility as a separate entity, a division with its own profit and loss center for accounting and justification. Such separate divisions and even groups within the basic organizational structure of the company often consider themselves autonomous, or at least partially so. Francis Schaeffer, in *Escape from Reason* (Ref. 7) suggests that we have perhaps conditioned ourselves to this "uncoupling" by education and practice. The tendency to study all our disciplines (art, philosophy, mathematics, music, engineering, etc.) in unrelated parallel lines and the high degree of specialization demanded to be expert in a given field contribute to the failure in life and business to understand the natural associations between the disciplines.

So far, this isn't too bad for the purposes of this paper, since we can draw organizational block diagrams and find ways and words to associate all the groups. But, the organization is run by people − not a mechanical implementation of the lines and words on the charts and job specifications; and people are not always altruistic or without aspirations to power and authority.

The computer itself provides a useful nucleus around which an organizational empire may be readily built. This type of thing along with sincere confusion between the computer as a technology or a tool can result in people managing the facility who have little practical knowledge of how it is actually being used. In fact, a batch type operation can be controlled (without disastrous financial results) by attention principally to accounting methods and only token management in the sense of understanding the process and controlling it by adjusting the appropriate variables based on this knowledge.

Management can't be blamed completely for this approach. The rapid and continuous change in the computer technology requires a lot of effort, even at the working level, to keep abreast of it. The justification of cost effectiveness in such a varied and difficult management/organizational environment must be tailored to the situation. Education of the appropriate managers is essential – it also takes time and money, which must be taken into account in the schedule and cost of implementing CAD and CAM. Ken Ruff states in his excellent paper (Ref. 8) that this education is so essential that management cannot assume the role of a referee of a "fair fight" to see which side will win but must know enough about the results and be biased in favor of the revolution (in methodology) or they should not entertain it.

One important factor in organizations structured as they are now is the difficulty of allocating the proper credit for an ROI that accrues to one group as a result of an expenditure in another group. For instance, Manufacturing may benefit considerably from a specific data structuring and classification and early capture of manufacturing related data in computer readable form associated with the engineering data. However, Engineering will have to spend money to do those things that will provide no direct ROI to their departments. Present accounting systems and sometimes top department personnel evaluation and financial remuneration policies generally will inhibit or at least work against such "beneficial sharing" of activity for the overall good of the company.

Batch Mode Computing

This has been the way of life for most computing facilities. It is effective and efficient for some types of work and some semblance of it will remain even if the most ambitious plans of the interactive or time-sharing advocates come to fruition. However, much of the computing work done today is inefficient with regard to the system (problem-user-computer) with a terrible waste of manpower.

The principal cause of this inefficiency is the effect of "turnaround time," which is the time involved in getting data into and out of the computer and interpreting the results.

Figure 3 (Ref. 9) shows the breakdown of the factors involved in getting one computer run through the machine. The term "turnaround time" is ambiguous in that it has been applied to all four of the explicit time spans shown in Figure 3. Engineering turnaround time involves the "apparent response time" plus the following two factors:

1) Data preparation from engineering symbols, names, and units to the form required by the program (before the "coding" shown in Figure 3).

2) Output must be valid engineering results; i.e., not data coding errors, operating system/program, or machine errors. An unstable solution because of a problem gain parameter is a valid engineering answer. It may not be an acceptable solution, but it provides the engineer with insight on how to modify the problem parameters for the next run. Included in this is the time to determine what the output means (a stack of printed output may take much longer to be assimilated than a plot or graphical presentation of the output).

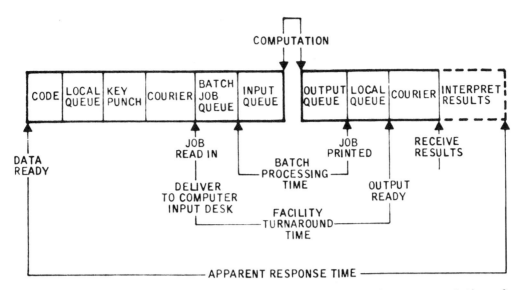

Figure 3. Computing requirements - response and turnaround time for scientific applications.

Until an engineer gets valid results from his program, he cannot make any engineering progress on that phase of his work. Therefore, engineering turnaround is measured from the time the data is ready for coding until valid engineering results are obtained. For example, if a program were submitted with one program source language coding error and one data coding input error, the turnaround time would be that shown in Figure 4. As can be seen, engineering turnaround time is a <u>function</u> of the apparent response time to get a single run through the computer. The iterative nature of the design process (Ref. 10 and 11) introduces another multiplication factor, resulting in many engineering turnaround times. Another facet that is also multiplicative is introduced through iterations caused by the interdisciplinary interactions in the design process (Ref. 10). It can be seen that a considerable amount of time is spent preparing input data or checking input data, output data, or program listings or dumps.

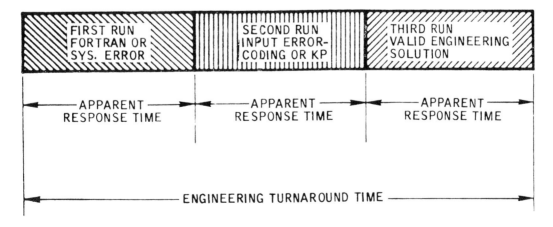

Figure 4. Example of engineering turnaround time.

While not very taxing mentally, this type of work is meticulous and demands close attention – which detracts from the time an engineer could spend on the problem itself. The time between runs is spent talking with other people, in transit between his work area and the computer input/output area, optimizing one's three-coin game at the coffee machine, and on other engineering tasks. Some time then is also spent "switching gears" mentally between jobs and computer runs. The end result is that highly trained, talented people, who are hired and paid on the basis of their potential, are often forced into a working environment that demands only a fraction of that capability and can contribute to the loss of the capability as well. Sometimes it is the loss of the person, who may go to a more personally satisfying job.

Interactive Mode Computing

Shortening the response time to "real time" (see Ref.9 for a good perspective on "real time") not only reduces the "wasted engineering manhours" but actually affects the design process as well. The problem-solving methodology will often change. The rapid, on-line feedback of the results of a parameter change allows the designer to maintain his mental momentum on that problem. This provides better insight into the problem itself and possible solutions. Creativity may be stimulated since, his attention is freed from much of the rote work and waiting associated with the batch mode of operation.

The interactive mode is a more complicated world on the computer side. Time-sharing operating systems, data banks, satellite computers, interactive terminals, tele-communication links, hardware and software interfaces, and engineer-programmer interfaces must be integrated into a smooth, reliable system. It is a system that may be more expensive in initial cost and in maintenance.

Some of the user requirements that characterize this interactive environment are:

The terminal must be available at all times during the first two shifts. This means an adequate number of terminals (one design-type terminal per five users and one analytical-type terminal per five to eight users is a goal to shoot for). It also presupposes sufficient memory, swapping capability, and I/O ports on the host computer supporting the terminals. Beware of a "reporting statistics" problem wherein some computer status reports equate system "up time" with terminal availability. These are not usually equal. For instance, a system with 40 terminals (20 hardwired, 20 dial up) and 10 dial-up autoanswer ports may have 98% uptime (host and terminals). But since only 30 of the 40 terminals can be connected to the computer at the same time the terminal availability to the user is only 73.5% ($3/4 \times 98\%$). In fact, only 50% of all the dial-up terminals can be "available" to the users at the same time.

A terminal cannot be scheduled 100% of its available time. There are two basic reasons for this user requirement; the first is concerned with not abusing the human resource, and the second with tailoring the use to the person's schedule.

1) There is a certain amount of time required to vacate a terminal area (with notebooks, drawings, etc.) and time required for log on and off. To completely schedule a terminal would require:

   a) Constraining an engineer's time and schedule to that of the terminal, and

b) Queuing up a $30 or more/hour resource (whose performance is adversely affected by waiting) to serve a $3 or less/hour resource (who just draws a little current while waiting)

It is not wise human factors practice and it is not sound financial practice to try to fully utilize a terminal at the expense of the user.

2) The problem solver (engineer, designer, analyst, etc.) activity is varied — review meetings, anlysis/design sessions, consultations, trips, fire drills on other projects, etc, etc. Flexibility and adaptability are desirable characteristics. Therefore, it is also desirable that some "open," unscheduled time be available on a terminal during the regular first shift time that he or she is at work.

Since efficiency and better use of human resources is the prime benefit from which time and cost savings derive, it is contradictory to have engineers standing in line waiting for the terminal. Further, it adds pressure to the user of the console and adversely affects the situation so carefully created where he can work naturally with the computer and concentrate primarily on his technical problem. Our current estimate is that never more than 60% of the available time should be "counted on" for analytical-type use terminals, and about 80% of available time on design-type use terminals. My experience has been primarily in a large aerospace/ground support equipment type company; where, typically, there are large complex problems to be solved that require a large mainframe computer. The first thought in this type of environment is usually "lets do it all on the mainframe," and to a point, this is a valid approach and a prime consideration. However, accessibility and usability to the end user mean not only physical location — a "friendly" user interface is also necessary. Putting a lot of users on-line interactively will usually overload a mainframe which is set up "system-wise" to do everything for everybody. The "functional richness" of such system software will be just too much overhead to efficiently or even satisfactorily handle the *short time constant demands of many interactive users. The decision to upgrade the mainframe or distribute some of the computational capability should be made with present user requirements and future plans in view. There should be a plan of computer equipment needs looking at least three years ahead. The company facility people should be a partner in making those plans.

Data must be easy to access and be protected. The user shouldn't have to be an accomplished programmer in order to get to his data or modify it. The user's programs and data need to be protected against unauthorized modification and against inadvertent loss or change by system hardware/software failures. This aspect of the on-line environment is very critical to the user's confidence in and use of the system. If it is difficult to use and his data gets lost or purged a few times, the user will go back to the manual methods to do his work.

The interactive software needs to have some tutorial help features and most especially to be checked out working software. Very little software, if any, comes "bug free," so involve the user in determining the features needed and in testing the system before acquisition and before putting any new mods/upgrades into production use.

---

*That is, the user is waiting for a response and expects it within a few seconds.

Data base management and configuration control of data and programs on the computer in machine readable form is a new and somewhat scary prospect for most users. They will need education as to their responsibilities and role in identifying, preparing, and validating data.

The user is still responsible for the end result. The interactive environment can be subtly misleading. With a few commands, a user at a terminal can cause a lot to happen and volumes of data to come out of the computer in neat graphs, etc., right now. It is the user's responsiblility to verify that the results are correct; "garbage in, garbage out," still works in real time too. In the batch mode of using the computer and in the manual method of problem solving, he usually had ways of checking results, consulting with others etc.; these may have to be modified to fit the environment, but should not be abandoned or left out because things happen quicker in the new methodology.

ECONOMIC FACTORS

Cost effectiveness is concerned not only with dollars but also with material, and the use of time and human resources. Noting the complex environment within which this cost effectiveness must be justified, it is immediately apparent that the more quantitative and dollar or cost-oriented the presentation is, the better the chance of success. This section will show, mostly by example, some of the basis for deriving the dollar costs and benefits associated with interactive computing in CAD/CAM.

Dollar costs are usually incurred in four ways:

1) Computer Hardware – CPU and peripherals, communication interface, and terminal charges.

2) Computer Support – Computer operations, system software maintenance, and accounting support. These are often combined with the hardware charges in a computer rate that varies as a function of the yearly computer work load.

3) Software Development – Application program design, coding, documentation, and maintenance.

4) Manhours – The user's personal time in the problem-solving process.

Benefits of using the CAD/CAM methodology may be found in one or more of the following six areas:

1) Reduced labor hours
2) Shortened schedule
3) Reduced material cost
4) Reduced manufacturing cost
5) Improved product – Performance, reliability, maintainability
6) Better management information – More and more timely

All of these areas can have a dollar value assigned but generally, some choice must be made as to which benefits will be utilized on a given product at the time. Therefore, there is seldom a "fixed" or unique cost benefit or saving to be derived. However, management will require some tangible measure of the return on their investment. This is usually obtained by comparing the total cost, labor hours, and schedule time between the old way and the new.

Computer and Support Costs

Hardware and support may be combined into a computer allocation charge that is passed on to the user in the form of a rate-per-usage unit. This is usually a direct charge; however, the cost distribution algorithm and whether any of the costs are allocated to overhead can have a significant effect on the cost effectiveness evaluation. In fact, initial developmental usage can be seriously affected by high rates. J. D. O'Neill has succinctly stated this in the following paragraph quoted from Ref. 12.

As John Marshall said, " 'The power to tax is the power to destroy.' " So is the power to cost. The accounting activities of significance to developing a new technology, such as computer graphics, are recording, costing and break-even analysis. The recording of machine usage is performed so that accounts may be charged. Accounts charged may be project, department or individual. Charging to individual accounts will be useful in gaging individual performance but will hamper the development of new technology. Most budgets are historically based. Project managers have a budget which allows little incentive for new methods. When a company hires highly educated, experienced personnel, gives them wide ranges of responsibility, and knows they are responsible, dedicated people, then it should not enmesh them in an accounting system which attempts to control their every movement and every second on a computer."

A Cost Allocation Work Order will usually be set up to collect the costs of the equipment and the charges of the users if they are to be billed back. The costs may be distributed several ways.

1) Put into a depreciation pool and put into general overhead

2) Charged directly to each user via an accounting procedure. These charges may be lumped or pro-rata if only a few users, or set up as a rate-per-usage unit if many users.

It must be noted that tracking, estimating, and billing the changes under (2) above does not come free. It costs the group operating the equipment and the users who all must estimate usage, authorize charges, and track utilization. Table 1 shows the typical items in a Cost Allocation Work Order.

Depreciation is figured on the acquisition cost plus sales tax plus freight and installation. Two typical methods are to straightline or use the sum-of-the years digits and is usually a corporate financial decision as to the method used. Table 3 shows a comparison of these two methods for a five-year depreciation life with first and last years counted as half years.

If the $226,603 in Table 1 is to be charged to overhead or a specific contract, then it can be billed monthly, quarterly, or whatever. If it is to be charged back at a rate, then a first cut at a rate has to be made by dividing the total cost for the year by the estimated usage units (for the type of graphic system hypothesized here, this is usually a "wall clock hour"). Since there are a finite number of hours in the day, there is a

Table 1. Typical Cost Allocation Work Order

Depreciation	$ 79,996	*
Maintenance	28,792	
Property Tax	4,791	
Communication	3,000	
Material	2,500	(paper, discs, mag tape, etc.)
Miscellaneous	1,000	
Subtotal	$120,079	
Overhead (30%)	36,024	
Labor (1.5 people)	70,500	(Operations, Sys. SW Support)
Total Cost:	$226,603	

*The values are derived from 4 terminal-turnkey Graphic Design system as shown in Table 2 using SYD depreciation for 1st year shown.

Table 2. Acquisition Cost/Turnkey Graphic System

		QTY	TOTAL PRICE
Configuration: Note: This configuration does not represent any specific turnkey system - prices are approximate and representative.	• CPU, MT Unit System Console, Comm Interface, Disc, System Software	(1)	$230,000
	• Graphic Terminal Work-Station - including Graphic CRT and Analog Table	(4)	120,000
	• Digitizer Table	(1)	25,000
	• Plotter	(1)	33,000
	• Application Software Package for P/C Board and Mech Design	(1)	40,000
		Total	$448,000

Table 3. Depreciation Schedule Comparison

Acquisition Cost	$448,000	
	26,880	Tax
	5,000	Freight and Install
Total Cost for Depreciation	$479,880	

Depreciation Period — 5 years (1/2 year front and back covers; 6 calendar years)

St. Line Method — 20% per year

SYD — 16.67%, 30.01%, 23.34%, 16.67%, 10.01%, 3.3%

YEAR	SYD	ST. LINE
1	$ 79,996	$47,988
2	144,012	95,976
3	112,004	95,976
4	79,996	95,976
5	48,036	95,976
6	15,836	47,988

limit to the number "wall clock hour" usage units. For instance, if one shift operation is desired, then eight hours per day times the approximately 250 working days in a year gives 2000 usage units (UU). But as previously discussed, 80% of that is all that should be reasonably counted on. You may get more billable usage than 80%, but that is a prudent number to use to count on for recovering the cost of operating the system. Therefore, using 80% of 2000 UUs is 1600; this times the four work stations is 6400 UUs for the year. Dividing that into the total cost for the year of $226,603 yields a target rate of $35.41 per UU. Table 4 provides a quick reference for the amount of time or UUs available and 80% of that time for several operational conditions. For example, if you used the ten hour/day, — four day/work for personnel and stagger the people, you get ten hours per day for six or seven days per week. So under ②Ⓑ in Table 4, there are 3000 UUs total, and 80% or 2400 UUs generally available. In this case the rate would be $23.60. If a regular, two-shift operation is predicted, then under ①Ⓒ we get 3200 UUs and a target rate of $17.70 per UU. This kind of exercise shows what kind of work load will be required to recover the cost (at the end of the year, the rate times the total UUs has to equal the total cost) and to produce a Usage Unit rate that will be cost-effective.

If you are fortunate enough to be able to allocate the computer costs into overhead (division, department, or corporate), you will be spared a lot of arguments, estimating fire drills, frustrations and the accounting expense. However, you will not be freed from the effort of determining, as best possible, what it costs to do the work. It is essential to know where and what all the costs are regardless of how you allocate them.

Assumptions   :   50 Weeks

                :   80% of available time can be billed.

Options:

(1)	5 Day Week	(250 D/YR)	
(2)	6 Day Week	(300 D/YR)	
(3)	7 Day Week	(350 D/YR)	
(A)	1 Shift	8 Hr./80%	− 6.4 Hr.
(B)	Prime Time	10 Hr./80%	− 8 Hr.
(C)	2 Shift	16 Hr./80%	− 12.8 Hr.
(D)	3 Shift	24 Hr./80%	− 19.2 Hr.

	A	B	C	D
1	2000/ 1600	2500/ 2000	4000/ 3200	6000/ 4800
2	2400/ 1920	3000/ 2400	4800/ 3840	7200/ 5760
3	2800/ 2240	3500/ 2800	5600/ 4480	8400/ 6720

Mainframes and analytical terminal costs can be similarly determined. On a mainframe, a rate is the usual method of recovering charges and the usage unit is a function of some internal computer charge distribution algorithm rather than wall clock time since many users may be time sharing on it. Note also in determining a configuration for a turnkey system, the number of work stations is a function of response time. For instance, a CPU may be able to connect up to eight work stations but it can effectively only handle four. This characteristic or capability of any system must be determined by the user running benchmarks (not vendor demos) of his own real work tasks.

Two interesting data points from our own experience relate to the usage level. In some design and documentation tasks, the use of procedure execution files allows a user to actually run two work stations at the same time. This is where a task has periods where interaction is minimal, and can result in high utilization of the hardware. The other point is that we have found that many people will come in on their own time — early, stay late, etc. — when they can use a system that gives them the satisfaction of producing that which they are capable. Their work/results becomes more fulfilling and less frustrating. This is particularly true in the analytical area where a short turnaround time really helps the problem solver reach a good solution. We are also at the point now where we are making time available — "free" — on a system on second shift for users to improve their proficiency at the terminal.

Software Development Costs

Programming for interactive graphics use involves some significantly different techniques from batch programming. In the batch mode, it usually sufficient to specify the equations to be solved, program options, and the format of the input and output. The program can then be coded and checked out with very little need for personnel help from the user. The user, however, is required to be much more involved in the interactive programming process. *How* he goes about solving a problem is important in determining when and how he wants to interrupt the process on the computer. Then there are considerations as to how to display the results and what options are desired as far as modifying the program and/or data and restarting the process. Superimposed on these program structure details are human factors considerations.

Two facts are immediately apparent: it will take longer to develop an interactive program, and it will be more expensive. More expensive in dollars, of course; but also in engineering manhours. One other factor in educating both programmers and engineers in interactive programming is structuring and managing data. Since the interactive user has a more flexible environment, he must be able to access, modify, and store his data in a more general, more random, and yet efficient way.

The turnkey graphics system comes with this software supplied for specific applications, i.e., drafting, mechanical design, printed circuit board layout, auto-routing, etc. The user may want to add some utility programs or work with the vendor to modify the supplied software (at some additional cost) to meet specific requirements. Some interactive analytical software packages can also be bought that run on a mainframe. Some front-end and back-end programs, like finite element modeling pre- and post-processors to prepare input and display output of finite element analysis programs, may run on mini or supermini computers. Some of these are even available in color graphics.

Most interactive analytical programs will have to be written by the user for a specific graphics language and terminal.

Interactive graphics programs can be grouped into three levels as far as capability and complexity:

1) Online plotting — A batch program generates a file of data that is then attached to a general-purpose interactive graphics plotting program. The user may vary the number of data points plotted, rescale the plots, select various coordinate grids, select variables to be plotted, and make comparison plots. However, the batch program must be rerun to change the output data.

2) Interactive I/O — Essentially, a batch program is slightly restructured — overlaid to reduce central memory requirements — the ability to change input parameters is added and the same output plotting as above.

3) Fully Interactive — The program is designed to take full advantage of the new capabilities of the graphic interface. The user can communicate in a graphic or topological way, as well as numerically. New ways of displaying data may be implemented — such as using different shades or tones to differentiate between stress levels, animation, etc.

We have taken our experience and compared it with other similar work to obtain the following representative program development times (costs) for three different levels of programming effort:

Level One — Modify batch program to produce a particular file(s) — possible some slight modification to general interactive plot program time includes checkout/debug.

> Manhours: one to three weeks
> Calendar time: one to five weeks

Level Two — If a general scheme can be set up such as using NAMELIST for input and the standard plot package for output, a very efficient process results. For example, this type of conversion was done for three-degree-of-freedom, dynamic trajectory simulation. An engineer wrote the batch program and an experienced graphics application programmer did the conversion (the biggest job was understanding the computation program and overlaying it). This whole task was done in about three months calendar time with two months of programming manhours and one manmonth of the engineer's time. Then a six-degree-of-freedom program was converted in about six weeks calendar time with only four manweeks programming time and two manweeks engineering time. Somewhat concurrent with the last task, the engineer converted a separation simulation program himself with four manweeks effort in about five weeks calendar time.

> Average manhours: four weeks to three months
> Calendar time: six weeks to four months

Level Three — Generalization here is difficult because of the range of problem sophisitication and programming expertise. Several examples may yield better insight:

Mechanical Design — Four-bar linkage synthesis. Engineer did programming. No previous program like it.

> Manhours: five manmonths
> Calendar time: seven months
> Size of program: 15 overlays; 4,000 cards

178

Structural Analysis — Engineer did programming with some professional programming help on data structure and special subroutines. About 30% of design time spent on data structure design and data manager implementation.

> Manhours: ten manmonths
> Calendar time: one year
> Size of program: 70 overlays; 150,000 cards
> Runs in $50,000_8$ ($20,480_{10}$) words of central memory

Control System Analysis — Root locus and frequency response. Application programmer did this task.

> Manhours: eight manmonths of programmer time; three manmonths of engineers time
>
> Calendar time: ten months
>
> Program size: 48 overlays and 11,000 cards

It should be noted that most programs are modified and/or added to several times following their initial use. This type of activity has resulted in additional expenditures from one quarter to one half of the original programming effort in our graphics experience. The program is usually not considered fully operational until a use period is completed and the second effort in programming, mentioned above, is done.

Since CAD/CAM activity is on-line, the data must also be available on-line and efficiently structured so as to minimize data handling cost and also not impact response time. This requires some data structuring for specific programs, and for general data storage, modification, and retrieval, the use of a Data Base Management System (DBMS). The creation of on-line data bases and their administration is a relatively new activity for engineering. It is not a trivial task and requires significant time and effort; items 1 thru 14 in the bibliography address this subject. Figure 5 indicates the general approach to data base design, and Figure 6 emphasises the role of the user. Often the user thinks that since the data base is stored in the computer, a computer specialist will just take the data and automatically generate a data base! Not so! The user is responsible for defining the elements, their logical relationship, validating the data to be entered, and specifying how he wants to access or query the data base. Then, the data base programmer can do a data base design and build the data base.

Since most turnkey systems have a specific and unique data base design, the problem of how to communicate between different systems and other data bases immediately arises. The brute force approach is to develop some programs to extract and convert data from one data base design to another and back (i.e., both ways) for each data base set that requires communication. This presumes an adequate and accurate knowledge of the data structure for each data base — a formidable task! Fortunately, a recent activity sponsored by the National Bureau of Standards called Interim Graphics Exchange Specification (IGES) is in the process of becoming an American National Standards Institute (ANSI) standard. This will provide a standard definition for graphics data in what is essentially a device independent file structure. A number of major vendors of turnkey graphics design systems have agreed to support this standard

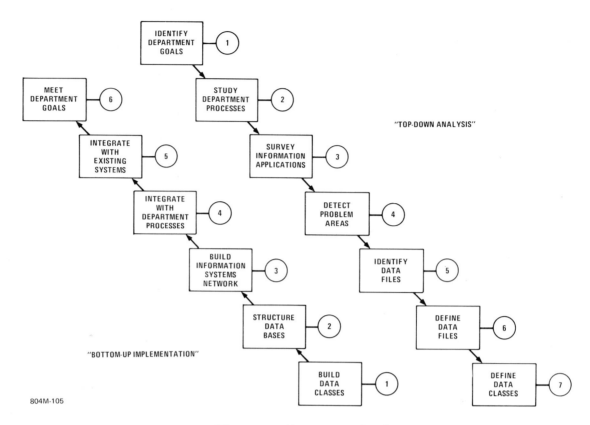

Figure 5. Data Base Design

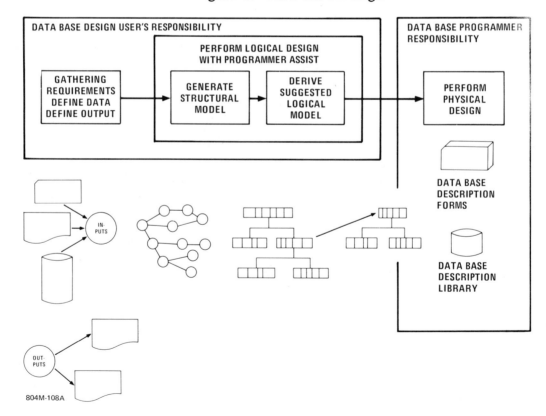

Figure 6. Design Details

in their systems. This will greatly facilitate the use of different systems within the same company and by subcontractors and others. Present experience and state-of-the-art in DBMSs favors establishing a primary centralized data base system which "feeds" or supports distributed computational capability. Copies of data are made and used at remote sites, but all updates must be reflected in the central, common data base system. This requires careful administration and control of data updates. It is also very desirable to have some way of indicating to a user who has accessed a portion of data information as to when it was last modified and whether or not someone with change authority has access to it at this time.

Graphics programming requires more consideration of the user and his personal involvement during the program design and development than for batch programming. Graphics programs must be smaller to minimize central memory requirements in the interactive mode and will have more actual coding due to the display requirements. However, since the user is now available to make decisions and supply his physical intuition and experience, some of the decision logic required in the batch program can be kept out. In our experience, the cost of programming for interactive graphics applications is on the order of 50% higher than for a batch program when programmers inexperienced in graphics are used, and about the same cost or up to 10% higher when programmers/engineers experienced in graphics programming are used.

Engineering Manhours

One of the principle benefits of the CAD/CAM methodology is the saving of time. Labor hours and schedule time are significantly reduced. The expression "time is money" is fine until something has to be entered in the accounting ledger, then some finite amount of money must be used.

Manhours expended represent definite amounts of money. Manhours not expended, or time saved, is also money, but the amount varies, depending on what is done with the unexpended manhours. A manager must decide how to take advantage of this time saved. For instance if a certain task can now be done with interactive graphics in four hours instead of 40, he might choose to do other tasks in the remaining 36 hours. In this instance, the time saving has a definite value, the manhour cost to do the task is one tenth the original cost. The manager may, however, wish to improve and refine the design now that he has almost an extra week and improved methods. The goal may be higher reliability, better performance, lower product manufacturing cost — whatever, in his estimate, offers the best benefit to his company at that time. The cost saving in manhours from the original task may only be one half or none at all, but the company does benefit from lower maintenance or penalty costs with a more reliable product (successful launch, surpassing performance goals, etc.). The return on the investment in this case is less tangible and further downstream, but nonetheless a real and valuable return.

The advantages of using interactive terminals are manifold. The benefits to the user are varied and depend upon which of the advantages he wishes to exploit. To illustrate, the reduction in time to do a given task may be regarded as an opportunity to exercise some management decision options not available before. Each option has its own payoff and can be selected in light of the current company situation in order to derive the maximum long or short term benefit to the company. As a consequence of these options and the present state of development and implementation, the quantifiable cost effectiveness of the use of interactive terminals has so far eluded a firm, empirical definition. Our experience has shown that engineering manhours are reduced with the use of interactive graphics. Tasks have ranged from one half to one twentieth of the original time. Figure 7 summarizes some of the advantages of saving time. The assumption made of an average of 5:1 time reduction in product development cycle stems from the Department of Defense Conference on CAD/CAM in Davenport, Iowa (Ref. 2); current results confirm this prediction.

REDUCE PRODUCT
DEVELOPMENT TIME BY 5:1

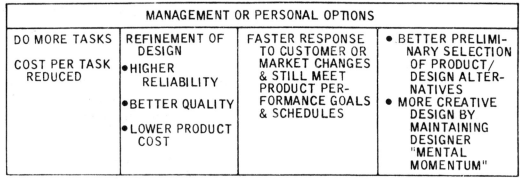

MANAGEMENT OR PERSONAL OPTIONS			
DO MORE TASKS COST PER TASK REDUCED	REFINEMENT OF DESIGN • HIGHER RELIABILITY • BETTER QUALITY • LOWER PRODUCT COST	FASTER RESPONSE TO CUSTOMER OR MARKET CHANGES & STILL MEET PRODUCT PERFORMANCE GOALS & SCHEDULES	• BETTER PRELIMINARY SELECTION OF PRODUCT/ DESIGN ALTERNATIVES • MORE CREATIVE DESIGN BY MAINTAINING DESIGNER "MENTAL MOMENTUM"

Figure 7. Options for using time saved.

Examples of Cost Effectiveness

The following are examples of the distribution of these various cost factors in actual applications and are examined to see what can be quantified as far as cost effectiveness is concerned. These examples are derived in part from personal experience and visits and discussions with contacts in other companies. An outstanding discussion of savings and the factors involved can be seen in Reference 13.

Printed Circuit Board Design

In addition to the detailed savings shown, less waste was obtained in drilled boards due to the better registration between layers as a result of the increased accuracy available on the automated system.

Analysis of Printed Circuit Board Design

	MANUAL			CAD/CAM			
	HOURS LABOR	ELAPSED TIME	COST	HOURS LABOR	COMPUTER TIME (UU)	ELAPSED TIME	COST
2:1 Taped up Artwork Master	240 Hrs	7 Wks	$ 6,000.				
1:1 Artwork Master				100 Hrs	80 Hrs	2.5 Wks	$5,380.
Photo Reduction to 1:1	4 Hrs	2 Days	$ 100.				
Accuracy			±.005				±.0005
Assembly Drawing	24 Hrs	1 Wk	$ 600.	1/2 Hr	1/2 Hr	1/4 Day	$ 31.
Drill Drawing	12 Hrs	3 Days	$ 300.	1/2 Hr	1/2 Hr	1/4 Day	$ 31.
N/C Drill Tape (Vendor)			$ 200.	1 Hr	1 Hr	1/2 Day	$ 62.
N/C Profile Router Tape				1/2 Hr	1/2 Hr	1/2 Day	$ 31.
N/C Automatic Insertion Tape				2 Hrs	2 Hrs	1/2 Day	$ 122.
Schematic (Avg. 6 F-Size Sheets per Job)	180 Hrs	5 Wks	$ 4,500.	60 Hrs	36 Hrs	12 Days	$2,796.
TOTAL	460 Hrs	70 Days	$11,700.	164.5 Hrs	120.5 Hrs	26.5 Days	$8,543.

Summary
Printed Circuit Board Design

	MANHOURS		ELAPSED TIME		COST*	
	HOURS SAVED	RATIO	DAYS SAVED	RATIO	$ SAVED	RATIO
Artwork Master	140 Hrs	2.4:1	4.5 Wks	2.8:1	$ 620.	1.1:1
Accuracy						10:1
Assembly Dwg.	23.5	48:1	4.75 Days	20:1	$ 569.	19.4:1
Drill Dwg.	11.5	24:1	2.75 Days	12:1	$ 269.	9.7:1
N/C Tapes						
Schematic	120	3:1	13 Days	2.1:1	$1,704.	1.6:1
TOTAL	295 Hrs	2.8:1	43 Days	2.6:1	$3,162	1.4:1

*NOTE: 1 Labor Hour @ $25 per Hour
        1 Computer UU @ $36 per Hour

Finite-Element Structural Model Analysis — Describing the input bars, shear panels, and nodes to the analysis program is a tedious job. A typical input deck may run 500 to 2,000 cards. Programs of this size and complexity offer many opportunities for input coding errors: misnumbered nodes, failure to right justify an exponent in an E-field, leaving out a shear panel, etc. Scanning the cards by eye (or even a listing of them) takes time, is boring, and is not likely to uncover all errors that may exist. The ability to view the model in its geometric presentation allows the engineer to detect errors in seconds that he might spend an hour looking for (and perhaps not find) on the cards themselves.

In Ref. 2, Lockheed-Georgia Company indicated that more than 500 hours of aborted Univac 1108 computer runs were avoided on a single aircraft wing using this kind of capability. First-year cost savings were estimated at $252,000. The interactive graphics version has the added advantage, over an offline digital incremental drum plotter, of being able to show (very rapidly) orthogonal views, perspective views, rescaled (blown-up) views of particular parts, to "peel off" parts to see subsections and to interrogate the geometrical picture to receive numerical data concerning the part selected and to change those parameter values at the CRT and then execute the program.

Our experience in developing three finite-element models (fuselage, empennage, and wing) is compared in Table 5.

The total cost savings on this task was $23,490 or a ratio of 5.4 to 1. The development cost of the program was about $35,000, including computer time and CRT time over a period of about 12 months. The structures engineer did the design and programming.

Table 5. Fuselage empennage, and wing model comparison.

	Batch	IGS	Benefits
Calendar Time	3 months	3 weeks	Kept schedule that could not have been made using batch technique. Also assisted other disciplines by providing results of structural analyses.
Manhours	13 manweeks $13 \times 40 \times 17$ = $8,840	5 manweeks $5 \times 40 \times 17$ = $3,400	Saved $5,440 in engineering labor cost. Reduced fatiguing rote work of engineer so he could concentrate on engineering problem rather than proofreading keypunched cards.
Computer Time	$20,000	$1,950	Represents about 40 hours of aborted runs on a CDC 6400 computer for the batch work. For the graphics, there was about $1,200 of computer time and only $750 (25 hours) of CRT time.

Software Documentation

Full Mil-Spec documentation of deliverable software requires many flowcharts. Due to the use of standard symbols and its topological nature, this job can be done very effectively on a graphics design system. It is not only very cost effective, but due to the volume alone it may be impossible to meet schedules manually. It might be argued that the power of a graphics design system is being wasted doing this type of simple job. It is true that this task only utilizes a portion of the capability of the system but –

1) It is <u>cost</u> effective

2) It supports a deliverable product

3) The graphic system is available and a different system with additional maintenance is not needed.

4) The high volume contributes to the work load and beneficially helps the rate at which the graphic system is charged.

The details of the savings are:

Category of Use	Manual Hours Required	CAD/CAM Hours Required	Time Ratio	Cost Ratio
		Labor/UU		
New Input	3 hrs/sheet	1.0/1.0	3:1	1.3:1
Minor Changes	1.5 hrs/sheet	.16/.16	9:1	3.8:1
Major Changes	3 hrs/sheet	.33/.33	9:1	3.9:1
Overall Savings*			7.6:1	3.4:1

*Changes represent over 92% of the activity.

Implementation of CAD/CAM can be justified on sound, quantitative, economic grounds. For some tasks, this could have been done eight years ago. The fact that the effective techniques of CAD are not as widely implemented as anticipated a few years ago points up the need to educate the users and their managers concerning the benefits of these tools. There is also the need to effectively educate both the technical and financial managers on the advantages of such a system and the methods of deriving cost figures for the changing elements in engineering, manufacturing, and business use of the computer.

Considering people, time, and money, the use of interactive techniques is shown to be very cost effective on a job basis. This saving now needs to be multiplied by many jobs and parallel management use. The increased use and integration of disciplines tends to be synergistic in benefits to the company.

All this will become reality only if all levels of management get involved. Like the salesman's song in *Music Man*, "you've got to know the territory." Management has the responsibility to know *how* the design and manufacturing process is carried on today. The designers and manufacturing people have a responsibility to know the characteristics of the tools they employ and to be involved in recommending and specifying needed characteristics and configurations for their activities.

Future

Two trends seem to be developing: one is organizational, and one is in computer hardware configurations. The engineering organization will probably see some changes after large-scale implementation of CAD. The outlook appears to be toward more generalists or multidisciplinary people who can take a task or design through almost all phases of analysis and design. Organizations can be smaller, with smaller specialists groups for research and methods. CAD techniques will bring greater return on the invested R&D dollar.

With the significantly decreasing cost and simultaneously increasing capability of minicomputers, there is developing a perceptible trend away from the super-large main computer to provide enough computer power to handle the complex work and varying work load in a large company. Some of the advantages are a more simple operating system on the mainframe - it handles mainly number-crunching and large data base management chores. Mini-computers handle input/output, graphic display, and data handling associated with such displays. More flexibiliy is available to the user in choosing peripheral equipment to meet specific project requirements (see also References 5 and 13).

Technically, the necessary computer hardware and software features exist, along with an adequate understanding of the design and manufacturing process, to have a wide-scale, profitable implementation of CAD and CAM in many companies, but:

KNOWING IS NOT ENOUGH
WE MUST APPLY.
WILLING IS NOT ENOUGH
WE MUST DO.

— GOETHE

REFERENCES

1. B. W. Boehm, "Keeping the Upper Hand in the Man Computer Partnership," Astronautics & Aeronautics, April 1967, pp. 23-28.

2. "Panel Reports for DoD/Industry Symposium on Computer-Aided-Design, and Computer-Aided-Manufacturing/Numerical Control," held at Davenport, Iowa, Rock Island Army Arsenal, 14-17 October 1969 Panel No. 3, State of the Art in CAD, by Roy M. Salzman of A. D. Little, Inc.

3. R. A. Philips, "Optimizing Man-Computer Interactivity" North American Rockwell Internal Technical Report —TM 571-23-7, 24 February 1970.

4. H. Sackman, and W. J. Erikson, "User Studies in Time-Sharing," System Development Corporation, Report No. TM-530/011/00, January 1968.

5. H. Lorin, "Distributed Processing: An Assessment," IBM Systems Journal, Volume Eighteen, Number Four, 1979 pp. 582-603.

6. P. Calingaert, "System Performance Evaluation: Survey and Appraisal," Communications of the ACM, Vol. 10, No. 1, January 1967.

7. F. A. Schaeffer, *Escape from Reason*, 1968 Inter-Varsity Press, Downers Grove Illinois.

8. Kenneth E. Ruff, "Managing the CAD/CAM Revolution," EMF Technical Paper MS72-910, 1972.

9. J. D. Aron, "Real Time Systems in Perspective," IBM Systems Journal, Volume 6, Number 1, 1967, pp. 49-67.

10. K. C. Bonine, "Implementation of An Interactive Graphic System for Computer Aided Design, Convair Aerospace Report GDC-ERR-1482, December 1969.

11. C. G. Kopp and J. B. Wertz, "Designer and Computer: An Engineering Partnership," Battelle Technical Review, February 1968.

12. J. B. O'Neill, "Computer Graphics As An Operational Tool," Presented to Computer Graphics 70 International Symposium, Brunel University, Uxbridge, England, April 1970 (Douglas Aircraft Company Paper 5672).

13. "Computergraphics, A Study for Designers of Printed, Integrated, and Hybrid Circuits," International Technology Marketing, Newton, Mass., 1978.

BIBLIOGRAPHY

1. Special Issue: Data-Base Management Systems, ACM Computing Surveys, Vol. 8, Number 1, March 1976

2. Ralph M. Flygare, "Distributed CAD/CAM With Data Base Management Common to both Engineering and Manufacturing," SME Technical Paper MS76-738, 1976

3. M. E. Sanko, "Data Structures and Data Accessing in Data Base Systems Past, Present, Future," IBM Systems Journal, Vol. 16, No. 3, 208-257, 1977

4. N. Raver and G. U. Hubbard, "Automated Logical Data Base Design: Concepts and Applications," IBM Systems Journal, Vol. 16, No. 3, 287-312, 1977

5. "Data Base Machines" Theme Feature, Computer, Vol. 12, No. 3, 7-79, March 1979

6. "Technology and Architecture for Data Management" Theme Feature, Computer, Vol. 12, No. 5, 8-48, May 1979

7. Special Issue on Data Base Machines, IEEE Transactions on Computers, Vol. C-28, No. 6, June 1979

8. Issue on Data Storage & Retrieval, ACM Computing Surveys, Vol. 11, No. 3, September 1979

9. Malcolm L. Stiefel, "Surveying Data Base Management Systems," Mini-Micro Systems, 94-104, November 1979

10. Gary H. Sockut and Robert P. Goldberg, "Data Base Reorganization Principles and Practice," ACM Computing Surveys, Vol. 11, No. 4, 371-396, December 1979

11. Papers from "Conference on Engineering and Scientific Data Management" Sponsored by NASA Langley Research Center, Hampton, Virginia, 23665, May 18-19, 1978

12. Harry Gebert, "Data Bases in Manufacturing Application Guidelines," SME Technical Paper MS79-831, 1979

13. "IPAD Information Processing" (Section 6); "Major Implementation Alternatives" (Section 7); "Data Management Systems Study" (Section 9) - Preliminary Information (10/31/77 8:00 am) Supporting The Full IPAD Preliminary Design Review presented by IPAD Staff Boeing Commercial Airplane Company/Boeing Computer Services, Inc. to the Industry Technical Advisory Board at St. Louis on November 29, 30 and December 1, 1977

14. "National Conference on Comparative Data Base Management Systems" Sponsored by UCLA Extension - Continuing Education in Management, Labor, and Business, 10995 Le Conte Avenue, Los Angeles, CA 90024

15. B. W. Boehm, N. D. Cohen, V. R. Lamb, and J. E. Reiber, "Developing Interactive Graphics Systems for Aerospace Applications," the Rand Corporation, presented at the AIAA Aerospace Computer Systems Conference, Los Angeles, Cal., 8-10 September 1969 (AIAA Paper No. 69-954).

16. A. W. Bowers, "Man-Computer Interactive Programming Concepts and Systems," Lockheed-Georgia Company, presented at AIAA Aerospace Computer Systems Conference, Los Angeles, Cal., 8-10 September 1969 (AIAA Paper No. 69-955).

17. D. B. Brick, "Interactive CRT Display Terminal, Parts 1, 2 and 3, Modern Data, May, June, and July 1970.

18. D. W. Peterson, "Design of Four-Bar Linkages Using Interactive Computer Graphics and Synthesis Curves," 11th ASME Mechanisms Conference, Columbus, Ohio; 1-4 November 1970

19. T. F. Reed, "WTVMAC A Graphics Program for Plotting Weight Versus Center of Gravity (Percent MAC)," GDC-ERR-1532, December 1970

20. S. R. Ruggio & K. A. Tyler, "Automation of Printed Circuit Board Generation," GDPD-ERR-70/019-2 December 31, 1970.

21. A. Karema, "Airplane High-Lift System Design by Interactive Graphics System," Integrated Systems Conference at Palo Alto, Calif., 17 and 18 February 1971

22. D. W. Peterson, "Design of Dead-Center LInkages for Airplane Landing Gear Retraction Systems," presented at 2nd Applied Mechanism Conference, Oklahoma State University, Stillwater, Okla., 7, 8 August 1971

23. K. C. Bonine, "Design Considerations for Continuous System Simulation Languages," presented at IFAC Symposium on Digital Simulation of Continuous Process, Gyor, Hungary, 6-10 September 1971

24. M. J. Cronk, "An Interactive Computer Graphics Program for NASTRAN," presented at NASA NASTRAN Users' Colloquium, LRC, 13-15 Sept. 1971

25. M. D. Prince, *Interactive Graphics for Computer Aided Design* Addison-Wesley Publishing Company, 1971

CHAPTER 9

APPLICATIONS

CAD/CAM Responds To A Changing Car Market

By Kenneth E. Ruff
Departmental Head
General Motors Corp.

CAD/CAM has enhanced General Motors ability to respond rapidly to shifts in the automotive market. The work involved in car body design and tooling is discussed. The CAD/CAM system currently employed is described. Its importance in streamlining interfaces is emphasized. The impact of the technology on response time for new products, the ability to satisfy regulatory requirements, and product quality is examined. An attempt is made to forecast the effect of computer technology trends on the evolving structure of the CAD/CAM system.

Introduction

Between 1900 and 1960 the automobile evolved gradually. It was transformed from a sportsman's curiosity into the principal means of transportation for most Americans. Improvements in efficiency, convenience and appearance occurred with certain regularity. Design and manufacturing progressed according to a plan.

Since 1960 changes have come rapidly as the industry faced many new problems. An initial challenge came from government regulations in the area of safety and environmental protection. In 1973 the emphasis suddenly shifted to a new concern for energy. Each of these new demands severely tested the responsiveness of automotive design and manufacturing. Instant invention was demanded but could not be forthcoming. Now, as ever, things take time. The responsiveness has, however, been remarkable as evidenced by the many changes that have taken place. Many factors have contributed to this speedy adjustment to a changing marketplace. Many of them have to do with the efforts of individual people. But technology has played a significant supporting role. At General Motors the emerging information technology called CAD/CAM has helped smooth the way. It helped place General Motors' first sub-compact, the Chevette, in the showrooms 2 years after the oil embargo signaled an imminent market shift. It also contributed to the rapid redesign of GM's basic car line into the smaller, lighter, more economical 1977 models available today. In this paper we will show some of the ways in which CAD/CAM has helped GM respond to a changing car market.

System Origins

The CAD/CAM technology that is in use today in GM results from the recognition in the late 1950's of the increasing importance of quick response. There was a great concern for the long lead times involved between vehicle concept and mass production realization.

The possibilities of employing the infant technology of numerical control and the early concepts of visual man-computer communication were recognized. At the GM Research Laboratories research in man-machine communication was carried out, while efforts to extend N/C technology for use in contour machining of car body tooling began at GM Manufacturing Development. The early promise shown in these projects resulted in a significant commitment of R & D resources to these two areas of exploration over the past 20 years.

Through the Research Laboratories DAC project and allied efforts, a high level of capability for aiding the designer in car body design activities was demonstrated. Mathematical research in the representation of sculptured surfaces was advanced to a point of effective utilization in computational algorithms essential both for design and numerical control. Data structures suitable for representing automotive curves and surfaces in computer storage were explored. In the numerical control areas, techniques for programming the regional milling of sculptured surfaces were developed.

These capabilities were integrated by Manufacturing Development into two complimentary systems, CADANCE and INCA. They provided an effective proving ground through which divisional designers, engineers and tool makers could test the operational feasibility of CAD/CAM. Extensive application and systems development was undertaken by Design Staff and Fisher Body to transfer the basic developments into productive use. The modern systems in use today by GM staffs and divisions are outgrowths of these combined efforts.

The Work Required

These systems provide computer assistance to a wide range of activities. The field of application is car body design and tooling. The functions included range from initial vehicle concept to the final tryout of production tooling.

Two major divisions of work are involved. The first is product definition. This is the set of activities that provide a complete physical description of the product to be made and all of its parts. In this case, the product is a car body. These product definition activities are associated with the CAD part of CAD/CAM.

The second major function is that of equipping the manufacturing facility to build the products at the required volumes and timing. Since car bodies are primarily made of sheet metal, most activities in this area are concerned with designing and building high volume sheet metal tooling.

We can identify five important sub-functions in the product definition area: functional specification of the vehicle; overall body design; detailed part design; design analysis and manufacturability analysis. Each of these has distinct techniques and problems associated with it, and they all must interact to resolve the total problem of product definition.

Functional specification involves the determination of space allocation for the driver, passengers, luggage, and the mechanical, hydraulic and electrical components of the vehicle. It also includes defining the driver's access to controls, his visibility; the comfort and safety of passengers and driver, and the ease of entry to the passenger compartment. The elusive aspect of appearance or styling, interior and exterior, is also important in the definition of a passenger car that is to compete in the free market place. Some of the functional specifications derive from market considerations, others come from government regulations. The car body is, of course, a component of the whole vehicle. Therefore, some of the requirements which it must satisfy are assigned in the process of overall vehicle specification.

Before the body functional specification has been finalized, work begins on the overall body design. This activity breaks down the body into its components. This breakdown may seem not to have changed greatly over the years, but there have been many changes and more are occurring as new materials are considered. In introducing plastics, for example, one plastic component will frequently replace several sheet metal parts. Overall design must also define the specific requirements which each component must satisfy. Some parts will primarily contribute to the strength or compliance of the body, others may be important to the appearance or as a mounting for mechanical gear.

Once parts have been generally defined and major functions assigned to them, a vast series of problem solving work must take place to define the specific internal physical form of each part. This is the detailed design activity. For each problem two outcomes are possible. Result number one - the problem is solved and a part is designed which meets all the requirements. Result number two - some requirement cannot be met, consequently design specification for some neighboring part must be changed. Because result number two is frequently the case, the design activity involves a great deal of communication among individual designers.

As a design proposal emerges for the body as a whole or any of its specific parts the adherence to functional specifications must be re-evaluated. Specific design analyses must be carried out to prove, for example, that the result is strong enough, rigid enough, and light enough to do its job. Overall, in fact, the design process involves the successive generation of proposals and their testing. For a rapidly moving design process much of this testing is analytical, but actual physical testing of prototypes is a necessary final step in many cases. One of the important contributions of CAD/CAM is to improve the functional analysis so that the costs and time of prototype testing can be reduced.

A final function within the product definition area is the analysis of the producibility of the design proposal. It is not enough that the car body and its parts fulfill all functional requirements. It is also essential that it can be built at the volume and cost levels specified. Therefore, part of the evaluation of the relative value of one design alternative versus another depends upon how well suited it is for production in our plants. We will get the final answers when we reach the production stage, but designs which appear to exceed processing capabilities are subject to special analysis during the product definition phase. If for example, it is concluded that a large deep sheet metal panel cannot be drawn, it may have to be redesigned as two separate pieces.

The entire design process from functional specification through detailing involves the constant interaction of people. A great deal of back and forth iteration is necessary to develop a good body design.

As this process nears completion, the job of creating the manufacturing capability begins. For the high volume production of automotive bodies this generally means providing very complex tooling. The work can be subdivided into three major activities. These are the overall process planning, tool design, and tool build.

The fabrication process which dominates car body manufacturing is sheet metal stamping. Other processes employed to a lesser extent include various types of plastic molding, fabric cutting, sewing, and strip trim rolling. The major assembly process employed is welding.

The process planning for fabrication and assembly focuses heavily on the specification of tools to be built for these processing steps. For example, for each sheet metal part a line of dies must be specified that will enable the part to be completely formed, trimmed and flanged. Presses of adequate size and capacity must be selected. For each welding operation holding fixtures and welding guns must be specified.

Once tools have been specified for a function, tool design can begin. One of the biggest jobs in this category is the design of the draw die and punch for a major sheet metal panel such as a fender or deck lid. The die must contain a cavity shaped like the final part, but in addition the surrounding surfaces which control the sheet metal as it is drawn into the cavity must be carefully designed. The determination of these die conditions is one of the most difficult die design activities.

The tool build activity is the largest and costliest of all the functions included in body design and tooling. The construction of the major sheet metal tooling involves the rough casting of the dies, rough machining, finish machining, grinding, filing and stoning the surfaces, benching and assembly of the parts and the tryout of the die-set in a press.

Figure 1 shows the approximate distribution of manhours between product definition, tool design and tool build. As it indicates, more and more people are involved as the process progresses from early concept to final realization in hard tooling.

Figure 2 shows how time is allotted for each of the functions. It is evident that reducing the time for product definition is important to smoothing out the work of tool construction.

Organizations, Roles and Interfaces

The activities of design and tooling which have just been described are carried out by thousands of people. They are members of several major GM organizations. Each organization has its peculiar role to play. But they must play in concert if the job is to be done well and on time.

The car divisions are at the top of the list. Each car division is responsible for the product it produces. Therefore, the entire process from vehicle concept to production must meet the car division's standards.

Nevertheless, the work of product design and tooling is shared by other units. The Design Staff at the General Motors Technical Center is one of these. It plays a major role in finalizing the functional specifications of GM vehicles. In the body area, the release by Design Staff documents this work. It displays a solution to the packaging and occupancy problems and trade-offs with aesthetic considerations. It defines the exterior vehicle shape and the passenger compartment and luggage space fairly exactly.

From the point of this design release, the work is typically subdivided between Fisher Body and the car division. The overall body design - everything from the cowl on back - is worked out by Fisher Body. The fenders, hood and everything forward of the cowl is designed and tooled by the car division. Clearly, close coordination between Fisher and the car divisions is essential to preserving the integrity of the vehicle design.

Each of these participating units has its own internal structure. However, a typical breakdown into major activities will include activities such as body engineering, die engineering, production engineering and tool manufacturing. The product design is completed in body engineering. Tooling is designed by die engineering and production engineering and built in the tool manufacturing facilities in-house or by outside vendors. This breakdown of responsibilities most closely parallels that of Fisher Body, the largest such organization. The division of responsibilities within each of the car divisions while somewhat less departmentalized is roughly similar. Carefully structured formal breakdowns like this organization's are essential to the management of the many people involved. They do, however, result in some formalization of information flow. There is, in other words, an interface between each pair of organizations. The CAD/CAM systems are intended to improve the flow of relevant information across all of them.

The Engineering Staff has major activities concerned with advanced product engineering and vehicle testing. However, within the context of body design and tooling we will focus on its role in the structural analysis of car bodies.

Off-line and complimentary to the major GM units mentioned above we have vehicle project groups. These are teams composed of members from the major participating units organized to coordinate the design activities for a line of cars. They make many major design decisions. However, within the realm of activities devoted to the car body they interface principally through their activities in structural analysis.

We have identified a dozen major GM units involved in the design and manufacturing process and have suggested that each internally will have four or five major sub-activities. From this it is evident that in taking the slash out of CAD/CAM we cannot concentrate our attention on a single design/manufacturing interface. Instead, we have many interfaces. There are at least ten or twelve of major significance.

There are two major factors that may normally be expected to impede information flow across these boundaries. These are geography and organizational separation. The first of these is by far the most important and the most readily impacted by technology.

In GM, the vast majority of design activities mentioned take place within the square mile area of the GM Tech Center. However, we must move out to a radius of 80 miles to cover all the prime domestic design activities. When we consider tool manufacturing as well as design, our inner circle expands to a 200 mile radius. If we consider the world car from which the Chevette emerged, we have to stretch as far as West Germany. Each of these degrees of localization provides the danger of progressively less efficient, less interactive interfaces.

Consider two people discussing an engineering drawing, and test in your mind the effect of these geographical influences on the fluency of their conversation. This is exactly the situation which must, in some sense, be repeated thousands of times in carrying out the design and tool manufacturing job. Geography is normally an impediment even when the two people are as close as adjacent buildings on the Tech Center site.

Each of the many interfaces linking groups of people has its unique requirements. However, there are certain characteristics by which they may be described. The major quantitative characteristic, bandwidth, gets considerable attention. And certainly, how much information can be transmitted in a given length of time is important. However, other characteristics are also significant. One of these is the degree to which the interface facilitates conversations.

Can people talk back and forth; can they interrupt each other; can they look at a common object, for example a drawing, and make references to it in their conversation. For people, face-to-face across a drawing board, all these questions can be answered, yes. But when one person is in Detroit and the other is in Lansing the conversation does not proceed so smoothly.

Another characteristic of an interface is the number of parties it can link. Two party conversations may not be enough. Can it support interaction between three people or organizations?

These few characteristics of an interface should illustrate the point that there are real limitations on what can reasonably be expected in interface efficiency.

The CAD/CAM technology involved in GM's system attacks these interface problems at several levels. First, it eliminates many small interfaces. This results directly from the fact that the scope of work done by one man is increased. The qualitative but essential communication which slowed down the pace now takes place more rapidly inside one head. And a single human brain is the most efficient information processing system we know.

Nevertheless, there are limits to how much a single man can comprehend. Many problems still require resolution through the interaction of several people. The system facilitates this type of job also. It does so by providing ready access to common data. The results of one man's work are available in the data base for review by another whose work depends on it. There is no transmission time required as there is in sending a drawing from one designer to another. The work can be available instantly as soon as the designer who originated it is willing. It is only necessary that each have access to a terminal which can address the same computer. This type of interface improvement impacts information flow for major organizations at the Technical Center. However, even at the Tech Center there are two major computing systems so that immediate access to a common data base does not apply to all interfaces.

The third level of interface improvement involves electronic transmission of data from one computer to another. While this is not as well developed as the other approaches, it is important in reducing time lags between geographically separated cooperating design activities and between design centers and manufacturing plants.

Hardware and Software Base

A brief look at the hardware and software used in the GM system may help to expose the richness of interfaces involved. The primary computer power for the CAD/CAM system is supplied by four IBM 370/168 computers at the Technical Center. The Research Laboratories installation is an 8 megabyte multi-processing system with about 5 billion bytes of on-line storage. Part of a second similarly scaled system is also used for N/C work. The Fisher Body computer is a 9 megabyte multi-processor with over 8 billion bytes of storage.

Over 60 design consoles, most of them IBM 2250's are serviced by these computers. These consoles are distributed throughout the staff and divisional design and engineering centers at the Technical Center.

We also have local mini-computers equipped with GT 48 graphic consoles that we call "network stations". They supply additional computing and graphic console capability for engineering and manufacturing sites such as Oldsmobile, several miles from the Tech Center. These units access the main computers via telecommunications to obtain critical data. It is then processed remotely for local use, using the network station mini-computer and CRT console. If results require changes to the main data base, the modified data is sent back again via telecommunications.

Some 30 plotters and drafting machines driven by computer generated tape or direct numerical control provide hard copy documentation of design work and assist in N/C tape verification.

In addition to a number of standard N/C machines used to cut tooling details there are some special devices, particularly at the Design Staff that help smooth the communication between people and computers. Among these are several point pickers for gathering coordinate information from clay models and a clay "nibbler" for N/C cutting of clay models. Also available is a variety of digitizing equipment for getting manually drawn design data into the computer.

A considerable variety of system software is necessary to handle all this hardware. The two large computer systems employ different operating systems. The machine at Fisher Body uses an almost standard IBM virtual storage system. The Research Laboratories machine is driven by a special version of TSS. Although many CAD/CAM jobs can be done on either system, there are particular jobs that can be handled more effectively on one system than the other. The question of standardization is under continual review and development work is underway which will lead to greater standardization. We do not, however, foresee identical operating systems for these two sites in the immediate future.

Closely related to the operating systems are the data management programs, access methods and the data structures which they support. Some of the design work done on the Research Laboratories machine depends upon associative data structures and association codes supported by the CADANCE system. However, the programs which support this work would generate an unnecessary overhead if applied to other tasks of a less global character. Ultimately, we expect to make these choices of approach independent of the specific installation.

One area which is in fact benefiting now from standard programs is that concerned with the graphic console driving codes. The so-called G-codes, developed by Research Laboratories, provide a highly flexible and effective set of programs for the design consoles. They are used by both of the main computer systems and in the network stations.

Telecommunications links between the variety of big and little computers within the system are still more notable for their differences than for their similarities. This is a simple reflection of the status of communication technology. It is certainly an area in which national and international standards efforts deserve support from the entire industrial community.

Applications

All these elements of system hardware and software discussed above merely create an environment in which the down-to-earth application codes used directly by the designers, engineers and part programmers can function in an effective integrated manner. The variety of application codes is enormous, and the relations among them provide for an apparently endless list of uses. I will try to show some of the typical design and manufacturing work done with their help.

One of the best developed computer aided design applications of the Design Staff is the transformation of the management approved clay model of an automobile exterior surface into a clean, consistent surface design.

Special equipment is used to rapidly measure the coordinates of points on key surface lines and sections and record this data on a computer readable media - typically punched tape. The machine shown in Figure 3 accomplishes this task more efficiently than former manual techniques. The accuracy is about three times better.

Next, the individual key curves of the surfaces are fitted mathematically. The designer works at a graphic console. He has a powerful battery of programs for constrained curve fitting and analysis at his disposal. He provides the knowledge to control them to produce clean curves that represent the true intent of the clay. Programs which analyze curve properties such as curvature help him to focus on local trouble spots.

Once the individual characteristic curves have been fitted and "sweetened" the designer concerns himself with the surface of which they are elements. He performs a "mesh" operation on the console which slightly re-orients the key curves in order to force them to a common surface. When this operation is completed the designer knows that each of a set of curves in one direction intersects each of a set in a perpendicular direction.

At this point he asks for a surface fit and obtains a mathematical definition of the surface on which these meshed lines lie. He then marries the surface boundary lines, testing that the space curves resulting from projecting them on his mathematical surface give desired boundary properties. If not, he does some adjusting until he achieves a compatible surface.

Once he has a complete mathematical model, he can cut sections through it in any direction and satisfy himself that, from every point of view, the surface is indeed what he intends.

The mathematical model that has been captured in computer memory as a result of this design process is the essential exterior surface specification. From it formal Design Staff release drawings are made for divisions requiring them, and the math model is released to those who will use it in their design work.

Sometimes the surface model also is used to derive N/C data to drive the clay "nibbler" to reproduce the surface in clay - usually on the opposite side of the approved clay model. This provides a 3-D verification that the intent of the clay remains in the math model and also allows an evaluation of the center of car conditions resulting.

Most of the car exteriors released by Design Staff now are done using these graphics design tools. The job is done faster and better than by former methods and the mathematical model makes a more complete definition available for those who need it.

This math model is used directly by Chevrolet, for example. They access the model developed by Design Staff directly through a graphic console at Chevrolet Engineering Center. Thus the improved interface between Design Staff and Chevrolet makes the results of the Design Staff work instantly available in complete detail.

Interior Panel design is an important design activity within Chevrolet that uses this information. Interior panels for the entire front end must be designed. The hood inner, for example, must mate to the hood outer. It must provide for hinging and latching, clearance for the air cleaner, and provide rigidity to the hood structure. Other panels include the fender skirt, fan shroud and radiator support. Chevrolet applied computer aided design to the work on all the front end sheet metal for the 1977 cars. CAD/CAM is applied in a similar but not identical fashion by the other car divisions for their front end work and by Fisher Body for all major panels of the body proper. In addition to the design work, these groups employ the computer to generate N/C data for machining master models of all of these elements. These models serve as part of the set of construction aids used by the die plant for building the tools to stamp out the production sheet metal parts. The N/C method of producing master models is today the dominant approach throughout GM. These models provide a proof of adherence to design specifications and a starting point for the manufacturing activities.

In addition to applications for layout and detailed design, there are extensive design analysis capabilities employed. For example, at Fisher Body an analysis of the visibility provided by the inside and outside mirrors is performed by computer graphics techniques. The results assure effective rear visibility for the vehicle operator and provide the necessary documentation to certify compliance with safety regulations.

The simultaneous demands for greater fuel economy and crash resistance have forced increased attention to the conflict between weight and strength. This has required more sophisticated analysis of car body structures. Computer technology has been applied effectively to deal with this problem. The structural analysis activities are centered at the Engineering Staff. From their design consoles detailed finite element breakdowns of car body proposals are made. These provide an effective way of preparing the complex data required for detailed structural analysis in the NASTRAN program - one of the fallouts of the space program for which our industry is indebted to NASA. Through proper interpretations the results of this analysis tells us whether the design proposal meets requirements. If not, it helps point the way to changes which will move it closer to an optimum point.

So far we have discussed primarily the CAD side of CAD/CAM. We have cited a few of the hundreds of applications in overall design, detail design and design analysis. The CAM aspects, as we have said, emphasize tooling. An early activity in the tooling area is that of die design. This happens after the functions of specific dies assigned to specific presses have been established. That assignment, which is a part of what we call die processing is not much impacted by computers. For that matter neither is die design - but we have high expectations in this area. In fact, many of the CAD tools designed for assistance in product design are almost what we need for die design. One of the features of die design which has in fact benefited enormously from the computer is the simple operation called die tipping. For each press operation used in making a sheet metal panel there is a preferred attitude or position of the part that makes the metal forming or trimming process work best. This tip must be determined for each of a line of dies. The start of the die design process is to layout the part in this preferred position. It has been common place at Fisher Body for several years for these tipped drawings to be done automatically.

Computer aids suitable for carrying out many of the more demanding tasks of die design are already available. But we expect some time to pass before these are perfected and in widespread use.

As indicated earlier, millions of manhours and months of lead time are expended in the construction of body dies. This is a principal target of our CAD/CAM efforts. While we have a long way to go before the CAD/CAM impact on this area is highly significant, there is a persistent growth in its application. The state-of-the-art use of N/C for point-to-point machining of die components is primarily limited by our rate of capital expenditure for N/C equipment. However, in the die contouring work, our advances are limited by the technology and our skill in transferring it into the production environment. Each year a number of die components are completely contoured on N/C machines. The 1977 Pontiac hood draw die shown in Figure 4 is one of a number of examples. It shows the high quality result of a well developed sculptured surface N/C capability. What it does not reveal is the fact that people using this capability are still finding technical limitations on the software tools. As a result, they are forced to use unwieldy work arounds to get the job done. Some of the CAD/CAM tools need improvement before they can routinely be employed profitably in a typical die construction activity.

The construction of welding fixtures is a job that makes more modest demands of the N/C technology. The Fisher Body production engineering activity uses CAD/CAM to assist in the design and manufacturing of welding fixtures used in its car body assembly plants.

The soft trim application, developed by the same group, is a simple illustration of a well integrated CAM sub-system. A design console is used to develop a 1 1/2 by 5 meter layout which arranges the various trim pieces to minimize waste material. Data for driving numerically controlled cloth cutting machines is generated easily from the console. The results are read onto a disc pack which is commonly accessible to the IBM 370/168 used for engineering and an IBM 370/158 devoted to more routine data processing. The data is transmitted from the 158 to a system 7 mini-computer at the trim plant. This computer serves as a DNC controller for the N/C cloth cutters. Because of this system N/C data is supplied to the plant within 3 days for changes that would formerly have taken two weeks. In addition to this response time improvement, it provides a significant productivity gain.

As a final illustration of a well integrated CAD/CAM sub-system, I would like to describe production engineering's Roll Die System. The manufacturing of metal trim moldings is accomplished by feeding flat strips of metal from a coil of raw material through a series of 10 to 20 sets of rollers. Each pair of these roll dies forms the metal a little more closely toward its final shape, typically some type of curved cross-section. In this application, the trim designer works out the detailed cross-sectional shape at the design console. Next, the roll die designer resolves the progression problem. He determines just how much forming can be accomplished at each station. As a result of his work, detailed cross-sections are defined as they will exist when the metal exits each station. These provide most of the variable information which the N/C expert needs to do his job. He now uses the light pen at a design console to select tools of his simulated lathe tool turret, and to indicate the beginning and end to each cut that the N/C lathe is to make in turning the set of roll dies. He completes his work by requesting N/C tapes to be written. They are produced automatically by the system in accordance with the information he has supplied during his session at the tube. At the plant the tapes are mounted on the lathe and one by one all the necessary roll dies are turned automatically.

In this application, the computer is used to aid in trim design, tool design and actual tool fabrication. It involves no loss of control by the people, yet it increases their productivity substantially, and cuts lead time drastically. This is CAD/CAM in a 2-D world. It is a routine application today. In the future we hope to have our 3-D CAD/CAM operating routinely in the same integrated fashion.

CAD/CAM Impacts

The material presented up to this point has been primarily descriptive. I have indicated the character and scope of the body design and tool manufacturing activities. I have tried to show that hundreds of people in many organizations are involved in these activities, and that they interface in many ways. Selected illustrations have been used to show that, in the main, body design at GM is computer aided design, and that at least some of our tool manufacturing is computer aided manufacturing. Technology should take no bows, however, unless all this results in an enhancement of our company's ability to meet people's transportation needs. To see that this is in fact the case, let's look at three kinds of impact. Let's consider the impact on response time for new products, the impact on our ability to satisfy regulatory requirements, and the effect on our quality.

Many factors combine to influence the quality of our sheet metal car bodies. The use of CAD/CAM for tooling affects only a few of these factors. Sheet metal symmetry and metal fit are generally affected. The symmetry improvement is a simple result of the left hand and right hand panels being produced by tooling which is at least partially generated from common design and N/C data. Because many steps in the tool manufacturing process have not yet employed numerical processing to any significant degree, however, this beneficial impact is sometimes diluted in subsequent steps.

The fact that most master models are built via CAD/CAM has significantly increased the assurance that the set of exterior panels is properly dimensioned to fit. Master models for the panels of a car are usually "cubed-up" so that the fit and flow from one to another can be observed visually. This makes it easy to verify that the independently developed detail designs have not destroyed the overall integrity of the body. This is one mechanism for coordinating the work of many individuals. It has shown us that the new design technology does maintain integrity better. Beyond that, when errors are shown up by the "cube-up", the system is able to respond with appropriate changes faster. We know, then, that the panels are now designed to fit better than ever. Once again, however, only a part of this benefit can be counted as a sure gain. Some of it may be lost in subsequent manufacturing steps.

The ability of CAD/CAM to assist in the sometimes frustrating process of meeting regulatory standards has been demonstrated. Among the efforts that have taken place to assure compliance with standards -- present, future, or anticipated -- we include work done in the vision area. Some of this deals with visibility of the exterior world provided by a system of inside and outside mirrors, windshields, sideglass, and backlites. Other work concerns the drivers view of the instruments, and the potential for their obstruction by the relationship between the seat orientation and the steering wheel position. Compliance analysis is accomplished through vision simulation, using typical CAD technology. In most cases, magnetic tapes of the resultant data serve as acceptable documentation for the Federal regulatory agencies.

Computer Aided Design has also played a prominent role in the air bag design, designs for 5 mile-per-hour impact bumper systems, and door side guard beam design. The fuel economy standards have created increased emphasis on weight reduction. As cited earlier, computer aided vehicle structural analysis has been an important factor in our ability to maintain strength while reducing weight.

In general, the ability of computer aided design to assist in designing for compliance to regulations and to readily develop acceptable evidence of compliance in the process has made most of these burdens more nearly bearable.

Finally, let's address the major question. Does the CAD/CAM approach provide the faster response time for which it was developed? The answer is yes. But there are qualifications.

Here are a few examples of specific activities and their attainable elapsed times with and without CAD/CAM assistance. Chevrolet's time to design a hood inner panel reduced by 5 weeks. Time to produce a hood master model cut 7 weeks; hood tooling time cut 12 weeks. Time from trim strip release until all roll dies are machined improved from 8 weeks to 2 weeks. Time to do panel tip drawings used to be several days; now done in a few hours. Time to complete structural analysis of a body; couldn't be considered without the computer.

These examples illustrate the possibilities. In general, productivity gains of individual elements are being used to obtain some combination of lead time savings, product improvement, cost reduction and decision time. An arrow diagram or PERT chart which attempted to depict all the design and tool build activities for a major new line of cars like the GM 1977 full sized cars would cover a big wall. It would be highly complex. If we colored the arrows red whose work is directly effected by the CAD/CAM system, we would see a lot of red color when we stepped back to look at it. However, there would still remain sizeable areas with little or no color in them. Certainly, not all the red arrows would lie on the critical path, though many of them would. Therefore, in the current situation of widespread but still incomplete use of CAD/CAM there is no uniformity of time savings spanning the entire job of design and tooling. Direct time gains are found primarily in the overall design and detail design areas. There is only a limited reduction in the tool design area and even less in tool manufacturing. However, the faster pace of design activities frequently allows earlier release of information to the downstream activities. This allows some leveling of peak loads in manufacturing. In effect it makes it possible for the manufacturing activity to do more work in parallel during a greater part of its cycle of activity. The result is an opportunity for better utilization of manufacturing resources. Hence the work is done in a shorter time.

Of course, complexity of the work relations is not the only factor which makes measurement of overall system response difficult. No two programs are ever alike. We can, at best, compare a current program with a former one of approximately equivalent scope. This is what has been done in trying to evaluate the impact on the full sized 1977 car program. The conclusion is that the major specification changes brought on by the energy crisis and made halfway through the program would have been impossible without the benefit of CAD/CAM.

Future Trends

The CAD/CAM system just described has been developing for nearly twenty years. Since it is a dynamic, growing environment, it is interesting to try to look ahead and envision its future shape. Because it is a computer based system, its future character may be partially revealed by trends in the base computer technology. The system was conceived at a time when the only reasonable architecture was the big central structure. A big computer with a big resident data base, all serving a population of nearby consoles was the central theme. Time sharing, of one kind or another, was the way to make this central serial computer serve many activities in parallel.

However, as the system progressed through its gestation period, the base technology advanced. The cost of CPU's and core memory has come down. Today's mini-computers are more powerful than the big machine on which this system was first developed. The effects of this trend are already seen as a centrifugal force beginning to move the raw calculating power out away from the computer center. As noted earlier, the GM system already has over a dozen satellite network stations handling a significant portion of the calculating effort. We can expect to see more such units performing more functions. And we can expect to see them stretched still further from the Technical Center, which is today the computing center. These changes are beginning to transform the computer system from a completely serial processor into a parallel processor displaying noticeable functional differentiation. Altogether this means more speed and greater responsiveness. And that is the mission.

This centrifugal force is trend number one. It is countered, however, by a strong centripetal force, the binding force of the common data base. To a considerable extent the satellite stations are tied inextricably to the big computer. They can function viably only by feeding on its data base. The centripetal force is a strong one because, at least at this time, it is hard to see how the essential integrity of the design data can be feasibly maintained except in a central system. This need for data integrity coupled with the high cost of interactive communication channels from the center to the periphery are the factors that must be weighed against the convenience, control, and parallel computation gains in determining which functions can best be done by the central computer, and which by the satellites. A critical point in the flight from the center would apparently be that point at which the sole function reserved for the once sovereign center is the maintenance and communication of data to and from the completely distributed parallel processing units.

Regardless of what seem inevitable changes in system architecture, we expect a continued expansion of the applications supported by the system. It was pointed out earlier that the die construction activity constitutes the overwhelming bulk of the work needed to prepare for a new line of vehicles. We noted also that this area has barely been impacted by CAD/CAM. In order to do so, we will need to improve the computer aided die design proficiency and the effectiveness of numerical control processing and programming assistance which the system provides. Given this, we can expect the use of N/C contouring for body dies to be accepted into production use as rapidly as the capital equipment base will allow.

Summary

As a result of almost twenty years of research, development, and systems implementation, General Motors now designs its cars with a computer aided design system, and has started to employ computer aided manufacturing in its tooling operations. Most of the major interfaces have been streamlined and simplified as a result of this technology. The slash has not been entirely removed from CAD/CAM, but it is considerably bent. The CAD/CAM impact on response time has been substantial. It is largely responsible for the fact that GM was able to make a major shift in design specifications for its full sized 1977 cars half way through the program. Future impacts of CAD/CAM are expected to be even stronger, and the range of effect even broader. As of car model year 1977, CAD/CAM has passed the test of responsiveness. The challenge ahead is higher productivity in manufacturing.

Tool
Construction
780
Product
Design
123
Tool
Design
97

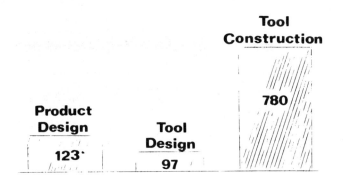

DISTRIBUTION OF 1000 HOURS
OF BODY TOOLING EFFORT

Figure 1

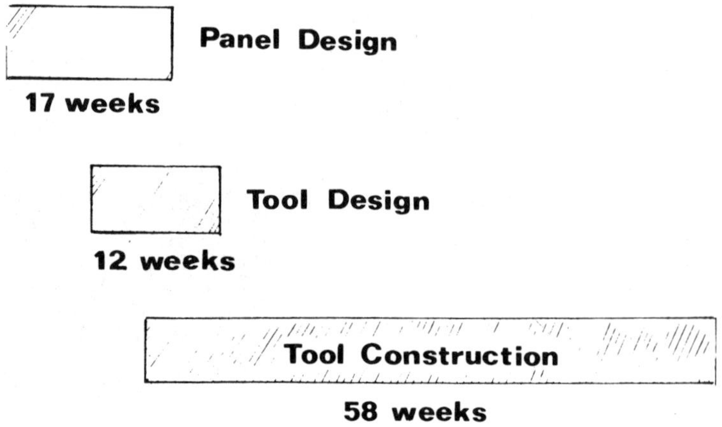

Panel Design
17 weeks
Tool Design
12 weeks
Tool Construction
58 weeks

MAJOR BODY PANEL
TIME DISTRIBUTION

Figure 2

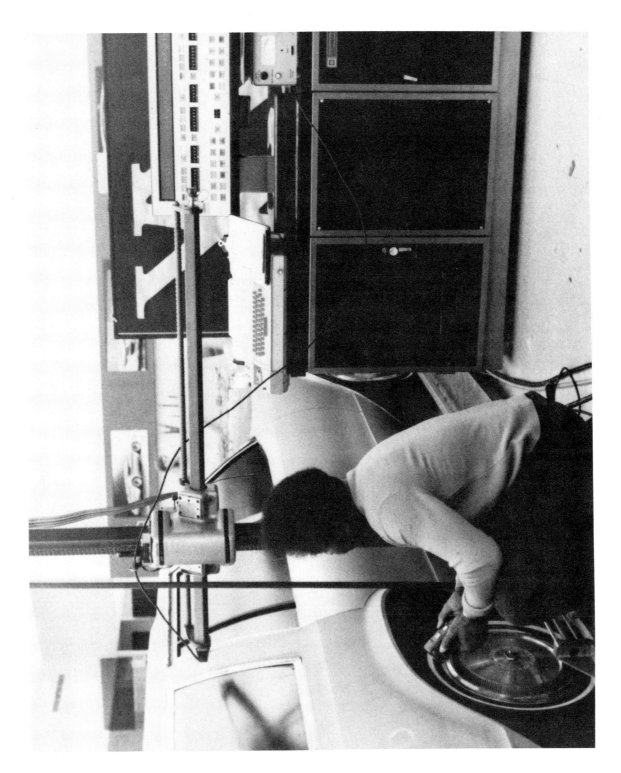

FIGURE 3

FIGURE 4

CAD/CAM For Automotive Die Design

By Hugh O. McCormick
Manager, Computer Programming &
Development — Ford Motor Company

Computer Aided Design methods have transformed the traditionally manual tool processing and designing of automotive body sheet metal stamping dies in Ford Motor Company. The production tooling is advanced through processing, draw development, die engineering, and construction by employing computer techniques. Interactive graphics and batch processing computer systems are used, each in applications best suited to their unique powers. Substantial production steel savings, improved standardization and timing are among the many benefits. This step in an integrated body design and tooling system is built on the base provided by computer aided clay model scanning and body product design.

INTRODUCTION

CAD/CAM, as used for body sheet metal die design, began development at the Ford Motor Company in the late sixties with the acquisition of computer aided equipment for clay model scanning, computer graphics designing, and numerically controlled drafting. These individual systems in concert with the ready availability of large scale batch processing computers in both the engineering and financial areas provided the nucleus for the formation of a totally integrated body design and tooling system.

We are going to examine the area of automotive die design by computer aided methods today. However, to put this part of the system into perspective, the evolution of the total system will be briefly explained.

The emergence of a new or restyled car in the market is preceded by a great deal of planning in many areas. The first evidence of these plans in three dimensional physical form is a clay model. This is a full scale result of the planning and is itself subjected to much examination and modification.

However, the story of CAD/CAM begins after this exhaustive process is complete and the clay model is presented for scanning. The scanning, which is measuring in order to transform the physical form of the model into digital form for subsequent use in the engineering and manufacturing area, has been improved through the application of new technology. The traditional method of manually measuring points and fitting templates has been replaced by automatic scanning in computer driven coordinate measuring machines. The scanner data representing the clay model is examined, modified if necessary, and drafted for visual verification all by computer aided methods. This data is transmitted to the body product engineering activity as a formal release of approved surface.

The body product designer discarding the manual design tools of sweeps, curves, compasses, and scales, turns to the sophistication of computer graphics. He performs the function of surface layout by smoothing the data and in turn, engineering the various body openings, joints, and associated flanges. Proceeding from this master exterior surface, the structural components are designed.

The transmission of this data representing the individual body panels is the input into our developing system of computer aided design of automotive tooling.

DIE PROCESSING

Die design is an integral part of the Manufacturing Engineering function that provides the tooling to produce body sheet metal stamping. The first step is processing, during which the manufacturing sequence is established, the operations to be performed are specified, such as draw, trim, flange, restrike, or pierce, the presses to be used are designated, and the position or tip of the panel in each die is developed.

It is in processing that the first major impact of CAD/CAM is evident. The display of the panel on the CRT has superceded the laborious and time consuming methods of the past. These involved examining the part drawing, the making of a soft wood model, and the vacuum forming of a plastic study model to portray the three dimensional aspects of the panel.

The data used to display the picture on the CRT screen is in three dimensional format. Therefore, using the speed of the computer the panel can be displayed in dynamic rotation, projected view, or cross section cut through any area. This capability precludes the need of physical study models.

The process engineer reviews the panel on the CRT evaluating the tip position for possible back angles that would inhibit forming, improper trim conditions, and other process functions normally performed at this time. The engineer can also exercise the option to prepare a drafting magnetic tape on all or any of the views or sections he may desire. This information can be transmitted to the numerically controlled drafting machine for preparation of study drawings. When the process procedure has been completed, the engineer will issue a set of process sheets specifying the final tips, die line up, and press assignments for manufacturing the panel in the assigned stamping plant.

DRAW DIE DEVELOPMENT

Concurrent with the processing phase the engineering and design of the draw die development is conducted, also on a CRT graphics display.

The draw development is the first step in the process of determining the shape of the drawn stamping which is subsequently trimmed, restruck, flanged, and pierced into the final panel shape. The main criteria for the draw development are:
1. Production of a quality panel.
2. Minimum blank size for optimum material utilization.
3. Minimum of subsequent die operations.
4. Utilization of existing press and automation equipment.

The intent of this presentation is not to discuss the complexities of engineering the draw development. The purpose is to illustrate the capabilities of the CAD/CAM software within the computer graphics system that provide the designer with many fast, accurate, and clever tools. It is our experience that, the designer, using the three dimensional data in dynamic rotation, changing views or cutting cross sections has a clearer insight into the physical shape of the panel and the development than in any other medium available.

The draw development engineer will begin his task by displaying the panel on the CRT. After a preliminary familarization period, the panel will be tipped to the recommended position. The panel will then be examined for compliance with die design standards such as back draft or closed walls, trim conditions, modification of surface for subsequent reforming to final shape, etc.

After this review, the engineer starts the design of the binder surface, the area used for clamping and restraining the sheet metal blank during the forming. Sheet metal when clamped into the majority of binder surfaces is still in the elastic range. The CRT menu provides geometrical functions such as arcs and lines to generate conic developable surfaces. There is an adjustable arc set at the front of the die, at the rear of the die and, if necessary, at the middle. When the designer is satisfied with the arc sets as compared to the drawn shape, he will command the computer to construct a binder surface through the arc set sections.

The engineer proceeds to evaluate the binder surface with several software functions all programmed with the capability to represent the binder surface, the draw die punch, and the interaction of the two to simulate the forming process.

1. He can cut sections through the punch and the binder, displaying the effect of the punch hitting the sheet metal blank. The CRT screen displays the depth of draw at the same time. There is an ability to stack these sections, so that there is simultaneous representation of the draw process at the front, rear, and intermediate section of the die.
2. By further menu pick, he can direct the computer to calculate and display the pattern of contact points as the punch incrementally descends.
3. Finally, he is able to display the vertical draw depth between the binder surface and the die cavity at any point designated.

This is an iterative process. If the hits don't propagate properly or the depths are shallow or deep, the engineer evaluates the condition and adjusts the binder surface through manipulation of the arc sets until the binder development is complete to his satisfaction.

The draw development engineer will at that point, coordinate with the stock layout engineer to perform the necessary calculations to arrive at the blank size. Again, if there is a cost penalty associated with the blank size, adjustments can be made to eliminate the cause.

After approval by the engineering supervision, the engineer commands the graphics computer to format the views and sections for drafting. This data is transmitted to the numerically controlled drafting machine to output the draw development designs. He then commands another program option to prepare hard copy outputs of both the hit propagation and the recorded draw depths.

Copies of the design and readings are then forwarded to the plaster shop for reproduction in plaster. After verification of conformance to the design, the plaster, in turn, is forwarded to a prototype supplier for soft tool evaluation.

The question at this point is; what are the advantages of computer aided design of draw developments. The computer graphics installations, the generating of the systems and applications software, the training, and implementation of the user programs obviously constitute major investments.

The advantages reside in the special powers of the computer, speed, accuracy, and transmission of comprehensible data.

1. The input of master draft quality data is readily available from the body design system on both a scheduled and request basis.
2. Library references and current standards are maintained for easy recall.

3. The data structure coupled with display techniques provides the equivalent of three dimensional viewing.
4. The reaction time to vary input parameters and view results has changed from days to seconds.
5. The ability to accurately scale and view from any perspective increases comprehension.
6. Lastly, substantial cost savings in the reduction of engineered scrap or offal have been identified providing a pleasing return on investment.

DIE DESIGN

After approval of the draw development design and concurrent with the soft tool evaluation, the next phase is the producing of the computer aided die design.

The die design program differs from the processing and draw development programs in that this software was written for large scale computer systems in a batch processing mode. This program employs analytic geometry packages. The main segment is the central design module which designs the castings complete based on the description of the part, or of the draw development. Standard components are positioned and oriented as specified and then integrated into the construction of the casting design.

The input to the program for a particular die is relatively simple consisting of the following:

1. Data representing the contours and outline of the part or development.
2. A few program instructions to specify features not automatically defined by t geometry of the part.
3. Press data file.
4. Picture file of standard die components.

The drafting module prepares the final output of the system on magnetic tape, which controls the N/C drafting machine in producing an engineering drawing of the die.

Describing the process in greater detail, the engineer first, prepares the data representing the part or draw development. This is prepared on the computer graphics by displaying the total network of lines and selecting a subset essential to the logic of the program as well as that customarily depicted in the final die design. The lines are coded as to their function, such as blank outline, punch opening, flange line, trim line necessary to the engineering of their respective dies. The line data and type is transmitted to a part storage file in the main computer to await further instructions.

Press data is digitized in sufficient detail for automatic resolution of size containment, shut height, fastening. This data is transmitted to a press library file in the main computer.

Standard die components are digitized and placed in a standard picture file. These are either accessed in their digitized dimensions or through logical instruction statements provided in the die specifications are revised to other dimensions. This area of the program is very versatile in providing many variations from a small library.

The designer compiles the set of instructions to the program by defining

1. Part number
2. Type of die
3. Press assignment(s)
4. Itemize standard components and provide location if necessary
5. Specific views and sections of die desired.

After a short run time the computer writes the drafting tape. The required views are drawn on the numerically controlled drafting machine. The die drawings in incomplete form are forwarded to the manual die drafting activity for finishing. This comprising a small amount of designing and a complete requirement of cross hatching, dimensioning and notation.

Again, what are the advantages of computer aided design, but specifically in this case, die design? The computer equipment investment is considerably less due to the time-share basis, but the software is more expensive.

1. The input of part data is readily available from the processing or draw development program.
2. All the data of the presses and components are available on single commands.
3. Use of standard components is rigidly enforced.
4. Time savings in that 2-3 weeks is reduced to 2-3 days.
5. Direct cost savings are realized, but indirect savings due to the accuracy of the system are substantial.

BLANK NESTING

The third and last area of CAD/CAM in die design is the blank nesting program. Blank nesting is the process of locating blanks as close together as is possible in order to optimize steel usage in blanking operations.

A brief description follows:

The engineer obtains a structural drawing of the part as early in the new program as possible. Using his experience, he "unfolds" the part and develops the required blank. The developed blank is then positioned on a coordinate measuring machine and digitized.

Latest steel cost information and other pertinent input data registered on magnetic disk packs are inserted into the computer system. The information used will be:

- Part number
- Part time
- Current date
- Engineering level of the part
- Type of material
- Metal thickness
- Production plant
- Financial planning volume, and
- Number of years which the part will be in production

The computer program will consider 6 different stock pricing structures. They include variations of coil and sheet stock.

The engineer, experienced in both the operation of the graphics system and methods of blank nesting, directs the computer to project the part on the CRT. The computer automatically nests the part in a single row. By rotating the blanks at predetermined intervals up to 180º, the nesting requiring the minimum amount of steel is displayed on the lower portion of the screen. Shown are:

- Rough piece weight
- Steel cost per piece and
- Steel cost for the life of the part

Each of 6 considered methods is listed according to rough piece weight per part. The top line shows the most economical method. At the engineer's command, a complete cost analysis of the nested part is recorded on the computer printer. The information recorded includes width of stock, base price of steel, and cost "extra" such as penalties for stock width, draw quality, pickle and oil, etc. Also shown for each of the 6 methods of procuring stock are total stock cost per hundredweight, rough piece weight, steel weight for the production life of the part, cost per pound, cost for the production life of part, and cost per piece.

The engineer, now using his experience and judgment in blank nesting, directs the computer in nesting the parts. He may scale up the areas where the webbing is most critical. In this way, he is better able to determine that only minimum webbing is being maintained — webbing being that portion of the steel that is left after the blank is removed. Using light pen commands, the engineer may cause more blanks to appear on the screen. They may be positioned in various relationships to each other. At the proper light pen command, the nested blanks and a cost summary are instantly shown. With each nesting, a cost analysis is recorded on the printer. This process is then repeated with as many different methods of nesting as the engineer deems necessary. The computer has nested in minutes what it would have taken days to do manually.

The engineer now elects to overlap the blanks and then determine the cost savings associated with the design changes or concessions which would be desired. Once all possible blank nestings have been analyzed, the cost reductions and the requested design changes or concessions, complete with life time cost savings, are reviewed with the product engineer for approval.

The remaining procedure is quite orthodox. All nesting methods with cost analysis are written into magnetic tapes. The selected methods are then transferred onto microfilm, and a hard copy is made. From magnetic tape, a full-size blank layout is made on an automatic drafting machine. This layout will be used for the design purposes.

To insure that all factors are taken into consideration, the die processor takes the selected blank nest methods and performs a complete value engineering study on each proposal. The most optimum blanking method, taking all factors as labor, maintenance, investment, and tool cost into consideration, is then selected for production.

The advantages of computer aided design.

1. Optimized nesting for best material utilization.
2. Quantifiable cost savings through product design concessions.
3. Documentation ease
    1. Computer system printer

2. Microfilm with COM
3. N/C drafting.

HARDWARE

There have been references to the equipment employed in the Metal Stamping CAD/ CAM. The specifics are as follows:

Computer Graphics

Lundy Model 32-300 Interactive Display with Light Pen and function keyboard Control Data System 17 Computer with Cartridge Disk and 9 track Magnetic Tape Unit.

Large Scale Computer System

IBM 370 installation linked by ASP RJE and TSO Terminals

Numerically Controlled Drafting

Gerber Model 4477/DMS High Speed Drafting System Coupled into the Data Management System.
Gerber Model 2075 Drafting System

Digitizing

Hewlett — Packard Computer, Table, and Plotter

Our immediate plans in the equipment field are:

1. Accurately forecast the capacity needs based on the manifold increases resulting from expanding capability and application in both the product design and the tooling areas.
2. Provide the communication network between all elements of the system and the data files.

SUMMARY

In summary, CAD/CAM is providing the designer and engineer with better tools to perform his job. The results are:

1. Substantial cost savings in production steel procurement by better Material Utilization through improvement in engineered scrap and nesting.
2. Reduced tooling costs by improved standardization and accuracy.
3. Improved timing through the ready availability of master data coupled with the response time of the computer.

CAM Systems In The Float Glass Process

By Richard R. Perryman
Manager, Manufacturing Engineering
Ford Motor Company

INTRODUCTION

With Computer-Aided Manufacturing systems becoming more and more popular, ones curiousity is aroused as to what is the big attraction for these systems. The Glass Division at Ford Motor Company has now seen about a decade pass since its initial efforts in computer process control. A review of what has happened through the years up to their latest installation - the Tulsa Glass Plant - gives at least one accounting of the effects of computer control evolution on an industrial environment.

The Glass Division at Ford produces float glass. The facilities required to produce float glass products are broken down into three areas: (1) Batching, (2) Glass Making and (3) Capping.

BATCHING FACILITY

The Batching Facility is where raw materials are stored and prepared into batch for delivery to the glass-making facility. Raw materials such as sand, dolomite, limestone, salt cake, soda ash, etc., are shipped in by closed rail cars and trucks. These materials are unloaded via underground hoppers, conveyors, and elevators to specific silos for storage, where they are readily available for weigh-up. Materials are precisely weighed up to an established formula in scales located below the storage silos, and then carefully discharged to a collection conveyor. The collection conveyor delivers all of the materials to a totalizer scale, where a cross check can be made of the material weigh-up. From here the materials pass to a mixer, where they are carefully blended into a homogeneous mixture. At this point the mixture is ready for delivery to the melting furnace.

GLASS-MAKING FACILITY

The Glass-Making Facility includes the Melting Furnace, Float Bath and the Annealing Lehr. Batch material is delivered to the Furnace and heated under natural gas firing to a temperature in excess of 2800° F. Having reached this temperature, the batch material transforms into a molten glass state. This glassy constituent is then gradually cooled as it passes through the refiner stage of the Furnace to a stabilizing temperature of around 2100° F., where it becomes ready for delivery to the Float Bath.

The Float Process involves the floating of a glass ribbon across a hugh, refractory-lined "Bath" of molten tin. The molten glass passes from the Furnace into the Bath and is allowed to flow onto the tin surface. The natural forces of gravity and surface tension cause the glass to take on the perfect flatness of the molten tin and attain a uniform nominal thickness of 1/4 inch across the width of the ribbon. As the ribbon passes through the Batch, this nominal thickness and ribbon width may be altered to accommodate product requirement by means of heating profile adjustments and mechanical attenuation of the ribbon. Finally, the glass ribbon is suitably cooled to a pseudo-plastic state in order to retain its final configuration prior to delivery into the Annealing operation.

Annealing is performed in a long oven called a Lehr. As the glass ribbon is transported through the Lehr on asbestos rolls, the temperature of the ribbon is first stabilized across its width and then carefully cooled through its annealing range. This is required to attain desirable strength characteristics in the glass. The Lehr has suitably partition flues above and below the glass ribbon to allow temperature-regulated cooling of the glass ribbon down to room temperature.

The glass ribbon of finished quality exits from the Lehr into the inspection area. As the glass passes through this area, it is inspected for various imperfections and marked for rejection accordingly.

CAPPING FACILITY

Following inspection the glass ribbon proceeds into cutting and packaging; collectively known as the Capping Area. Here, the glass ribbon is cut down into rectangular sizes as required to fill requested orders. This is accomplished by first scoring the ribbon laterally to one set of prescribed dimensions, then longitudinally to the corresponding prescribed dimensions, and, finally, separating and routing the resulting brackets to their respective take-off points for removal and packaging. The glass is then ready for direct shipment to the owner.

HISTORY OF COMPUTER CONTROL

The history behind Process Computer Control at Ford Glass started in the glass-making area. Early in 1965, when Ford began making preparations to switch its existing plate glass facilities over to the new float glass process, a serious look was also taken at the advancements which were taking place in process control. The use of computers in industry for process control was in its infancy and, although somewhat clumbsy in its initial applications, showed some encouraging potential. Among these pioneers in computer control, the one that drew most appeal to Ford was IBM; who in joint effort with Owens Corning Fiberglas had applied an IBM 1710 System using a DDC software package to a fiberglas furnace. Subsequent discussions with IBM resulted in the selection of IBM 1800 System using an adapted version of the new DDC package.

The first Ford installation went into the Dearborn Glass Plant, which launched early in 1967. As an initial effort it was quite ambitious having over 500 analog monitoring points and 80 direct digital control loops. Basically the computer functionally replaced the use of various analog readout, recording and controlling devices used in similar installations and simply emulated their functions. A good deal of effort was spent initially to insure that this was indeed achieved. These accomplishments themselves were rewarding because of certain benefits inherent particularly to computer control. First of all, control loops were found to be more easily "tunable" because of flexibility in algorithm selection and control constant resolution (this was particularly true with, surprisingly, the control loops having long dead times and slow responses.) A better job of both monitoring and controlling was also attributed to the improved precision and accuracy of the computer over standard analog devices. Also, along this line, a general overall upgrade of instrumentation resulted due to the added attention of computer interfacing. All-in-all this first adventure into the realm of Computer Process Control was deemed a success and had a strong influence on opening the door to future endeavors.

Subsequent installations followed until by December, 1969, all four of the then existing Ford Glass Lines had computer control on their glass-making operations. The evolutions that took place with each of these installations plus other subsequent upgrades established the precedence for the Tulsa lines.

The changes that have taken place since that initial installation might appear subtle to the common observer, and yet have been extensive in many respects. The fundamental concepts and philosophies of DDC control are still very much intact and remain the nucleus of the system's function; however, the operating system itself has taken on a totally revamped appearance. Originally the system operated in a virtually dedicated environment which restricted the system to its absolute basic functions. Today the system operates in a multi-programming environment which not only allows on-line generation and "swapout" of the fundamental functions, but includes extensive versatility in generating, compiling, and executing additional foreground and background operations, making optimal usage of core image partitions and system idle time. This versatility has opened the doors to the imaginations of many engineers and analysts who have implemented countless methods for capturing, analyzing, evaluating, and reporting information. The results have been a sizeable growth in cascade and supervisory control, more sophisticated reporting media, more extensive historical data collection and more thorough diagnostic measures. This extended utilization is also reflected in the hardware configuration which has seen a 20% growth in process I/O, 50% growth in core, 1000% growth in bulk storage, and peripheral add-ons such as CRT's, which can visibly display any of this information on a moment's notice.

The Capping Area, which got its computer start in latter 1969, has gone through a similar dynamic evolution. Its original concept was basically a direct take-off from a previous hardwired digital logic system, whose functions required some upgrading. These upgrades included: (1) consolidating the primary operator and cordwood operator functions into a single operator's task, (2) providing a more positive method of "tracking" glass through the Capping operation and (3) providing an improved method of operator communication with the system. The result was a mimi-computer system which functionally met these objectives on a cost competitive basis.

This new system performed the task of making the assigned single or double primary cuts, tracking the glass to the cordwood machines, making the corresponding cordwood cuts and, finally, delivering the glass to the routing section - all through the single request of one operator. This simplification of a one-time complex task was made possible because of the facility to preload the system with the specifics of a given order and, upon a single keyboard entry, initiate processing its execution. "Tracking" of the glass through its various stages was greatly improved by the addition of verification sensors at strategically located points along the glass travel path. These sensors coupled with appropriate logic made it virtually impossible to get out of sequence; even in the event of on-line breakage, a particularly vulnerable situation in previous operations.

It did not take long at all for this initial Capping System to begin experiencing operational evolution. As a bonus, a provision had been included to allow a "single shot" function; a one-time demand cut of a specialty selected sized sheet. This provision was added primarily to allow cutting large sized architectural sheets on a selective bases to avoid costly defect losses. This provision proved to be a decided advantage in the operation. However, an even bigger benefit was found by adding a new logic function that accommodated coupling the "single shot" to a standard two-size cut in some repeatable fashion to allow a three-size cut pattern. This offered more flexibility in balancing line operation by allowing a mix of up to three different sizes.

Today, the Tulsa Capping System, a third generation approach to Ford computerized cutting, handles up to sixteen different sizes at any one time. These sizes are cut on a balancing basis and directly computer routed to their assigned takeoff points. The order schedules, which are prepared in advance, are entered into the system via cards and processed in an automated fashion. Orders are individually processed to pre-established takeoff points where scrap is carefully monitored to insure accurate order switchover. Production reports are generated each hour and at shift end to recap order processing status and to determine yield performance rates.

Changes, placing added emphasis on operating reliability, are also apparent. The one-time single mainframe system now is configured with six mainframes; a master system mainframe feeding five slave mainframes which directly control the cutting equipment. This was primarily done to isolate responsibility to each mainframe and allow independent operation in the event of any individual mainframe failure. The system now also has an extensive repertoire of alarm messages which will pinpoint almost all equipment failures or operation deficiencies and allow the operator to take quick corrective action.

The Batch House is the most recent facility to adapt a computer system in its domain. It got its start in the latter part of 1972 at the Nashville Plant when the existing facility began approaching its practical capacity limitation and it became necessary to make some improvements.

Again the initial computer system was a simple outgrowth of an already existing conventional system with a few added embellishments to justify its incorporation. In the case of the Batch House, there were three major improvement factors sought: (1) faster batching cycles to allow increased throughput (2) more precise and consistent weigh-up and mixing to insure optimal melting performance, and (3) more dependable and reliable equipment to guarantee better uptime.

At this same point in time, suppliers of conventional scales systems, were making some initial inroads in utilizing computer control in their more recent system designs. Having performed the initial ground work in developing the fundamental software and hardware interface modules, it was a fairly straight-forward effort to incorporate the specific features needed to get the required improvement factors.

Faster batching cycles were acquired through the use of adaptive weigh-up modules. These program modules have the inherent ability to dynamically update the fast-to-slow feed switchover point and adapt to prevailing affecting conditions (i.e. silo fill level, material density, humidity, etc.). This allows maximum use of the fast feed rate thereby resulting in minimal weigh-up cycles. In addition maximum overlap of sequential functions (i.e. weigh-up, discharge, totalizing, mixing, etc.) was achievable; again to allow the overall throughput to be maximized. Better precision of material weigh-up was achieved because of the ability to again dynamically update the feeder shutoff point. This provides the ability to automatically compensate for weigh-up affecting variables such as scale heel buildup and material "tailing" after shutoff.

Finally, the computer-based system has proven to be a more reliable system in terms of fewer hardware malfunctions. This has been primarily due to the fact that the closed, integrated logic packages in these systems are simply less vulnerable to the inherent dusty environment of a batch facility.

The subsequent Batch Control Systems installed in Tulsa have expanded their scope beyond the original concept of batch material weigh-up and mixing. These systems now incorporated the monitor and control of the raw material unloading operations. This includes the auto selection of unloading conveyors and diverters to insure correct routing of materials to their respective storage silos. This is verified by a logic cross check to a plug box attached to the delivery rail car or truck. The system also weighs the materials as it is being unloaded to storage. This information is used in conjunction with batching data, to maintain a dynamic raw material storage inventory, as well as to verify stated capacities on materials delivered.

In addition, the system now includes such features as direct monitoring of furnace feeder hopper fill status, automatic bad batch reject points within the batching cycle, and scale weigh-up calibration cross check. Finally like the other systems, its repertiore of diagnostic and error messages has also been expanded to aid in operational troubleshooting.

In reviewing the history of computerizing our Float Glass Facilities, it is interesting to note the similarities in progression that each area has gone through. Initially, each system was implemented in lieu of some existing conventional system, motivated on the premises of added improvement features. In all cases this meant first achieving across-the-board interface compatibility between process and computer system just to establish functional equality to prior conventional methods. Then, having accomplished this, proceed to incorporate the improvement features and substantiate their stated justification. These objectives, although by no means menial and demanding the full, concentrated effort of some very dedicated and capable people, nevertheless were attainable.

However, it is apparent that the benefits did not end there. The true adaptability advantages in each of these systems began to fully surface after the flurry of reaching their initial goals. For example, like practically everything else, it took no time at all for portions of these systems to show some degree of obsolescence, even in some cases during the implementation stages. Fortunately the modular construction of these systems, both in the hardware and software sense, lends itself quite readily to last minute changes without jeopardizing critical cost and timimg schedules. Also, as has already been shown, subsequent installations and upgrades have seen continual change ranging from major design revisions to accommodate new operation concepts to broadening reporting and diagnostic functions, all toward a superior operating facility. In all cases these evolutions were handled with relative ease as compared to what would have been involved having the counterpart conventional systems.

In all, it appears that the key attraction that computer systems have is adaptability. It has been demonstrated that computers are not only adequately adaptable for use in a manufacturing environment, but are possibly the only equipment adaptable enough to take on the newer and more dynamic challenges facing a manufacturing facility today.

Interactive Design And Three-Dimensional Modelling Applied To Vehicle Lamp Manufacture

By J.N.S. Deane
Manager—Engineering Department

and

M.F. Hessey
Principal Research Officer in Computing
Lucas Industries

A system which has been developed for the computer aided design and manufacture of automotive lighting is described. The system allows inter-active design of the lamp surfaces using computer graphics, and a math-ematical model of the resultant lamp is stored in the computer. This can be used to generate drawings, to drive a specially developed model making machine or to produce tapes for numerically controlled machine tools. Substantial benefits in accuracy and reduced lead time have resulted from the development of these facilities.

INTRODUCTION

The authors' organisation began work on computer aided design, as applied to the description of the shapes of engineering components, in 1970. Prior to that date their use of computers had been extensive, but in the engineering field had been mainly concerned with product performance analysis rather than with product shape description. At the time that the work was started there were no commercially available CAD packages which were regarded as suitable. The potential advantages being claimed for the use of CAD – faster, more accurate design, automated draughting, output for nc machines, cheaper design, fewer designers, fewer skilled designers – also did not seem to have been adequately proved. As a result of this it was decided to undertake our own research work to evaluate the techniques, and to produce a CAD/CAM system which might suit the needs of the company. From past experience of 'general purpose' computer programs it was felt that it would be preferable to carry out such work with respect to a particular product, rather than aim immediately for a system which would claim to be suitable for any design work. It was believed that in this way a much more practical system would result, and that it would be more feasible to introduce it in stages rather than to have to wait for a total 'package'. This would also result in greater designer involvement during development.

From the start great emphasis was placed on the fact that the system should be an aid to designers, and was in no sense an attempt to achieve design by computer. For description of surfaces, some of which are required to be aesthetically styled, design by computer was not practical, but the use of computer graphics and other computer aids were potentially of considerable value. It was also seen as a clear aim that the system should not merely aid the initial product design, but should also lead to a means of quickly, and directly, generating from the design data the necessary models and prototypes, and aiding production.

The product chosen to be the main subject of the project was automotive small lamps. Lamps represented an ideal subject for the application of computer techniques for a number of reasons:

1. They are complex three dimensional shapes designed to present an aesthetically pleasing appearance, and are difficult to represent unambiguously on a conventional drawing.

2. Automotive lamps are designed frequently, a new design being required for almost every new model of road vehicle.

3. Although the shape of every new lamp is different, they constitute a family of shapes, the basic design characteristics being the same.

4. Because of the difficulty of describing the shape on a conventional drawing it is not easy to attain the required accuracy by normal design methods.

5. There is often a problem in designing the lamp, producing models and prototypes and making production tooling within the time available. Reduction of lead time is therefore one of the most important potential benefits of CAD/CAM methods.

The CAD/CAM system provides the following facilities:

1. Interactive design and viewing of surfaces on a computer graphics display.

2. The ability to produce accurate drawings to scale. In view of the potential output of manufacturing information direct, these drawings would be used primarily as visualisation aids and for checking, rather than being required for production. Hence they would not need to be fully dimensioned.

3. A means of producing models and prototypes for customer approval within a very short space of time.

4. The production of tapes for nc machine tools to be used in making the injection moulding or casting tools.

Although the system was developed with particular respect to automotive small lamps it was regarded as important that it should be suitable for other products in the future with as few modifications and additions as possible.

As described above the product chosen for the initial investigation of CAD techniques was automotive small lamps.

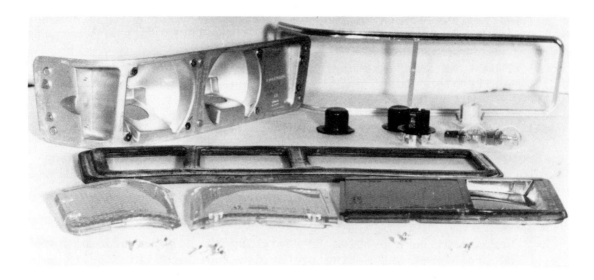

Figure 1

Components of a small lamp

Figure 1 illustrates a typical small lamp assembly. In considering the use of CAD techniques to describe the surfaces of such a lamp it was found that three essentially different design activities existed, each of which required a different computational approach. These three divisions of the design are the body moulding base surface, which is the surface of the lamp which mounts on the vehicle body panel; the reflector pockets, which collect light from the bulb and reflect it through the lens; and the exterior lens surface, which is visible and is usually a styling feature on the vehicle.

Body Moulding Base Surface

The body moulding base surface is required to mount accurately on the vehicle body panel, although it is separated from it by a rubber gasket of constant thickness. Customers generally use one of two methods to define the shape of the body panel to which the lamp is mounted:- dimensioned drawings or models. In the case of the model this may be examined with a three dimensional measuring machine. Thus in either case the co-ordinates of points on the panel surface are available. Using conventional design methods it is necessary to use this data to construct the offset surface which will be the body moulding base surface, that is, to allow for the gasket thickness. A number of section drawings would be used to describe this shape. Using CAD the procedure is to obtain a mathematical description of the car body panel surface in the computer, and from this to generate automatically the offset surface and any necessary drawings.

In order to achieve this the co-ordinates of the points defined on the drawing of the panel (or measured off the model) are input to a computer program which has been developed for this work. This performs a least squares fit to the data and produces a description of the surface in terms of bi-parametric cubics, or Coons patches. The number of patches used is defined by the designer, taking account of the complexity of the surface. A small number of patches provides sufficient accuracy for this work, three patches having been used on the majority of jobs undertaken to date. The co-efficients of the patches are converted into Bezier polynomial form in order to maintain compatibility with other programs in the suite and are then automatically stored. They can then be accessed when a further program is run to examine the surface which has been obtained. This program allows the panel surface to be inspected on a graphic display unit (Figure 2), and permits any rotation, magnification or shift of the surface to be performed.

Figure 2

Graphic display unit

Sections, perspective, isometric, stereo and a variety of other views can also be provided. All pictures produced on the display may be dumped on a graph plotter to any required scale (Figure 3).

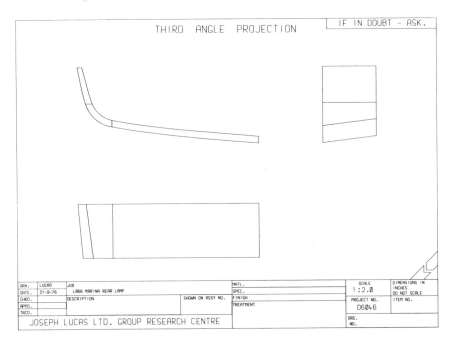

THIRD ANGLE PROJECTION   IF IN DOUBT - ASK.

DRN.	LUCAD	JOB		MATL.			SCALE	DIMENSIONS IN
DATE.	21-9-76	L866 MARINA REAR LAMP		SPEC.			1:2.0	INCHES
CHKD.		DESCRIPTION	SHOWN ON ASSY NO.	FINISH			PROJECT NO.	DO NOT SCALE
APPD.				TREATMENT			D6046	ITEM NO.
TRCD.								

JOSEPH LUCAS LTD. GROUP RESEARCH CENTRE   DRG. NO.

Figure 3

Drawings of   Morris Marina lamp mounting surface

The offset for the rubber gasket can be specified as any thickness and all the viewing facilities can then be used on this new surface, which is the body moulding base surface. As mentioned previously, the drawings are produced as a visualisation aid and for checking. No attempt has been made to dimension the drawings, since the computer representation of the surface will itself be used to produce the component.

Reflector Pockets

The reflector is required to collect light emitted from the bulb and to reflect it through the exterior lens. The main reflecting surface is a paraboloid. Focal length and focal point must be chosen to obtain sufficient light collection. The selection of these two values could be carried out with the aid of analysis programs, but although such programs have been developed they have not yet been integrated into the CAD system.

As can be seen in Figure 1, a reflector pocket is made up of a number of intersecting plane, conical and parabolic surfaces. The computer representation of this component therefore depends on a complex data structure describing the way in which these mathematically simple surfaces are connected, rather than a simple data structure describing a mathematically complex surface, which was the case for the body moulding base surface. For this purpose a program has been specially developed, which is particularly intended for handling the surface connection problems associated with reflector pockets.

The program is run interactively from the graphic display unit. Input consists of co-ordinates of points defining the hole in the car body surface through which the pocket is to fit. A draw and draft angle are then input, together with the space available behind the lens. These are used to generate a tapered box, which represents the envelope within which the pocket is to be fitted. This can then be modified to include conical sides and the parabolic dish may be specified in terms of the focal point and the focal length. The program can then automatically intersect the pocket with a body moulding base surface, which results in a mathematical representation of the entire body moulding, and which is stored in the computer. At all stages of the design process use can be made of the same graphic display and plotting facilities as were described previously. Figure 4 illustrates a drawing of a body moulding surface and three reflector pockets produced in this way.

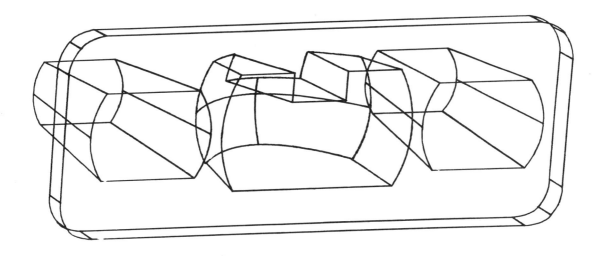

Figure 4

Reflector Pockets

Lens Surface Styling

The procedure used in applying CAD to the design of the exterior lens surface depends on the quantity of data supplied by the customer. In some instances the shape of the lens may be fully defined by drawings or a model, in which case the procedure used to represent the surface will be the same as was described for the body moulding base surface. In other cases only the feature lines are defined in detail, and detailed styling is left to the lamp designer. Since the styling procedure will be interactive the program which has been developed for this type of work makes extensive use of the graphical display unit for both input and output. Initially the lens boundary and feature lines are defined by the co-ordinates of points on a number of sections - usually six sections are sufficient for even complex lenses. These fixed points are then displayed for a section on the display, and the designer styles a smooth section line through them. The section will be represented as a Bezier polynomial, the shape being modified on the graphic display by moving the Bezier polygon vertices. During the design of such a section any specified section or sections which have already been designed may be displayed simultaneously, to ensure a smooth progression in shape. When the designer is satisfied with all the sections which have been designed, a Bezier net is generated from the section data. This, being in the same form as the representation stored for a base surface, can be accessed by the viewing and drawing programs described previously.

In addition to being a styling feature on the car the exterior lens is also required to distribute light from the reflector. Programs are available for the optical design of the lensing, and these will in due course be integrated into the CAD system.

MODELS AND PROTOTYPES

When dealing with the complex three dimensional surfaces found on automotive lamps it has been found that CAD and the use of a graphical display screen are extremely useful. The ability to produce many drawings is a very valuable visualiation aid. However, the display screen is still only two dimensional, and the best way of visualising such three dimensional surfaces is to be able to see and handle the object, or a model. Models would also be extremely useful in obtaining customer approval of a lens surface design, or for checking a body moulding for fit on the customers vehicle body.

The existence of a three dimensional mathematical model within the computer provides the means of generating such a physical model very rapidly on completion of a design. This can be achieved by driving a three axis plotter or providing a tape for an nc machine. In practice no three axis plotter is commercially available, and the use of a production nc machine is inappropriate for rapidly producing a model or visualisation aid for the following reasons:

1. Production machines are unlikely to be available at short notice.

2. Models do not require to be produced to great accuracy, so that the nc machine will be under utilised.

3. A soft material can be used for a model. A conventional nc machine may not be able to take full advantage of the speed at which this can be cut, and will not have provision to collect dust which may be formed in machining.

4. The cost of an nc machine reserved for this work in order to be available when required would be excessive.

For these reasons it was decided to develop a machine especially for model making, or three dimensional plotting, for use in a CAD environment. Experience had been gained of a simple machine of this type at Cambridge University in 1973, although that machine was slow, operated in a special room and had restricted workpiece size. The machine which has now been designed and built at Lucas is shown in Figure 5.

Figure 5

Model making machine

The overall size of the machine is approximately 1.2m by 1.4m by 1.8m, and the cutting head and workpiece are fully enclosed by the bodywork. This feature was necessary since many soft materials will produce dust when machined, which is required to be contained. This is particularly true of the polyurethane foam which has been used most frequently. As a further precaution extraction apparatus is attached to the bottom of the cabinet. The front and rear covers are of Perspex to permit inspection of the work during machining. Three axis control is provided, and a modification is to be made to facilitate accurate re-setting of the angular position of the cutting head by hand.

The machine is capable of movements of 60cm by 45cm in the horizontal plane, and a vertical movement of 30cm. This is more than adequate for any current lamps, and will allow its use in producing models of a variety of other products. Each axis is driven by a stepper motor, resolution being 12.5 μm. In retrospect this accuracy is unnecessary, and 25 μm would be more appropriate, with a corresponding increase in speed. The axis drive is by open loop control. Any loss of steps on the motors is checked by means of counters fitted to each axis. In practice errors are rare. The control unit used for the machine has been developed around a microprocessor, and currently data is read in from paper tape. The paper tape is generated by an interactive program which uses the surface mathematical representation as input, together with data specifying cutter size, direction of machining and accuracy. It is planned to link the microprocessor controller directly to the computer which currently generates the tape and so provide direct numerical control and eliminate the tape and reader.

The machine is basically a simple, cheap, lightweight numerically controlled milling machine. It is capable of machining a vareity of soft materials, those that have been used to date being polyurethane foam, polyethylene, wood and nylon. Models of lamp surfaces cut in polyurethane foam can typically be produced inside two hours on the machine.

The machine has been used to produce models of a wide variety of lamp surfaces designed using the CAD system. Figure 6 shows an example of one such surface - the Rover 3500 front lamp mounting surface.

Figure 6

Rover 3500 side lamp mounting surface model

Both right and left hand models can be generated from the surface representation, and the model may be produced in either male or female form.

Models produced in this way can form an aid in prototype production, this being particularly true of the exterior lens surface. Figure 7 shows a model of a car rear lamp and a vacuum forming taken from it to produce a prototype.

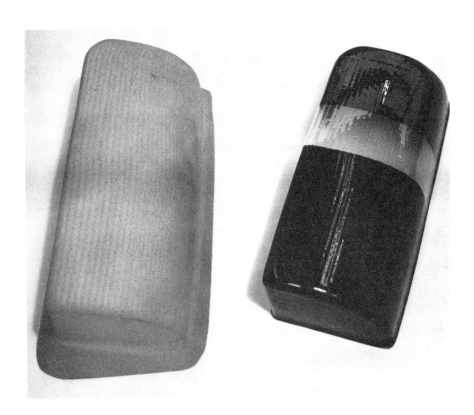

Figure 7

Rear lamp model and prototype

Such vacuum formed prototypes can be used as space models, and, although they do not include full optics, may also be useful for initial testing.

The machine, like the majority of the CAD/CAM system which has been described, is not only applicable to the development of automotive lamps. It has been used to make a wide variety of other three dimensional surfaces, as will be mentioned at the end of this paper.

COMPUTER AIDED MANUFACTURE

Once the design of the lamp has been approved the lamp has to be put into production. The mathematical model of the surfaces held in the computer has already been shown to be usable to generate tapes for a model making machine, and in a similar way tapes can be produced for a conventional nc machine tool. At present tapes are produced in a format to suit an Olivetti Auctor CNZ machine (Figure 8), but in fact the format could be modified to suit any machine.

Figure 8

3 axis nc milling machine

Currently work is in progress to modify the CAD output to a form compatible
with the APT CLFILE, so that existing machine tool post processors can be
used to generate tapes in the correct format.

Since lamps are a high volume production item, the nc machine is used to
produce injection moulding and diecasting tools. The lamp surface data is
used to cut the tool cavity, and further programs have also been developed
to facilitate generation of cutting tapes for shut-off faces. In general
in producing tooling it is necessary to allow for material shrinkage. This
is another way in which the use of the computer model is of great value,
since all the data can be automatically scaled to allow for this before
generating the tooling tapes.

Figure 9 shows three stages in the use of the CAD/CAM system for the Ford
Cortina Mark III rear lamp.

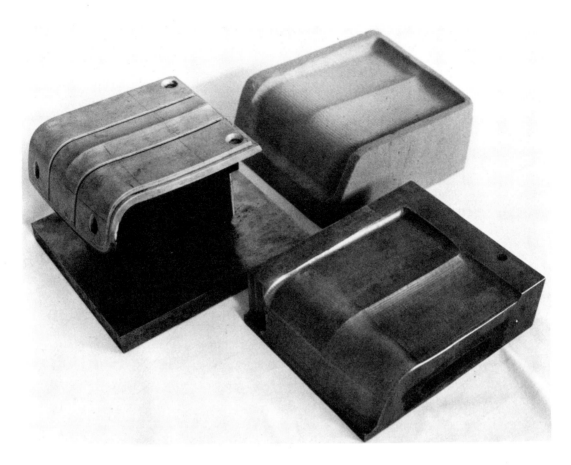

Figure 9

Ford Cortina Mark III rear lamp

On the left in the background is the lens model supplied by Ford, defining
the shape required for the lens, and on the right is a polyurethane foam
model of the same surface reproduced by the CAD system and cut on the model
making machine. In the foreground is the same shape cut in steel on the
Olivetti nc machine.

DISCUSSION

The system which has been described was developed as an integrated facility
for computer aided design and manufacture of automotive small lamps. It
was originally developed in a research environment, but great efforts have
been made to make it easy and convenient for ordinary designers to use. To
this end designers have been involved in the testing of the individual
programs, and in instigating modifications. The completed programs have now
been applied to routine design work, and it is hoped to install computing
facilities within the factory design office itself in the near future.
Although the programs were originally developed on a minicomputer they have
now been fully implemented on the company's internal timesharing service, so
that the capital cost of equipment required in the design office is limited
to a graphical display unit.

Figure 10

Model of an aircraft engine fairing

Designers have adapted to using these computer aids with little difficulty. The system covers the design of the major areas of the lamp, but at present does not deal with details such as fixing bolts. Although there are time savings at the design stage these are relatively small. The real benefit arises through the ability to produce accurate models and prototypes extremely rapidly, and to produce the tapes for nc machines used in tool making. The design of a base moulding or a lens surface can typically be completed, and models made, within two or three days. This is far faster than is possible by conventional methods, and similar or greater gains are offered in the toolmaking area. Accuracy of the system is also greater, particularly in the transition from design to manufacture, where the ambiguities of conventional drawings and the interpretation of the pattern maker are eliminated.

The costs of using the system probably balance those of conventional methods - that is the direct costs of men and computer time as against men. The real benefits lie in the better service which can be given to the customer in accuracy and turnaround. Since toolmaking is more rapid it is often not necessary to start this operation immediately, as the vehicle will not go into production for a period. This extra time means that there is less risk of late changes to the vehicle body necessitating expensive modifications to the tooling. Unfortunately these benefits are not easy to quantify in financial terms, but would be expected to result in increased business and consequently greater income.

Although the system was developed for automotive small lamps it has now been successfully applied, with minimal modifications, to a large number of other products. Unfortunately space prevents discussion of all of these in this paper. Examples are headlamp lenses and reflector assemblies, particularly those made of plastic (DMC), aircraft engine fairings (Figure 10), a brake adjusting mechanism and even a water closet cistern.

ACKNOWLEDGEMENTS

The authors wish to thank the directors of Lucas Industries Ltd for permission to publish this paper. Also gratitude is expressed to British Leyland and Ford for permission to publish photographs of lamp designs.

CAD/CAM For Closed-Die
Forging of Track Shoes and Links

By Taylan Altan, C.F. Billhardt and N. Akgerman
Battelle Columbus Laboratories

A computerized method has been developed (a) for designing blocker and
finisher dies for forging, and (b) for manufacturing blocker dies via
numerical control (NC) machining techniques. The computer-aided design
and manufacturing (CAD/CAM) method, developed in this project, has the
capability of designing dies for not only track shoes and links, but also
for a myriad of nonsymmetric forgings, provided die design can be performed
by analyzing the forging cross section by cross section.

INTRODUCTION

Many land and amphibious vehicles require large quantities of track shoes
and links. These are made from various steel alloys by closed-die forging,
followed by finish machining. A considerable portion of the manufacturing
cost is incurred in producing the die sets (generally both roughing and
finishing dies are needed), and in the material scrap resulting from the
forging flash. Excessive die wear and unexpected breakage often add to
these expenses.

The design of the dies, especially the roughing or blocker set, is an intui-
tive art, highly dependent on the skill and experience of the designer.
After a best-judgment design is completed, a model is handmade in wood,
plastic, plaster, etc. This is then traced by a tracer milling machine to
produce the die cavity, or an EDM electrode from which the die is to be
made. These various steps require skill and experience on the part of the
craftsmen, and can take considerable time. After the forging dies are completed, additional time and money is needed to test and refine their
geometry.

Among the factors to be considered, or calculated, in designing a forging
process are the forging volume and weight, the volume distribution, flash
dimensions, flash and scale losses, loads, stresses, and energies to be
encountered, and the selection of forging equipment [1,2]. These same factors must be considered for both preforming (often more than one) and finishing operations. Computations of variables, such as the volume or volume
distribution are generally made by dividing the part into basic geometric
subelements, such as spheres, cones, cylinders, rectangles, etc., for individual evaluation. Such procedures are inexact at best, require a great
deal of time, and provide many opportunities for human error. Other variables may be determined strictly by judgment and/or experience. The application of practical computer-aided techniques in forging is expected to
eliminate the tedious and repetitive computation and drafting work required
by the die designer. Thus, the designer can devote his attention to more
significant design tasks requiring judgment, selection, and decision making.

CAD/CAM OF FORGING DIES

Computer-Aided Design of Preforming Dies

In many forge shops, preform or blocker dies are designed by experienced die designers, mostly by intuition and by using empirical guidelines. Recently, preform design has been computerized for rib-web type forgings[3]. A review of rib-web type structural parts reveals that almost all structural cross sections can be divided into basic components of L-shapes, as shown in Figure 1, where 10 different L-shapes form the cross section of a forging. Hence, once a generalized design procedure for the basic L-shape is set up, the computer-aided technique can easily combine the basic modules in a building-block manner to obtain preforms for many parts. Further, by modifying certain design parameters, such as the ratio of the web thickness of the preform to that of the finish part, different preform shapes can be designed for different materials to be forged in different forging machines.

Since track-shoe cross sections do not exhibit the "L" modularity of structural parts, one is forced to assume a global approach to preform design and consider a given cross section as a whole. A literature survey was conducted comparing finish die designs to the corresponding preform designs in order to develop mathematical guidelines suitable for automating preform design. These guidelines yield an acceptable preform some of the time, although not always. Therefore, extensive interactive capability was implemented so that the experience of the user can be brought to bear on the computations to obtain an acceptable preform. The computational speed of the computer and the visual perception of the designer complement each other in producing a preform design.

Computer-Aided Design of Finish Forging Dies

Apart from the geometry of the forging, it is the flash configuration that determines the finish die geometry. Flash dimensions directly influence the stresses and loads encountered by the dies during forging. When the stresses exceed the allowable levels, dies either crack or permanently deform. By varying the width and thickness of the flash, the stress distributions and the peak stress can be varied. A thicker flash will result in a lower peak stress. A shorter flash land will also have the same effect.

In determining the flash dimensions, the designer makes a compromise between the maximum allowable stresses on the dies, the capacity of available equipment, and the amount of excess flash material needed to fill the die. This decision is best made by using an interactive system which gives the user the opportunity to quickly evaluate the effect various flash geometries have on die stresses and loads.

THE DEVELOPMENT OF THE CAD/CAM SYSTEM FOR NONSYMMETRIC FORGINGS

System Concepts

The CAD/CAM approach used in this program is outlined in Figure 2. The system of computer programs developed is called TRACKS. Early in the development of the TRACKS system, it became apparent that perception played a vital role in preform design. Die designers base their decisions not only on volume distribution, but also on the relationship between the geometric features of a given cross section. Perception is nearly impossible to program, especially when the geometry under consideration does not exhibit any modularity as in track-shoe cross sections. Designers, on the other hand, can perceive the subtle geometric relationships between the features of a cross section at a glance. Thus, interaction between the man and the machine was required. This was best achieved via interactive computer graphics. The best hardware for this task is a refreshed graphics tube with a light pen. Such an interactive graphics terminal might be connected to a time-sharing service. However, due to the high volume of data required for graphics, in order to be responsive, such a system should possess high data transmission speeds. High data rates are usually not readily available on time-sharing systems. Instead of a time-sharing computer, a minicomputer was used. This choice, although slower in performing arithmetic, has the following advantages:

- Stand alone unit, dedicated to shop operations
- Extremely powerful graphics capability
- Relatively inexpensive hardware.

The major hardware components, shown in Figure 3, used by TRACKS are:

- PDP-11/40 with at least 28k of memory
- One disk drive
- VT11 display processor and graphics tube
- Keyboard terminal.

System Capabilities

The actual software employed reflects the functional outline of Figure 2. As is the custom in conventional die design, TRACKS works with cross sections. Initially, a data file containing the sections that are to be considered during design, is created.

Given a forging drawing, a die designer selects the sections he wants to work with. A draftsman would then obtain the coordinates describing these cross sections. ,Another means of obtaining accurate descriptions of the cross sections would be an APT part program. This approach would be especially attractive if the finish die is to be NC machined. Then parts of the same APT program can be used for both NC machining and sectioning purposes.

Design is performed one cross section at a time; sections need not be ordered consecutively on the data file. Once a cross section is read in and processed, it is displayed to the user, who then has the option of stress analysis, preform design, switching to another section or stopping. Similarly, in each phase, various options are presented to the user. It is possible to cycle through the various phases testing different design options. The light pen is used extensively as a natural tool for interaction between man and machine. The light pen is used to point to objects on the screen as well as to move the dies up and down in order to visualize how the preform fits in the finishing dies.

The CAM phase can be entered after preform designs are completed, or if a file of preform cross sections are available, it can be executed immediately. Given a cutter diameter, the CAM phase blends the cross sections and calculates the cutter paths necessary to machine the preform surfaces. Finally, an NC tape file is generated which can be punched onto paper tape and taken to an NC machine for manufacturing a model or an electrode.

It is possible to produce various intermediate preform designs (blocker designs) by using the preform design output file as the input to TRACKS. The usual sequence of operations is shown in general block form in Figure 4.

System Limitations

The system of computer programs, TRACKS, has a number of limitations which a potential user should be aware of. These limitations do not affect the application of TRACKS to track shoes and links; however, they will limit the immediate applicability of TRACKS to some other forgings. It is believed that most of these limitations can be removed by the addition and/or modification of appropriate subroutines. These known limitations include:

(1) At present, TRACKS cannot handle cross sections which exhibit plane-strain metal flow and which have a flash land on only one side. Two kinds of metal flow, axisymmetric (radial flow) and plane strain (parallel flow), cover most of the flow patterns in a given forging. Cross sections of a forging represent either axisymmetric or plane-strain metal flow. Each cross section can have a flash land on one side or on both sides. Thus, potentially, four types of cross sections are possible. At present, axisymmetric cross sections with flash on one side and on both sides, as well as plane-strain cross sections with flash on both sides can be handled by TRACKS. The ability to handle plane-strain cross sections with flash on one side could be added in the future, if required by the users.

(2) At present, only preforms for plane-strain cross sections and not those for axisymmetric sections can be manufactured by TRACKS. The manufacture of preform templates for round parts would involve the addition of a new subroutine.

(3) Ideally, TRACKS should be able to handle a mixture of
     plane strain and axisymmetric cross sections, be able
     to place them correctly in space, and calculate the
     blends in between and determine the cutter paths for
     NC machining. At present, TRACKS can only produce NC
     tapes for parallel plane-strain cross sections. To
     implement the ability to handle a mixture of cross
     sections would require considerable additional effort
     and may not be necessary in most practical cases.

APPLICATION OF "TRACKS" TO CAD/CAM OF TRACK-SHOE FORGING DIES

The TRACKS system of computer programs was tested by applying it to the
T-130 track shoe. The upper surface of the T-130 is shown in Figure 5.
The five cross sections (labeled 2-6), used in this application, are
depicted by the dotted curves in Figure 5.

Data Preparation and Input

Each cross section of a forging is represented by a polygon. The polygon,
in turn, is described the x,y,z coordinates and the associated radius at
each vertex. These data are obtained from the finish forging drawing and
tabulated by a draftsman. A disk file of the data for use by TRACKS is
created using program ENTRDT. The data could also be prepared as punched
cards or tapes.

Load and Stress Calculations

Load and stress calculations are made using the cross-section data for the
forging. Using the "depth" of a cross section, the forging load acting on
that cross section is calculated. The sum of all these loads per cross
section gives the total forging load.

At the start of stress calculations, each cross section is displayed to the
user at the cathode ray tube (CRT). The user is asked by the computer to
point to the cavities, or ribs, of the cross section so that a metal flow
model can be determined by the computer program. Figure 6 illustrates a
flow model with the "shear surfaces" along which metal flows after the die
cavity and all the ribs are filled. The user is also asked to input (a)
the friction factor, f, (b) the flow stress, $\bar{\sigma}$, of the material to be used
under the particular forging conditions, and (c) the flash dimensions.

The friction shear stress, τ, at the die-forging boundary is expressed as
$\tau = f \bar{\sigma}$. The friction factor, f, is usually determined by conducting a ring
test under forging and lubrication conditions, similar to those encountered
in production[1,2]. In mechanical press forging of steel components with
graphite-based lubricants, f has been found to be between 0.2 and 0.3[2].
In estimating the stresses and the load for forging the T-130 track shoe,

the friction factor, f, was estimated to be f = 0.25 at midrange of values measured for practical conditions.

The flow stress, $\bar{\sigma}$, of the forging material is primarily influenced by the rate of forging, i.e., strain rate, $\dot{\bar{\varepsilon}}$, and the forging temperature, θ. In the present program, the flow stress, $\bar{\sigma}$, was estimated from experimental data available from previous studies[2]. The T-130 track shoe is forged from AISI 4140 steel. There are no published flow-stress data at forging temperatures available for this alloy. However, under forging conditions, the flow stress of this material is close to that of AISI 1045 on which flow-stress data are available. The maximum load is measured in the finish forging stage, which is the third station in forging the T130 shoe with a mechanical press. The first two stations are preblocking and blocking, or preforming. In finish forging, the stock temperature can be expected to be about 2000 F. The amount of deformation, or strain, $\bar{\varepsilon}$, is relatively small and is in the order of $\bar{\varepsilon}$ = 1. The strain rate, $\dot{\bar{\varepsilon}}$, is between 16/sec to 20/sec, as measured in earlier investigations[2]. Thus, for AISI 1045, using θ = 2000 F, $\bar{\varepsilon}$ = 1, and $\dot{\bar{\varepsilon}}$ = 18; the flow stress, $\bar{\sigma}$, is estimated from the data, given in Reference 2, to be $\bar{\sigma}$ = 15,000 psi.

Using f = 0.25, $\bar{\sigma}$ = 15,000 psi at 2000 F average forging temperature, the computer programs calculate 3500 tons as the total load required to forge the T-130 track shoe. This figure is based on a flash geometry of flash width = 0.250 inch, flash thickness = 0.125 inch. This track shoe is forged in a 4000-ton mechanical press. Thus, it appears that the calculated load values are well within acceptable engineering tolerances.

Estimating Forging Energy

The energy required to produce a forging is the area under the load-displacement curve. Experimentally, the energy may be found using an X-Y recorder. Generally, the displacement value, obtained from a linear potentiometer, LVDT, or similar device is recorded on the X axis. The load value is obtained from strain bars on the press columns and is recorded on the Y axis. The energy is then found using a polar planimeter or by numerical integration.

To calculate the energy required for a forging analytically, it would be necessary to calculate the load on each section for each increment of stroke. Due to the complexity of the parts considered in this program, with their many cavities, calculating the load at other than full closure appears to be an impossible task. If possible at all, making such a calculation would require an extreme amount of computer time.

Because of the problems in determining the energy required for the real forging, a simple model of the forging die cavity is generated[4]. This is shown in Figure 7. The height and width of the linear portion are given by:

$$\bar{H} = \text{Total Volume/Total Plan Area} \qquad (1)$$

$$\bar{W} = \Sigma\ (W_I * D_I)/\Sigma\ D_I\ , \qquad (2)$$

where W_I = the width of Section I, excluding flash

D_I = depth of Section I (plane strain)

= $\theta \cdot R_{CG}$ for Section I (axisymmetric strain).

As shown in Figure 7, the model has a linear-center section which is taken to be in plane strain. At each end, there is a semicircular section which is considered to be in axisymmetric strain. The perimeter of the section is entered by the operator subject to the condition that:

$$P \geq 2 \ \Sigma \ D_I + \pi \cdot \overline{W} \ . \tag{3}$$

From this, the depth of the model is found as:

$$\overline{D} = (P - \pi \ \overline{W})/2 \ . \tag{4}$$

The inequality in Equation (3) is used to account for irregularities in the perimeter of the actual part. In the track shoe considered in this program, there were several places where one section was offset from another, thus adding considerably to the perimeter. Because load is considerably influenced by the amount of flash and the amount of flash is directly related to the perimeter, it is necessary to model the amount of flash as accurately as possible.

The three dimensions, $\overline{W}$, $\overline{H}$, and $\overline{D}$ which are used to describe the cavity of the model, are thus all derived as weighted averages from the actual part. The flash height and width in the model are taken as those used in determining the load for each section.

The billet area to be used in the model is chosen as the maximum cross section of any of the sections analyzed. To this is added a percentage for flash and other losses. The billet is assumed to have a square cross section and thus has a side dimension of

$$B = (\text{Section Area}_{max})^{1/2} \ . \tag{5}$$

To ensure filling at the ends of the model die, Figure 7, the billet is assumed to have a total length of $\overline{D} + B$.

Starting with the original billet size, the energy model calculates the load on the die cavity of Figure 7 at seven stroke positions. The first position is when the upper die contacts the billet, just as deformation starts. The second, third, fourth, and fifth positions are at various stages of die fill. At the sixth position, the cavity is filled and flash is extruded just to the edge of the flash land. At the seventh and last position, the forging stroke is completed.

By knowing the original billet size and fixing the forging width at each step, the height of the forging can be found by maintaining volume constancy. The displacement at each step is the difference between the original billet height and the forging height. The flow model assumes that the free surface of the billet remains as a vertical plane throughout the forging

process (no bulging). Strain rate and temperature effects are also neg-
lected.

Using this approach, the energy necessary to forge the T-130 track shoe
from a round-cornered square forging stock is estimated to be about 5400
inch-tons. Considering that the maximum forging load is estimated to be
about 3500 tons, the calculated value of the energy appears to be quite
reasonable.

Preform Design

After calculating the load on each finish section, each section was modified to create the preform geometry. In general, many of the small details
of the finish forging cross section were eliminated and radii were enlarged
to permit easier metal flow from the billet into the preform die. The
finish and preform geometries for Sections 2-2 and 4-4 of Figure 5 are
shown in Figures 8 and 9. The other sections were modified in a similar
manner.

The preform design is constructed on the cathode ray tube (CRT) screen by
interacting with the computer via the light pen and the keyboard. The features of the finish die geometry are used to create the preform die geometry.
The computer is used to perform all the necessary arithmetic; the designer
performs all the decisions that require visual perception.

Figure 9 illustrates the capability of "opening and closing" the dies on
the screen. The user can "move" the upper and lower dies, as well as the
preform, on the screen using the light pen. This gives the designer the
ability to visualize how his preform fits into the finish dies, especially
the location of the initial contact points (pickup points) which have a
bearing on expected die fill.

As the preform design for each cross section is completed, the geometry is
saved on a disk file for subsequent use by the CAM section.

NC Machining of the Preform Surface

After the designs of the preform cross sections are completed, the CAM
section of TRACKS is entered. The major input to this section is the file
created by the preform design section. In addition, the desired draft angle
between adjacent cross sections and the cutter diameter are also input.

The preform surface was generated, based on a 7-degree draft between adjacent sections, and a 2-inch vertical feed at the start and end of the cut.

A plot of the upper surface cutter center-line path is shown in Figure 10.
Figure 11 shows the wood preform model which was produced. The model was
made in two steps. It was first rough machined using an 0.500-inch diameter
ball mill, and then finished with an 0.250-inch diameter ball mill. Separate tapes for each cutter size for both the upper and lower surface were

used.

In Figure 11, a block can be seen behind the large "horn" projection.
This was added to prevent the horn from breaking off from the main body
while being machined. It should be noted that NC tapes were made for only
half the track shoe since the track shoe is symmetric around the X-Z plane.
The other half of the preform model can be machined by using the mirror
image function of the numerical controller on the NC milling machine.
Thus, Figure 11 is only for one-half of the upper surface blocker for the
T-130 track shoe.

SUMMARY AND CONCLUSIONS

In this project, a system of computer programs for computer-aided design
and numerically-controlled machining of preform forging dies was developed.
This system is implemented as a stand-alone system on a minicomputer. It
is capable of calculating the expected forging load, the stock volume
required, the plan area and average forging pressure. In addition, the
system is capable of designing preform cross sections via interactive
graphics and determining the cutter paths for NC machining blocker dies.

Although the system was developed for track shoe forgings, it is completely
general in its applicability. Track shoes do not exhibit any geometric
modularity; therefore, the computer programs were written so as to be able
to handle most any cross-sectional geometry. Thus, not only track shoes
and links, but also crank arms, gear blanks and other forgings could be
processed through TRACKS.

Load and energy calculations are useful not only in forging press selection,
but also as an indirect guide to estimate die life. Stress calculations can
guide the designer in determining the optimum flash dimensions. Although
restrictive flash geometry is desirable to promote die fill, it also results
in high die stresses. The stress distribution determined by TRACKS could be
used as a guide for preventing die breakage. In the ideal case, the stress
distribution would be needed as part of the input (boundary condition) to
computer programs for analyzing the stress state within the die in order to
prevent premature die failure.

Our survey of preform design techniques showed that there are some general
guidelines, but no one method that is applicable to all forgings. Accordingly, preform design must utilize the experience of the designer. CAD
techniques speed up the calculation and drafting portion of preform design
and they enhance accuracy and reproducibility. Since manipulation of
geometry is the major activity of the design process, interactive graphics
is the most natural way of establishing communication between the computer
and the designer.

NC machining of a preform appears to be economically attractive since the
geometry is already in machine readable form. Also, the geometry is truly
defined only on the cross sections. The surface in between the cross sections is left to the die maker to "blend in". Approximately 80-90 percent
of this blending can be done satisfactorily by computer programs and by NC

machining. This approach speeds up the die manufacturing process and ensures high reproducibility in die making. After NC machining most of the preform surface, the 10 to 20 percent of the metal removal that is left is best done by hand.

The system of computer programs, TRACKS, should be considered as only a starting point in updating existing methods of forging die design and manufacture. Additional work needs to be done in implementing such a system, in evaluating the results, and for modifying the system as needed so that CAD/CAM application in forging becomes a routine procedure, used daily under production conditions.

ACKNOWLEDGMENTS

This paper is based on a program sponsored by the Army Tank Automotive Command, Warren, Michigan, and by the Army Materials and Mechanics Research Center, Watertown, Massachusetts, under Contract No. DAAG46-75-C-0041. The program manager at AMMRC was Mr. R. A. Gagne, and the liaison engineer at TACOM was Mr. G. B. Singh. The authors gratefully acknowledge this contractual support and the assistance of Messrs. Gagne and Singh.

REFERENCES

(1) Altan, T., et al., "A Study of the Mechanics of Closed-Die Forging, Phase I", Final Report prepared by Battelle's Columbus Laboratories for AMMRC, Watertown, Massachusetts, September, 1970, Contract No. DAAG46-68-C-0111, AD711-544.

(2) Douglas, R. J., and Altan, T., "A Study of Mechanics of Closed-Die Forging, Phase II", Final Report prepared by Battelle's Columbus Laboratories for AMMRC, Watertown, Massachusetts, November, 1972, Contract No. DAAG46-71-C-0095.

(3) Akgerman, N., Subramanian, T. L., and Altan, T., "Manufacturing Methods for a Computerized Forging Process for High-Strength Materials", Final Report prepared by Battelle's Columbus Laboratories for Air Force Materials Laboratory, Wright-Patterson Air Force Base, Ohio, January, 1974, Contract No. DAAG46-68-C-0111.

(4) Billhardt, C. F., Akgerman, N., and Altan, T., "Computer-Aided Design and Manufacturing for Closed-Die Forging of Track Shoes and Links", Final Report prepared by Battelle's Columbus Laboratories, for Army Materials and Mechanics Research Center, Watertown, Massachusetts, July, 1976, Contract No. DAAG-46-75-C-0041.

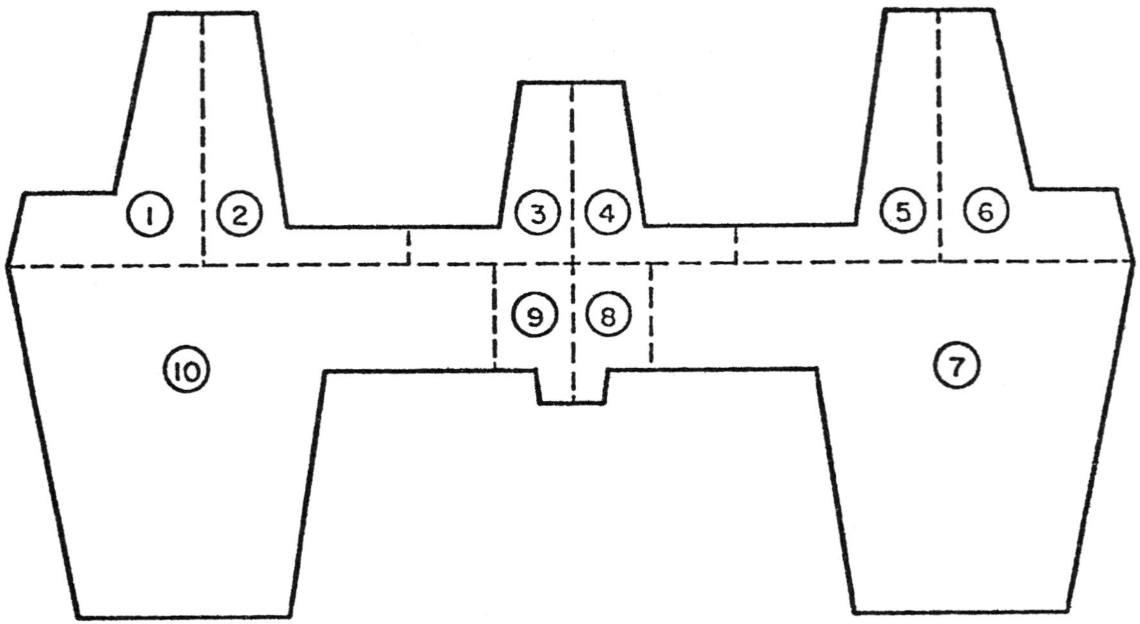

FIGURE 1. DECOMPOSITION OF A RIB-WEB TYPE FORGING CROSS SECTION INTO ITS COMPONENT L-SHAPES

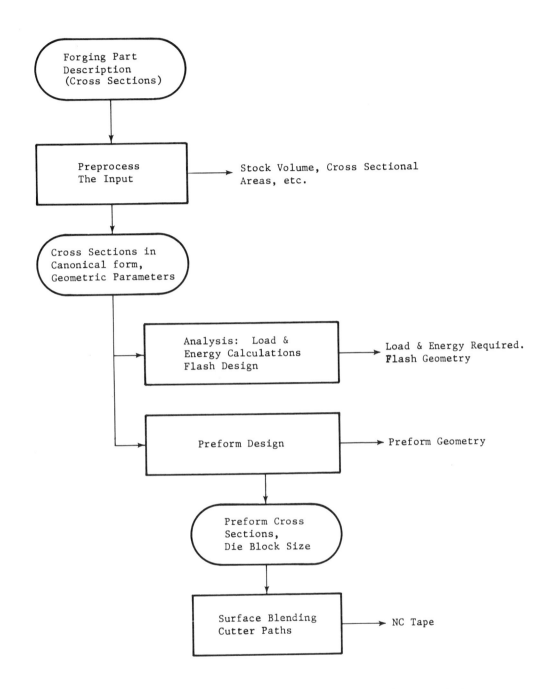

FIGURE 2. FUNCTIONAL OUTLINE OF THE CAD/CAM SYSTEM
FOR TRACK-SHOE FORGINGS

FIGURE 3. PDP-11/40 MINICOMPUTER SYSTEM WITH REFRESH GRAPHICS
DISPLAY TERMINAL USED IN DEVELOPING THE "TRACKS"
SYSTEM OF COMPUTER PROGRAMS

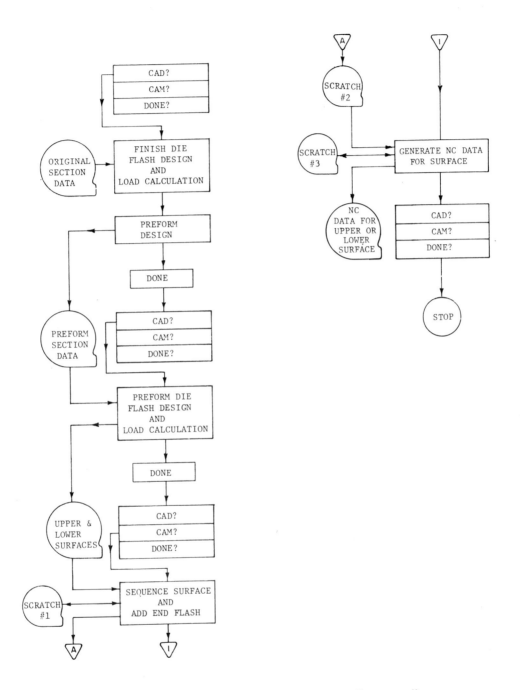

FIGURE 4. GENERAL OPERATION OF "TRACKS"

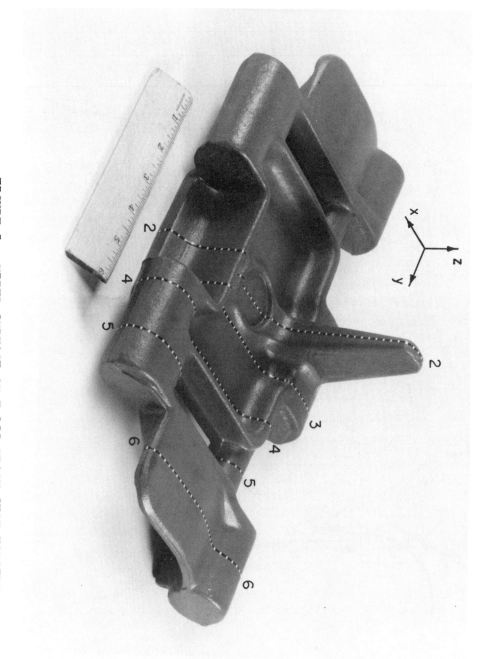

FIGURE 5. UPPER SURFACE OF T-130 TRACK-SHOE FORGING

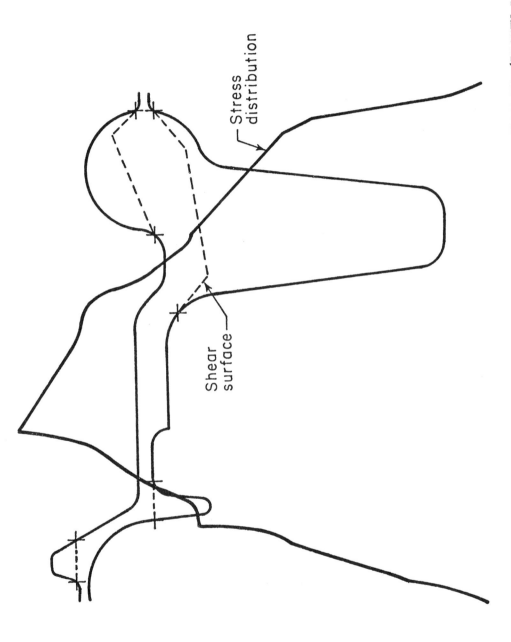

FIGURE 6. TYPICAL FORGING CROSS SECTION, THE SHEAR SURFACES OF THE FLOW MODEL (BROKEN LINES), AND THE CALCULATED STRESS DISTRIBUTION FOR A GIVEN MATERIAL AND FLASH DIMENSIONS

253

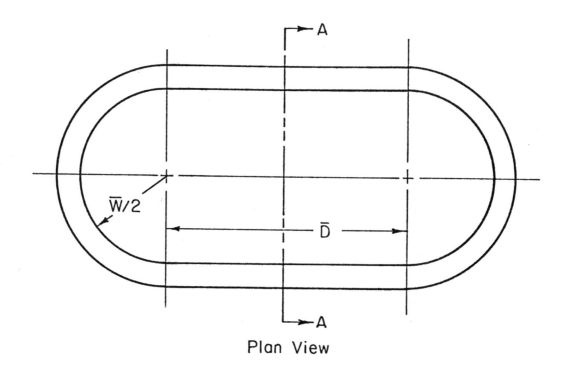

Plan View

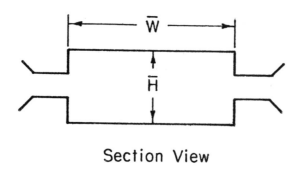

Section View

FIGURE 7. ENERGY MODEL DIE CAVITY

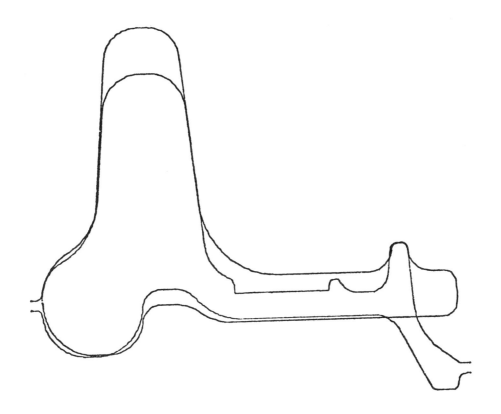

FIGURE 8.   T-130 TRACK SHOE, SECTION 2-2.   PREFORM SECTION
AND FINISH DIES (Dies Closed)

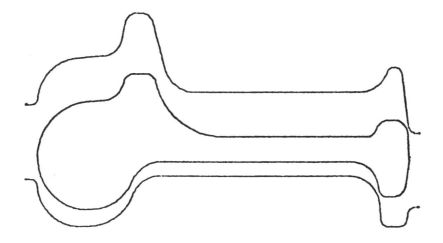

FIGURE 9.   T-130 TRACK SHOE, SECTION 4-4.   PREFORM SECTION
AND FINISH DIES (Dies Open)

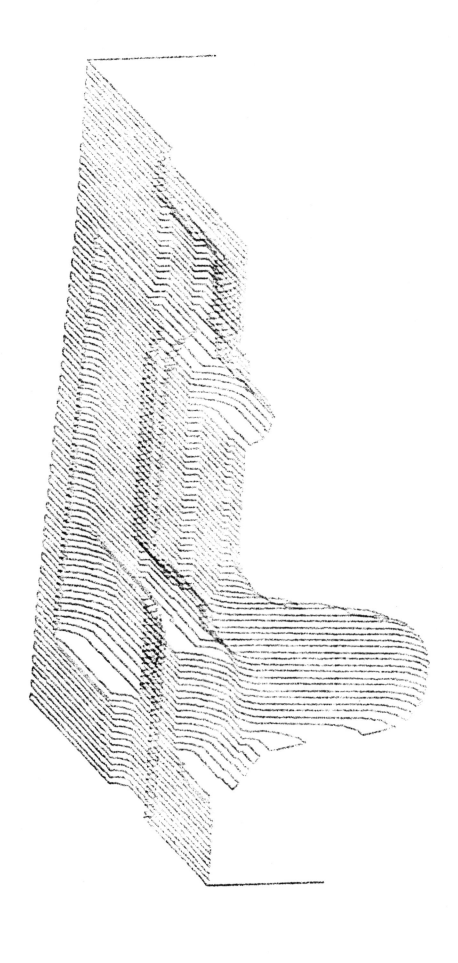

FIGURE 10. T-130 TRACK SHOE PREFORM CUTTER PATHS FOR 0.5-INCH BALL MILL (Upper Surface)

FIGURE 11. NC MACHINED WOOD MODEL OF T-130 TRACK-SHOE UPPER SURFACE PREFORM

CAD In Airframe Design

By Marvin D. Wehrman
Structures Engineering Manager
Boeing Commercial Airplane Co.

The Boeing Company has expanded the use of computers to include the preparation of engineering drawings. The system utilized is a combination of large host mainframes and minicomputers. This combination is tied together with a network called the CAD/CAM Integrated Information Network (CIIN) which allows data to be transferred between machines and also to be stored and retrieved from a common Geometric Data Base (GDB).

Engineering drawings are produced using a combination of general and special batch APT (Automatically Programmed Tool) programs on the mainframes and then completed on the interactive computer graphics (ICG) system. Drawings are also originated on the graphics computer. Data can be accessed from either system and this data is available to other design groups like Payloads, Controls, Hydraulics, Power Plant, Electrical, etc., as well as Manufacturing.

Introduction

The Boeing Company began using computers in the building of airplanes in 1958. At that time Manufacturing created APT programs to describe parts shown on Engineering drawings. Also Engineering created computer definition for external loft lines. That data could then be used to create a punched paper or mylar tape and make machine parts. This procedure is known as numerical control (N/C).

Boeing used special batch APT programs on the YC-14 (an Air Force transport aircraft designed in 1972) to make Engineering drawings for wing inspar ribs, wing leading edge ribs and some body frames. The computer-defined geometry of these assemblies allowed the prototype wing box to be assembled without the use of unplanned shims. This procedure for creating drawings was an extension of the N/C technology which used the computer to drive a pen in lieu of driving a cutter to make a machine part.

In 1974 the Boeing Commercial Airplane Company brought in the first interactive computer graphics systems. The advent of interactive graphics to The Boeing Company marked the beginning of a new epoch in computer aided design because of its reciprocity. This dimension allows designers to "talk back and forth" -- to interact -- with the computer and to realize the results of their work immediately. The use of interactive graphics has magnified the scope of the use of computers and the effectiveness of batch programming, has narrowed the gap between Design and Manufacturing and has opened up new possibilities for excellence in all design projects (i.e. Structures, Systems, Payloads and Propulsion).

The 767 Project (Boeing's new twin-engine, 200-passenger commercial jet transport) is using computers to perform an increasingly large volume of its design work. This work is accomplished in three ways. (See Figure 1.) Two of these methods rely on direct access to the large host computers housed in the data centers at the Boeing Renton and Kent facilities. The third means of computer usage includes primarily the on-site stand-alone minicomputer system. There are specific tasks which work best with each of these applications. (See Figure 2.)

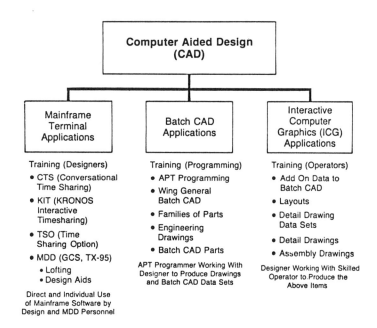

Figure 1.   CAD work is accomplished in these three ways. The first two, Mainframe Terminal Applications and Batch CAD Applications, rely on direct access to the large host computers. The third, ICG, includes primarily the on-site, stand-alone minicomputer system.

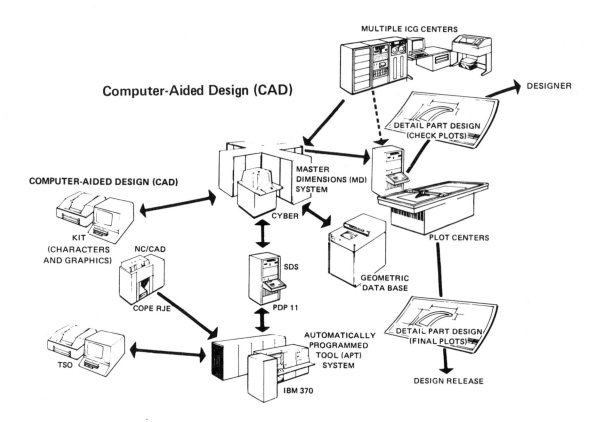

Computer-Aided Design (CAD)

Figure 2.   This chart shows the flow of data through the systems used by the 767 CAD organization.

Conversational Time Sharing (CTS), Kronos Interactive Time Sharing (KIT), Time Sharing Option (TSO) and Master Dimension Definition (MDD) lofting programs all serve as design aids in mathematically defining the components of the airplane. The general and special batch APT programs contain a tremendous amount of geometry which Manufacturing is able to use for tooling and fabrication of parts. These programs are located in the large host mainframes.

The third method, Interactive Computer Graphics (ICG) encompasses all the graphics and annotation functions.

What We Have Learned

The Boeing 767 Program enjoys the advantage of the experiences of previous aircraft programs' utilization of computers in design. There now exists a documented history to assist Engineering in determining the percentage of CAD penetration (the amount of computerization).

Part cards and drawing sheets are   indications of the amount of design work and geometric entities. Historical data for the design of existing Boeing airplanes and the YC-14 is available for analysis and comparison. This data has been accumulated in four major areas of endeavor: Structures, Systems, Payloads and Propulsion. We (the 767 Program) are achieving our planned CAD penetration of approximately 18%.

There also exists for our benefit the successes and failures of other efforts and experiences from which to plan direction. Developmental work has been done with various kinds of interactive systems. Each of these systems is more successful in certain applications than in others. This conclusion was reached in part by studies and partly through trial and error. We have gained from our experiences in the real-time, production environment.

We are learning the most effective combinations of interactive and batch, of divergent types of graphics systems and plotters, and of manual and computerized drafting.

More generally, we have learned that computers are very powerful in terms of geometric manipulations, especially for self-checking capabilities. We've learned, as with any tool, that there is a right way and a wrong way to use computers. We try to find applications that are productive and build on those, and to eliminate situations which are not productive. Where it takes longer to accomplish the task by computer than by hand--for example, single end-item parts--it would take more time to build it up on the computer than for a drafter to do it by hand. With assemblies or multiple usages of parts or where the data set is beneficial to Manufacturing we turn to the computer.

The use of computer aided design in The Boeing Company has been a slow, gradual process over the years, incorporating each change and technique that has been successful.

How Structures Design Is Using Computers

In January of this year when the Mockup of the Model 767 was assembled, the Mockup organization judged it to be the most outstanding mockup the Commercial Airplane Company has built. The Mockup Shop attributed this success to the completeness and accuracy of the drawings. For example, a separate CAD drawing was produced for each body frame, rather than a typical frame with a list of exceptions.

Conversational Systems

The large host computers, housed at the Boeing Renton and Kent, Washington, facilities, are used primarily in two ways by the Structures group: direct access to call up conversational design aid programs, and general batch and special batch programs.

The 767 Project uses as design aids some universally-available programs which are located on the large host computers. These programs are accessible through the Conversational Timesharing System (CTS) and the Kronos Interactive Timesharing (KIT) programs. These conversational programs do not require a special computer skill and are used in much the same way as a calculator to perform a variety of time-consuming and complex mathematical tasks for the engineer. Even though this data is stored at remote sites (40 to 50 miles away) it can be accessed from terminals at the 767 site located in the Everett, Washington plant.

General Batch Programs

The batch process, using the APT language, is a parametric design--or design geometry generation--process that produces drawings based on design parameters in combination with the MDD (lofting) programs. In this mode some parts are stored on the computer so that Manufacturing Engineering can access the structural geometry of the aircraft parts. The primary advantage of the batch process is its capability. Batch programming is effective for contour-related families of parts, such as inspar ribs, body frames, leading edge ribs, etc.

During the development of the YC-14, batch programs were initiated which pioneered the use of Batch CAD. However, due to geometry differences and software construction these programs were not readily usable on subsequent aircraft design programs. Following this experience Engineering began creating several large general programs which incorporated macros (parts or components which are pre-programmed). The general programs could then be adapted to any Boeing commercial aircraft configuration. These first general programs were for wing box structures (Figure 3) and body monocoque (Figure 4).

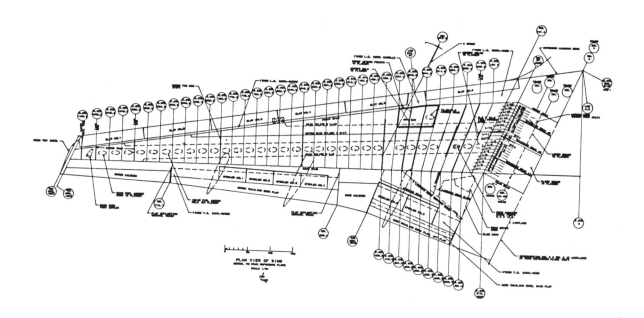

Figure 3.   Wing Centerline Drawing.

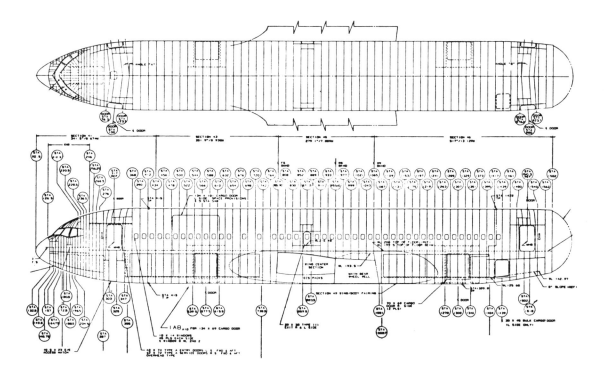

Figure 4.   Body Centerline Drawing.

For two years a team of Batch CAD programmers were able to accomplish a tremendous amount of upstream work, eventually moving on site at the Everett plant to work on the 767 Project. Wing inspar structure, body monocoque and nacelles were defined. Additional family-related programs were also programmed in order to provide layouts and drawings for other items such as the wing leading edge and trailing edge. The general batch programs for the wing were modified further (same program, revised geometry) in order to support the Mockup releases for the empennage. Initial support of the empennage structure was minimal. However, as the vertical stabilizer was relofted and revised late in the program as a result of design changes, the program was of considerable value in support of the redesign effort.

Now a data base of general and special batch programs is on file whose worth is immeasurable. Using a combination of batch programs and interactive graphics, drawings such as skin panels and stringers can be manipulated to be presented on standard engineering drawing forms. These large parts (some 65 feet long) would be unmanageable to detail entirely in a batch mode to produce full-scale drawings.

<u>Special Batch Programs</u>

Special batch programs -- those which have had to be especially

created and not taken from the stockpile of previous programs -- were
written for the fixed leading edge, the leading edge slats, the fixed
leading edge machined ribs, and the trailing edge flaps. These are ideal
special batch programs because they are families of look-alike contour-
related parts. (See Figure 5.) The basic geometry for either the actuators
or the tracks can then be combined with the contours for a perfect geometric
fit. A program for a whole series of leading edge ribs and slats can be
created with the contour as the only basic variable.

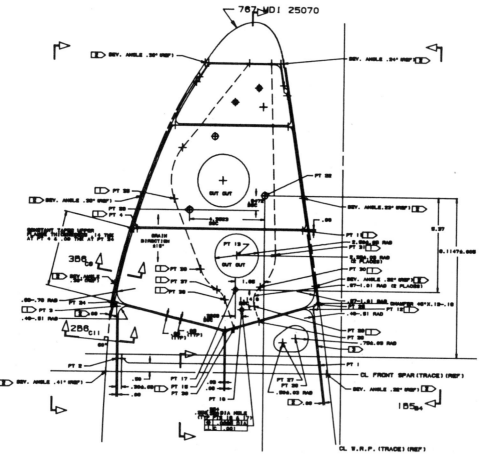

Figure 5.   Leading Edge Rib.

Special batch programs become very powerful to the overall
development of structural design and have a high productivity rate for
families of parts.

Interactive Computer Graphics

The design of an airplane generates a number of large, unwieldy
drawings when dealt with at full scale. For this reason certain activities
in the design phase can be handled on a graphics plane, with the aid of
a visual, interactive device.

Interactive computer graphics (ICG) systems are used in a variety of ways. While Batch CAD can generate multiple look-alike drawings rapidly, there are certain phases of drawing development that lend themselves better to an interactive visual mode.

ICG encompasses several main functions: a visual real time display, the production of a data base of engineering parts designs, the development of a pattern library, the maintenance of a data management system, and the use of a plotting system. These functions operate on the minicomputer system configuration, with communications links between the ICG and large host systems for storage, access of APT and MDD programs, and communications between ICG systems. The systems provide the capability to generate, store, revise and verify geometry.

The 767 Project uses a number of batch and ICG combinations varying in their ratios. For example, wing inspar ribs were begun with a general batch program, then brought onto the ICG system for completion. (See Figure 6.)

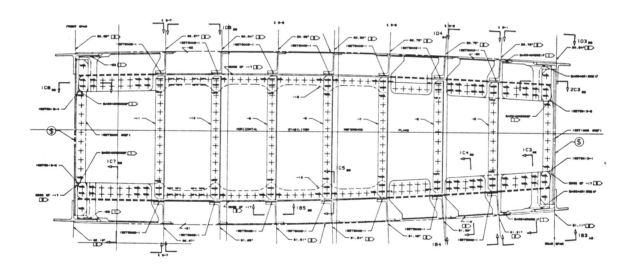

Figure 6.   Wing Inspar Rib.

We're using interactive graphics in a lot of areas. Payloads, as an example, uses extensively the leveling capability of the interactive graphics system to assist in the design of aircraft interior arrangements. Graphics entities can be separated on different levels, or locations, on the disk at the discretion of the user. An example of this technique is when Payloads engineers insert seats, lavatories, galleys, etc., each on a different level. Using this method, Payloads can custom build interiors for each airline depending on their requirements.

With this capability the designer can manipulate data on one level without disturbing data on another level.

Some drawings are started through the batch process, then labeled and dimensioned at the graphics terminal. An example of assemblies which are built from scratch on the interactive graphics system are floor beam assemblies. (See Figure 7.) The leveling capability works for floor beams in the same way it does for Payloads. We put fasteners, webs, stiffeners, cords, and cutouts on different levels. All levels can be called up as a composite at any time for assembly and installation drawings.

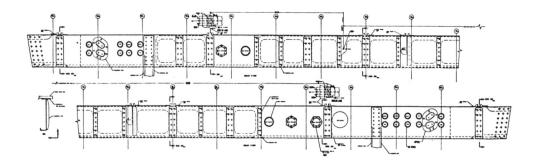

Figure 7. Composite Floor Beam.

We've used interactive graphics on the aft pressure bulkhead. (See Figure 8.) An engineer with less than a year from graduation using existing 747 pressure bulkhead drawings and instructions from his lead engineer produced 14 sheets of stable mylar drawings on the ICG for the Mockup which was faster and more accurate than creating the Mockup drawings by hand. Further activities on the ICG include the penetrations for fuel lines, air lines, and wiring which run through the bulkhead back to the auxiliary power unit (APU) and the control surfaces in the empennage.

The value of complete computer-generated drawings cannot be over-emphasized, especially in structural definition such as body frames that interface with Payloads and Systems.

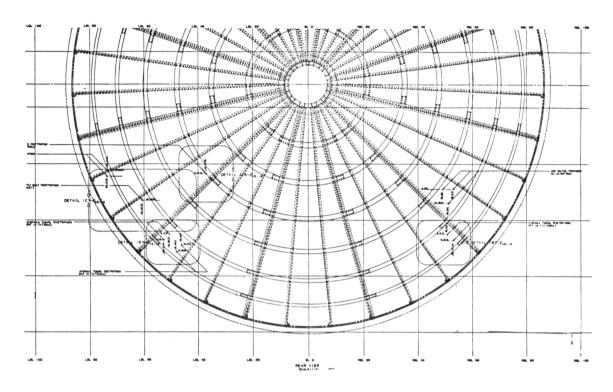

Figure 8.   Aft Pressure Bulkhead.

How It Is All Tied Together

Though the activities using computers take place in several different forms (interactive graphics, batch programs, lofting programs, conversational systems), Boeing has devised a method for tying the data together. Through a link and a data storage device called the CAD/CAM Integrated Information Network (CIIN) these functions can relate to one another. Engineering can now call up or send data stored on other systems, like or unlike, on the large hosts, or from Manufacturing. (Refer to Figure 2.)

For many years such data as Master Dimensions Definition (MDD) and Batch CAD programs were passed back and forth via magnetic tape. Then, when interactive graphics came on the scene, the need for a more efficient, less primitive method for exchanging this data was apparent. At the same time, during the early and mid 1970s, processing became less expensive. Minicomputers and intelligent terminals became feasible.

Design work on the 767 exists in a heterogeneous environment, but is becoming centralized through the distributed communications capabilities of CIIN.

Common Geometric Data Base

We have established a common geometric data base (GDB) whereby geometry can be input to the data base from Structures, and be used by other groups such as Systems, Payloads, or Power Plant, as needed to go through the design process. From these disciplines within Engineering, the data is available to Manufacturing to build tools and parts from released data sets.

Conclusion

It has been an exciting and difficult year for the 767 design group, but the difficulties have been tempered by the successes. Never before has the need for effective interplay between unlike systems and processes been so pronounced. Some of the problems have stemmed from the human aversion to change. People have been reluctant to change their ways of doing things. This problem has been partly alleviated through training and the increasing success of CAD systems.

The Boeing 767 Project, in its endeavor to bring all of these domains together with the aid of the computer and a dedicated work force, is committed to building the best airplane ever built. In the future, we intend to capitalize on our experience and increase the amount of CAD penetration.

BIBLIOGRAPHY

1. Beeby, W. D., _The Application of Computer Aided Design to the 757 and 767_ (New York: AIAA Aircraft Systems and Technology Meeting, 1979).

2. Braithwaite, W. W., _Boeing's CAD/CAM Integrated Information Network_ (New York: AIAA Aircraft Systems and Technology Meeting, 1979).

3. Klomp, C. W. et al, _The Concept of an Interactive Graphic Design System (IGDS) with Distributed Computing_ (Los Angeles: AIAA 1975 Aircraft Systems and Technology Meeting, 1975).

APPENDIX

PRODUCTION'S DIRECTORY OF COMPUTER SERVICES *

. . . computer suppliers, software houses and consultants offering services related to the application of computers in manufacturing

* Revised and Updated Annually by PRODUCTION Magazine, Bramson Publishing Company, Box 101, Bloomfield Hills, MI 48013

Advanced Systems, Inc.
1601 Tonne Road
Elk Grove Village, IL 60007
(312) 593-1790
Produces and distributes video assisted instruction material in areas such as data processing, manufacturing, management engineering, etc.

Allan Hannas & Associates
P.O. Box 8
Summit, NJ 07901
(201) 277-3458
Management consulting, information systems design, for physical distribution, materials management, inventory control, production scheduling, purchasing.

American Software, Inc.
550 Pharr Road
Suite 630
Atlanta, GA 30305
(404) 261-4381
Master scheduling software packages, MRP. System evaluation studies.

Applicon, Inc.
154 Middlesex Turnpike
Burlington, MA 01803
(617) 272-7070
Minicomputers, peripherals and terminals for end users. Software for NC programming and interactive nesting. Three dimensional general purpose interactive graphics systems.

Applied Information Development
823 Commerce Drive
Oak Brook, IL 60521
(312) 654-3030
Minicomputers, mainframes for OEM and end users. Master production scheduling, costing, capacity planning, MRP order entry, BOM inventory, data collection. Training, consulting.

Arista Manufacturing Systems
7830 Silas Creek Parkway Extension
Winston-Salem, NC 27106
(919) 725-8504
Manufacturing systems including master scheduling, MRP, manufacturing standards, inventory record control, shop floor control. Education, training, consulting.

Arthur Andersen & Co.
69 W. Washington
Chicago, IL 60602
(312) 346-6262
Standard software for manufacturing and financial planning and control. Inventory simulator programs used to evaluate savings resulting from system and/or policy changes.

ASK Computer Services, Inc.
730 Diesel Drive
Los Altos, CA 94022
(415) 969-4442
Inventory control, BOM, MRP, work in process, purchasing, and capacity planning software packages designed for Hewlett-Packard minicomputers.

J. Baker & Associates, Inc.
5135 West Golf Road
Skokie, IL 60076
(312) 677-9760
Mainframes, minicomputers, peripherals and media for end users. BOM processors and warehouse distribution software. System evaluation studies, and design.

Basic Four Corp.
14101 Myford Road
Tustin, CA 92680
(714) 731-5100
Minicomputers, peripherals, terminals, media and supplies for end users.

Basic Timesharing Inc. (BTI)
870 West Maude Avenue
Sunnyvale, CA 94086
(408) 733-1122
Minicomputers for OEM and end users. Timeshare (multi-user) systems based on minicomputers.

Boeing Computer Services Co.
177 Madison Avenue
Morristown, NJ 07960
(201) 540-7700
Interactive, on-line integrated manufacturing planning and control systems including BOM, master scheduling, inventory control, purchase order control, shop order control and more.

Brandon Consulting Group, Inc.
505 Park Avenue
New York, NY 10022
(212) 935-6290
System evaluation studies, feasibility studies. Seminars in the selection of software and service contracts, legal issues in hardware contracts, financial optimization.

Bristol Information Systems
84 North Main Street
Fall River, MA 02722
(617) 679-1051
Minicomputers, peripherals, terminals, media and supplies for end users. Standard and special software development, inventory, order entry, BOM, shop floor controls.

Burroughs Corp.
Burroughs Place
Detroit, MI 48232
(313) 972-7000
Mainframes, minicomputers, peripherals, terminals, media, supplies for OEM and end users. Complete range of system development, software support, consulting, and training for manufacturing applications.

Business Controls Corp.
507 Boulevard
Elmwood Park, NJ 07407
(201) 791-7661
Standard software packages for inventory control, MRP, BOM, order processing costing. Special system development.

Calma
527 Lakeside Drive
Sunnyvale, CA 94086
(408) 245-7522
Minicomputers, peripherals and terminals for end users. Complete turnkey, interactive graphics design systems, automated drafting, automated BOM processors.

Centech, Inc.
10385 North Dearlove Road
Glenview, IL 60025
(312) 299-6788
Interactive NC tape preparation systems including processors and post processors.

Cincinnati Inc.
P.O. Box 11111
Cincinnati, OH 45211
(513) 367-7100
MRP software and systems for end users.

Cincom Systems, Inc.
2300 Montana Avenue
Cincinnati, OH 45211
(513) 662-2300
Manufacturing application software, closed loop systems. Stand alone and/or supportive education programs, user training. MRP, BOM, etc.

Computer Covenant Corp.
790 Farmington Avenue
Farmington, CT 06032
(203) 677-6563
Standard software packages for production scheduling, labor distribution, job costing, materials inventory.

Computervision Corp.
201 Burlington Road
Bedford, MA 01730
(617) 275-1800
Minicomputers, peripherals, terminals, media and supplies for end users. Complete turnkey interactive graphics display systems used for drafting and design of discrete parts and mechanical assemblies. NC tape preparation systems using interactive graphics.

Comserv Corp.
3050 Metro Drive
Minneapolis, MN 55420
(612) 854-2020
Minicomputers, mainframes for OEM and end users. Advanced manufacturing, accounting and production systems, distribution order entry, interfaces. Consulting, specifications, education and training.

Control Data Corp.
8100 34th Avenue, South
Minneapolis, MN 55440
(612) 853-8100

Mainframes, minicomputers, peripherals, terminals, media and supplies for OEM and end users. Wide range of application software including automated drafting, geometric modeling, and NC packages. Factory automation, inventory/production control.

Data General Corp.
15 Turnpike Road
Westboro, MA 01581
(617) 366-8911
Minicomputers, peripherals, terminals, media and supplies for OEM and end users. Broad based systems engineering and consulting in inventory control, materials management, and receivable materials management, etc.

Data Systems Div.
Sierra Research Corp.
P.O. Box 222
Buffalo, NY 14225
(716) 631-6200
Turnkey minicomputer and microcomputer systems and peripherals for OEM and end users. Factory data collection, machine monitoring, WIP inventory control, material tracking, time and attendance, simulations.

DCD Co.
Div of Borg Enterprises
1615 West River Road, North
Minneapolis, MN 55411
(612) 588-0551
Software packages and special software development in job costing and inventory control, special evaluation and justification studies.

Digital Equipment Corp.
146 Main Street
Maynard, MA 01754
(617) 897-5111
Mainframes, minicomputers, peripherals, terminals for OEM and end users. Distributed processing systems, direct process control, shop floor data collection systems.

Digital Scientific Corp.
11425 Sorrento Valley Road
San Diego, CA 92121
(714) 453-6050
Minicomputers for end users.

Diversified Systems, Inc.
131 Caledonia Northeast
Grand Rapids, MI 49505
(616) 452-3969
Software for automatic screw machine shops, stamping and fabrication facilities featuring production control, inventory control, work in process, loading, job cost.

General Automation, Inc.
1055 South East Street
Anaheim, CA 92803
(714) 778-4800
Minicomputers, peripherals and terminals for OEM and end users. Factory data collection, process control, and NC software packages. Special software development and implementation, turnkey project management.

Gerber Scientific
90 Spruce Street
Hartford, CT 06101
(203) 644-1551
Minicomputers and mainframes for end users, peripherals and terminals for OEM. Multi-user interactive graphic design and data management, NC tape preparation systems.

Hewlett-Packard
11000 Wolfe Road
Cupertino, CA 95014
(408) 257-7000
Minicomputers, peripherals and terminals for OEM and end users. Standard materials management, inventory control, and MRP software packages. System development.

Honeywell Information Systems
200 Smith Street MS 486
Waltham, MA 02154
(617) 890-8400
Factory management, production scheduling and control and inventory control including workcenter data management, capacity requirements planning, order costing, shop floor control and more.

I

IBM Corp.
Old Orchard Road
Armonk, NY 10504
(914) 765-1900
Mainframes, minicomputers, peripherals, terminals, media, and supplies for OEM and end users. Production, inventory control, management and accounting systems. Shop data collection, direct process control.

ICL Inc.
Turnpike Plaza
197 Highway 18
East Brunswick, NJ 08816
(201) 246-3400
Minicomputers and peripherals for end users. Production control for small and medium manufacturers, BOM, inventory control, requirements planning, WIP, shop controls.

IIT Research Institute
10 West 35th Street
Chicago, IL 60616
(312) 567-4000
Special software development. On-going multi-client project to develop programs for manufacturing applications: computer aided line balancing, generalized assembly line simulator, computer aided batch scheduling.

Incoterm Corp.
Subsidiary of Honeywell
65 Walnut Street
Wellesley Hills, MA 02181
(617) 237-2100
Mainframes, minicomputers, peripherals and terminals for OEM and end users. Special communications networking to handle in-plant data collection—time and attendance reporting, work in process tracking.

Information Automation, Inc.
925 Westchester Avenue
White Plains, NY 10604
(914) 948-4300
Minicomputers, peripherals and terminals for end users. Software packages for factory data collection, machine monitoring, automated incentive programs, other manufacturing applications.

Information Displays Inc.
150 Clearbrook Road
Elmsford, NY 10523

(914) 710-1281
Minicomputers, peripherals, plotters, displays, and digitizers. Turnkey interactive graphic design and display systems for machine and production tooling design, plant layout.

Integrated Software Systems (ISSCO)
4186 Sorrento Valley Blvd
San Diego, CA 92121
(714) 452-0170
Computer graphics software for a broad range of special applications. Data representation graphics and software, DISSPLA® and TELL-A-GRAF®.

Interactive Information Systems
P.O. Box 37403
Cincinnati, OH 45222
(513) 761-0132
Systems OEM for DEC and Hazeltine products. MRP, scheduling, order entry, BOM, work measurement systems, inventory, automated process planning, shop floor data collection, consulting, training.

Interface Mechanisms Inc.
4405 Russel Road
Linnwood, WA 98036
(206) 743-7036
Peripherals for end users. Bar code readers and printers for inventory control and production tracking applications. Consulting, training.

M

Management Assistance Inc.
300 East 44th Street
New York, NY 10017
(212) 557-8387
Minicomputers, peripherals and terminals for end users. Software for inventory control, order entry.

Management Science, Inc.
4321 West College Avenue
Appleton, WI 54911
(414) 739-3616
Work measurement, performance audit and costing software.

Mandate Corp.
300 East Ohio Building
1717 East Ninth Street
Cleveland, OH 44114
(216) 861-8100

Broad range of management system software packages including product data control, costing, MRP, inventory management, shop floor controls, and labor efficiency.

Manufacturing Data Systems Inc.
4251 Plymouth Road
Ann Arbor, MI 48105
(313) 995-6000
In-house and time shared NC tape preparation systems, parts classification systems, automated process planning, software development.

Manufacturing Software & Services
6761 Bramble Avenue
Cincinnati, OH 45227
(513) 271-4900
NC tape preparation software, post processors, complete systems.

Manufacturing Software Systems Inc.
P.O. Box 278
Williston, VT 05495
(802) 878-5254
MRP software evaluations. Covered are the logic of MRP and supporting systems and downstream systems to MRP.

Martin Marietta Data Systems
300 East Joppa Road
Baltimore, MD 21204
(301) 321-5744
Manufacturing systems including production scheduling, performance reporting, inventory control, purchasing, costing, order processing. Financial control and engineering control. Remote computing services.

Microdata Corp.
17481 Red Hill Avenue
Irvine, CA 92705
(714) 540-6730
Mainframes, minicomputers, peripherals and terminals for OEM and end users. Broad based systems consulting and system evaluation.

Mid-America Computer Corp.
Thorndale at York Road
Bensenville, IL 60101
(312) 595-4100
Minicomputers, mainframes, peripherals, media and supplies for end users. MRP, scheduling, order entry, BOM, inventory, automated process planning, shop floor data collection, capacity planning, costing and more.

Midec Inc.
1000 RIDC Plaza
Pittsburgh, PA 15238
(412) 963-6011
Manufacturing systems using Tandem computers. Modules include engineering and production, order entry, accounting, purchasing, payroll and personnel.

Mitrol, Inc.
1050 Waltham Street
Lexington, MA 02173
(617) 862-6350
Industrial management systems including inventory/production control, MRP, capacity planning, purchasing, cost control, engineering, sales and marketing, financial planning.

NCA Corp.
388 Oakmead Parkway
Sunnyvale, CA 94086
(408) 245-7990
Manufacturing management systems designed specifically for DEC minicomputers. Systems include inventory control, purchasing, BOM, work order status, MRP and more.

NCR Corp.
1700 South Patterson Boulevard
Dayton, OH 45479
(513) 449-2000
Mainframes, minicomputers, peripherals, terminals, media and supplies for OEM and end users. Software and services including BOM, inventory control, MRP.

NCR Data Pathing Systems Div.
370 San Aleso Avenue
Sunnyvale, CA 94086
(408) 734-0100
Minicomputers, peripherals and terminals for end users. Turnkey systems for labor reporting, inventory control, WIP tracking, tool control, production scheduling and loading.

Northern Telecom Systems Corp.
Box 1222
Minneapolis, MN 55440
(612) 932-8000
Formerly Data 100. Minicomputers and peripherals for end users. Software sold by distributors. Consulting, training.

Northrop Data Systems, Inc.
1160 Sandhill Avenue
Carson, CA 90746
(213) 637-1533
Turnkey interactive minicomputers with special software for end users. Inventory control, production control, MRP, capacity planning.

Olivetti Corp. of America
500 Park Avenue
New York, NY 10022
(212) 371-5500
Minicomputers, peripherals, terminals, media and supplies for OEM and end users. Standard software for computer assisted part programming, inventory control, job costing, and accounting applications.

Precision Patterns, Inc.
55 Oak Street
Norwood, NJ 07648
(207) 767-1200
Precision parts nesting system for cutting operations.

Prime Computer, Inc.
40 Walnut Street
Wellesley Hills, MA 02181
(617) 237-6990
Medium to large scale general purpose interactive computers for end users.

Process Computer Systems, Inc.
750 North Maple Road
Saline, MI 48176
(313) 429-4971
Microcomputers, peripherals, media and supplies for OEM and end users. Direct process control, scheduling, work measurement systems, inventory, shop floor data collection, graphics systems.

Professional Computer Resources, Inc.
2021 Midwest Road
Oak Brook, IL 60521
Jobshop resource management systems including inventory control, job accounting, purchasing, capacity planning and standard accounting functions.

Qantel Corp.
3525 Breakwater Avenue
Hayward, CA 94545
(415) 783-3410
Minicomputers, peripherals and terminals for end users. On-line manufacturing planning and control systems, product data management, order entry, MRP, scheduling, inventory, control, forecasting, labor reporting.

Rath & Strong, Inc.
21 Worthen Road
Lexington, MA 02173
(617) 861-1700
Standard and special software development: MRP, inventory control, shop control, standard data, balance capacity, rework control, quality control, organization development.

Scientific Time Sharing Corp.
7316 Wisconsin Avenue
Bethesda, MD 20014
(301) 657-8220
Integrated controls systems including forecasting, inventory control, scheduling, MRP, shop floor control, warehousing and distribution.

The Service Bureau Co.
500 West Putnam Avenue
Greenwich, CT 06830
(203) 622-2000
Manufacturing management system including master scheduling, net change, MRP, inventory control, BOM, purchasing, shop floor control, capacity planning.

A. O. Smith Data Systems Div.
P.O. Box 584
Milwaukee, WI 53201
(414) 447-4472
Inventory planning and manufacturing activity planning, purchasing, inventory and stores control, customer order servicing, plant monitoring and control, cost planning and control.

Software International Corp.
2 Elm Square
Andover, MA 01810
(617) 475-5040
Manufacturing resource planning software systems, material requirements planning, shop floor control with capacity planning software. Consulting and education/training.

Sperry Univac Division
Sperry Rand Corp.
Box 500
Blue Bell, PA 19424
(215) 542-4011
Mainframes, peripherals and terminals for end users. Minicomputers for OEM and end users. Full range of control systems support including special, standard, and turnkey systems for MRP, forecasting, inventory maintenance and accounting, WIP, etc.

The Standard Register Co.
Dayton, OH 45401
(513) 223-6181
Label preparation systems.

Summagraphics Corp.
35 Brentwood Avenue
Fairfield, CT 06430
(203) 384-1344
Graphic displays, intelligent digitizers for OEM and end users.

Systems Management, Inc.
10400 West Higgins Road
Des Plaines, IL 60018
(312) 298-3840
Control and information systems including BOM, inventory control, order status, MRP, WIP, costing, capacity requirements planning, shop floor control, business control systems.

Tandem Computers, Inc.
19333 Vallco Parkway
Cupertino, CA 95014
(800) 538-9360
Computers and minicomputers for OEM and end users. Data base, distributed, data communication and multi-terminal systems for a wide range of applications.

Techware Computing Co.
9620 Executive Center Drive
St. Petersburg, FL 33702
(813) 576-3734
Minicomputers, peripherals, terminals, media and supplies for end users. "CAM-TECH" series of computer aided NC tape preparation programs for NC turret punches, presses, shears.

Tektronix, Inc.
P.O. Box 500
Beaverton, OR 97077
(503) 682-3411
Modular computer graphics hardware and software for mechanical design, analysis, drafting, NC tape preparation. Multi-user systems, remote graphics workstations, intelligent workstations for OEM and end users.

Texas Instruments, Inc.
13500 North Central Expressway
Dallas, TX 75222
(214) 238-2011
Minicomputers, peripherals, terminals for OEM and end users. Minicomputer based distributed processing hardware. Direct process control, engineering support systems.

Threshold Technology Inc.
1829 Underwood Boulevard
Delran, NJ 08075
(609) 461-9200
Peripherals and terminals for OEM and end users: voice recognition systems for NC programming, inspection.

TNO, Org. for Ind. Research, Inc.
176 Second Avenue
Waltham, MA 02154
(617) 890-4030
Group technology, shop layout, and NC lathe programming software packages, software development in automated process planning.

K. W. Tunnel Co., Inc.
Valley Forge Plaza, Suite 690
1150 First Avenue
King of Prussia, PA 19406
(215) 337-0820
Standard production and inventory control software packages, project management, studies, group technology.

University Computing Co.
1930 H. Line Drive
Dallas, TX 75247
(214) 655-8894
NC tape preparation software and services, NC postprocessors.

Versatec
2805 Bowers Avenue
Santa Clara, CA 95051
(408) 988-2800
Printer/plotters, media and supplies for OEM and end users.

Wang Laboratories
1 Industrial Avenue
Lowell, MA 01851
(617) 851-4111
Mainframes, minicomputers, peripherals and terminals for OEM and end users. Interactive management systems and inventory control.

Westinghouse-Industry Systems Div.
200 Beta Drive
Pittsburgh, PA 15238
(412) 782-1730
Mainframes, minicomputers and systems for OEM and end users. Terminals for end users. Standard software for DNC, software and systems development for milling, turning, assembly, test, and warehousing.

Xerox Computing Services
5310 Beethoven Street
Los Angeles, CA 90066
(213) 390-3461
Timesharing services for complete manufacturing closed loop systems. MRP, scheduling, order entry, BOM, inventory, shop floor data collection. Consulting, training.

This directory is intended to provide PRODUCTION readers with basic descriptions of CAM related services offered by the listed organizations. All computer suppliers are not listed, and many companies listed offer capability beyond the scope of this directory. Contact the supplier to obtain more details concerning services available.

INDEX

France, 10
Future, 3-13, 115-131, 186-187, 205-206

G

General batch programs, 262-263
Glass-making facility, 218-219
Graphics, 91-112, 164, 184, 217, 227, 259
Grinding, 3, 153

H

Hardware
   bases, 199-200
   die design, 217
   economic factors, 172
   integration of new technology, 31
Hierarchical approach, 69-87
History, 219-223
Human limitations, 27
Hungary, 135-143
Hydraulic tubing, 94-98

I

ICAM, 17-65
Improved control concept, 43
Indirect costs, 28
Industrial robots, 21, 23, 30, 52, 57, 135-136, 147-160
Informational data banks, 25-26
Integration of new technology, 31-32
Interactive computer graphics, 264-266
Interactive design, 224-237
Interactive design system operation, 123
Interactive mode computing, 170-172
Investment casting foundry, 152
Italy, 10

J

Japan, 7, 8, 10, 30, 69, 149
Job satisfaction, 13

K

Kit parts programming, 20

L

Labor costs, 4, 10
Labor resistance, 147
Labor standards, 20

Landing gears, 98
Layout, 93
Lens surface styling, 229-230
Loft, 100
Logistics management, 27

M

Machine tools, 3, 4, 129
Macrovie of CAM, 20
Maintenance, 47, 142-143
Make/Buy criteria, 20
Management control, 20
Manufacturing control, 35
Material costs, 172
Material handling, 35
Material storage, 35
Metrology—interchangeability, 3
Milling, 234
Milling machine center, 20
Multiechelon systems, 73-74
Multilayer hierarchy, 79
Multi-level software, 143

N

NC, See: Numerical Control
Netherlands, 7, 8, 10
New technology, 31
Noise level, 6, 8
Nonsymmetric forgings, 240-242
Norway, 7, 8
Numerical Control
   advanced developments, 131
   Air Force involvement, 17
   contour machining, 193
   drafting machine, 214
   F-18 aircraft, 104
   "family tree" concept, 93
   industrial robots, 153-154
   instruction, 26-27
   machining of preform surfaces, 245-246
   printed circuit board design, 183
   programming, 69, 99, 129
   tape, 80, 120, 249
   three-axis milling machine, 234

O

Online plotting, 177
On-line variable program (versatile) automation, 7
On-line moment-by-moment optimization, 7
Operations summary, 20
Opinion survey, 11
Optimization, 3
Organizational hierarchies, 73-74
Output per man-hours, 10

P

Personnel, 137

Physical machining, 3
Planning, 93
Preform design, 245
Preforming dies, 239
Presses, 6, 152
Problem-solving system, 166
Process control, 20
Product design, 208
Production engineering, 3-13
Productivity, 4, 69, 92
Productivity rates of change, 10
Programs, 6-8
Project technology listing, 57

Q

Quality assurance, 35, 99
Quality control, 93, 105

R

R and D, See: Research and Development
Reflector pockets, 228-229
Reporting features, 20
Research and Development, 143
Resistance to change, 147
Response time, 166
Return on Investment, 17
Robots, See: Industrial robots
ROE, See: Return on Investment

S

Scheduling, 20
Selling, 135-143
Sheet metal, 20, 30, 44, 53
Shop floor use, 23, 41
Social incentives, 5-6
Social well-being, 8, 11
Software
    architecture model building, 23
    bases, 199-200
    development costs, 177-181
    documentation, 185
    economic factors, 172
    ICAM evolution, 21
    integration of new technology, 31
    interactive communication problems, 25
    model simulation, 23
    multi-level, 143
    programs, 164
    robot-DNC systems, 156-157
Strategy, 6-8
Structures design, 261-262
Sub-assembly planning, 20
Surfaces, 3
Sweden, 10
Switzerland, 10
System design, 139-142

T

Technical support, 20
Technology assessment, 8-9
Tests, 35
Three-axis NC milling machine, 234
Three-dimensional modelling, 224-237
Tool construction, 208
Tool design, 93, 129, 208
Tooling, 99, 102-103
Tools, 141
Track-shoe forging dies, 242-246, 249
Training, 138
Transfer line, 80

U

United Kingdom, 10
United States, See: U.S.
U.S. rates of change of productivity and labor costs in manufacturing, 10

V

Vehicle lamp manufacture, 224-237

W

West Germany, 7, 8
Wheel-well, 98